The Public and the Private
in Aristotle's
Political Philosophy

The PUBLIC
and the PRIVATE
in ARISTOTLE'S
POLITICAL PHILOSOPHY

Judith A. Swanson

CORNELL UNIVERSITY PRESS

Ithaca and London

First published 1992 by Cornell University Press.

International Standard Book Number 0-8014-2319-8
Library of Congress Catalog Card Number 91-55528
Printed in the United States of America
*Librarians: Library of Congress cataloging information
appears on the last page of the book.*

⊗ The paper in this book meets the minimum requirements
of the American National Standard for Information Sciences—
Permanence of Paper for Printed Library Materials, ANSI
Z39.48-1984.

TO DRM

CONTENTS

Acknowledgments

Most helpful in the production of this book were the comments provided by the then anonymous readers selected by Cornell University Press. Thomas L. Pangle's remarks compelled me to revise some of my arguments. David R. Lachterman suggested that I respond to several particular interpretations; as a result the book addresses issues it might not have otherwise. I am grateful to both for their suggestions. A first, very different draft was read by Joseph Cropsey, who also read a late draft of the Introduction; by Nathan Tarcov and Russell Hardin; and by Ian Shapiro, who also read a subsequent version of Chapter 4. Mary P. Nichols gave useful comments on a draft of Chapter 2. Research assistance was provided by Michael Jones, Susanne Klepper, and Lisa Toland. For introducing me to political philosophy, I acknowledge in particular Timothy Fuller, the late Michael Oakeshott, and Joseph Cropsey.

An Earhart Foundation Fellowship and a Josephine de Kármán Fellowship from the Aerojet-General Corporation enabled me to begin the manuscript that evolved into this book; a lectureship in the Department of Political Science, Yale University, enabled me to write a draft; teaching seminars on Aristotle at Yale, the University of Georgia, and Boston University gave opportunity for reflection; a Boston University Faculty Research Grant helped me to complete the book. Except for the arguments I explicitly credit to others, the interpretation is my own.

J. A. S.

A NOTE ON TRANSLATIONS
AND TEXTS

I have translated portions of Aristotle's *Politics* from the text edited by Alois Dreizehnter, consulting the translations of Ernest Barker, Carnes Lord, W. L. Newman, and H. Rackham. In translating from the *Nicomachean Ethics* I used the text edited by Franciscus Susemihl and consulted the translations of Terence Irwin, H. Rackham, and W. D. Ross. My translations of Aristotle's other works were generally from the texts provided by the Loeb editions; I consulted the Loeb translations and those of the Clarendon Aristotle Series. For full and specific references, see the Bibliography. Any emphasis in quotations of Aristotle is mine. Quotations of Plato's *Republic* and the *Laws* are from Allan Bloom's translation (New York: Basic Books, 1968) and Thomas L. Pangle's translation (New York: Basic Books, 1980), respectively. Translations of commentary in French are my own. The quotation from Joachim Ritter's *Metaphysik und Politik* in the Appendix, "Premises of Interpretation," was translated with help from a Berlitz Language Center.

I use the following abbreviations for Aristotle's works:

AC   *The Athenian Constitution*
DA   *On the Soul* (*De Anima*)
EE   *Eudemian Ethics*
GA   *Generation of Animals*
HA   *Historia Animalium*
Met *Metaphysics*

MM   *Magna Moralia*
NE   *Nicomachean Ethics*
Oec   *Oeconomica*
PA   *Parts of Animals*
Ph   *Physics*
Pol   *Politics*
Rh   *The "Art" of Rhetoric*
Top   *Topics*

References to Aristotle's texts are to the Bekker line numbers as found in Dreizehnter's edition of the *Politics*, Susemihl's edition of the *Nicomachean Ethics*, and the Loeb editions of other works. I also refer to the chapter and section divisions found in the same editions. References appear in order of importance; clusters of references are intended to be considered together (though some numbers may refer to the same point).

The Public and the Private in Aristotle's Political Philosophy

INTRODUCTION

The central topic of this book is the meaning of privacy according to Aristotle. I propose that Aristotle's political works present a vivid and substantive conception of the private. It is widely believed, though, that political philosophy did not take an interest in privacy until the emergence of classical liberalism in the seventeenth century. Most interpretations of Aristotle's political philosophy in particular indicate that he regards the private only as a precondition to the public; commentators argue or assume that he equates the private with the household.[1] What accounts for these misreadings? Two possible sources are Aristotle's usage of the word *idios* and classical liberalism. The word *idios*, "private" or "one's own," usually means in Aristotle's corpus simply what is not common, public, or relative to the regime.[2] From this meaning one might infer that Aristotle treats the private only in contradistinction to the public.[3] Modern expositors may infer that Aristotle

---

[1] For a famous example, see Hannah Arendt, *The Human Condition* (Chicago: University of Chicago Press, 1958), 37.

[2] H. Bonitz, *Index Aristotelicus*, 2d ed. (Graz: Akademische Druck–U. Verlagsanstalt, 1955), 339. Thus, *bios idios* is a way of life that is not "the common way of life of the city [*koinon tēs poleōs*]" or is not politically active (*ouk ekoinōnēsan praxeōn politikōn*) (*Pol* 1265a26, 1273b27–29).

[3] It is also inaccurate to suggest, as Arendt does, that Aristotle ("the Greeks") thought privacy idiotic, presumably because one meaning of *idiōtēs* is "ignoramus" (*Human Condition*, 38). It should be noted now, since I make several references to *Human Condition*, that Arendt does not always make clear whether she means to include Aristotle among "the Greeks" and "the ancients" (by which she seems to mean the Greeks and the early Romans); and at times, especially in her second

1

equates the private with the household because they are familiar with the liberal tradition's formulation of the private as a "sphere." In any case, Aristotle's conception of the private includes both the household and the meaning of *idios*, but it goes beyond both; for the private is constituted of activities that cultivate virtue and discount common opinion.

It is not that Aristotle never characterizes places as private; rather, in his estimation what defines a site as private are the activities that ordinarily go on within it. If the activities promote virtue uncompromised by prevailing morality, then the place is private. Similarly, the number of persons involved in an activity does not in itself determine whether it is public or private. For example, a multitude of people can transact business with one another. Number of agents is a determining feature of private activity only if the quality of the activity suffers when more than a limited number participate.

Because Aristotle maintains that virtuous activity may require agents to make choices and that actualizing virtue may even mean right choice making, he understands the private to include the opportunity and the resources needed to make virtuous choices, or privacy. Insofar as privacy is opportunity to actualize virtue, it presents opportunity not to act virtuously or at least not to actualize one's potential. This sense of the private, the private conceived in terms of choice, comes closest to the modern notion. As I show in Chapter 4, this is the respect in which Aristotle understands economic activity to be private.

Whether actualized or not, every form of private activity has, Aristotle suggests, a *telos* of its own. Raising children, interacting

---

chapter, she conflates Homer's, Plato's, and Aristotle's views. She approaches justifying her presentation when she claims that Plato and Aristotle sometimes express public opinion. She asserts, for example, that "in his two most famous definitions [of man as a political and a speaking animal], Aristotle only formulated the current opinion of the *polis* about man and the political way of life." And later, "these aspects of the teachings of the Socratic school . . . sprang not from actual experience in political life. . . . But the background of actual political experience, at least in Plato and Aristotle, remained so strong that the distinction between the spheres of the household and political life was never doubted" (*Human Condition*, 27, 37). I generally refer only to Arendt's commentary that is explicitly on Aristotle; but because she embeds her commentary on Aristotle in her commentary on "the Greeks" and "the ancients" and sometimes treats Aristotle's thought as representative of "the Greeks," I occasionally regard her remarks on "the Greeks" as including Aristotle. For discussion of the general question of the relation between Aristotle's work and his culture, see the Appendix, "Premises of Interpretation."

with one's mate, overseeing servants, transacting business, keeping friends, and philosophizing all require virtue of some kind, and each activity can be perfected. By trying to perfect such activities, human beings realize their own potentials. Achieving virtue requires discounting or being insulated from common, diluted conceptions and misconceptions of virtue. To live only according to prevailing expectations precludes discovery of one's potential. For Aristotle, the raison d'être of privacy is to enable one to turn away in order to achieve excellence.

This point raises the second topic of this book: the relation between the public and the private. Traditional accounts of Aristotle's political philosophy, especially Hannah Arendt's, maintain that he exalts the public realm over the private—a view usually derived from the assumption that he equates the private with the household and the household with the realm of necessity. On this view, Aristotle believes that the private opposes the public as necessity opposes freedom.[4]

In this book I dispute that interpretation. Insofar as Aristotle indicates that private activity requires pulling away from the drag of common opinion, he presents the private in opposition to the public. But insofar as he suggests that private activity in the form of, say, friendship or philosophy can transform common opinion into right opinion, he believes that the private serves the public. His account suggests, moreover, that human beings carry virtue earned in private into the public, whereas the human propensity to cherish what is one's own and desirable (*Pol* 1262b22–23) protects the private from being corrupted by opinions learned in public.

The public should accommodate and if possible facilitate the private, according to Aristotle. By way of law, ruling, and education, the public should provide opportunities and resources to cultivate virtue. By facilitating the forming of families, for example, a regime encourages kinship, a kind of friendship and moral virtue; by allowing a free market, it invites citizens to cultivate judgment and self-restraint; and by furnishing a liberal arts education, it promotes moral and intellectual virtue.[5] Private endeavor repays the

---

[4] Arendt, *Human Condition,* 27.

[5] See also Richard Mulgan, "Aristotle and Political Participation," *Political Theory* 18, no. 2 (1990), 198. Although I agree with Mulgan that Aristotle thinks the private should be "a concern of the community and its laws," I maintain that Aristotle wants regimes to keep in view the difference between interfering in and facilitating the private.

public: families provide future citizens, the economy effects distribution, and the educated are able to rule and teach. A regime should aim to bring about such a dynamic equilibrium between the public and the private, for then it will be self-sufficient, "what is best" (*Pol* 1253a1).

Why should members of contemporary liberal societies take note of Aristotle's recommendations regarding the public and the private? Perhaps because the liberal conception of the private and of its relation to the public is wanting. The distinctively modern liberal view of privacy arguably derives from Hobbes and Locke in particular.[6] Hobbes contributes to the modern view of privacy in arguing that nature, by both imposing on human beings and arranging no escape from the desire for self-preservation, sanctions one's resistance to threats:

> If the sovereign command a man, though justly condemned, to kill, wound, or maim himself; or not to resist those that assault him; or to abstain from the use of food, air, medicine, or any other thing, without which he cannot live; yet hath that man the liberty to disobey.
>
> If a man be interrogated by the sovereign, or his authority, concerning a crime done by himself, he is not bound, without assurance of pardon, to confess it.[7]

Nature figuratively shields each individual with the right to self-protection. Shielded by this right, each individual inhabits a "private world"—necessarily distinct from the worlds of others in that its raison d'être is that individual's security.[8]

Because self-defense cannot reliably ward off threats to self-preservation, Locke observes that individuals need a legal "fence" to prohibit all threats, including any from the ruling power. Locke not only seals the sphere around each individual (by replacing natural

---

[6] Hobbes's political theory, though not itself liberal, was instrumental in the rise of liberalism; see Andrzej Rapaczynski, *Nature and Politics: Liberalism in the Philosophies of Hobbes, Locke, and Rousseau* (Ithaca: Cornell University Press, 1987), 11–12, 25–29, 63–65.

[7] Thomas Hobbes, *Leviathan or the Matter, Forme and Power of a Commonwealth Ecclesiasticall and Civil,* ed. Michael Oakeshott (Oxford: Basil Blackwell, 1946), XXI.142; see also XIV.84, and Rapaczynski, *Nature and Politics,* 49, 75–76, 83.

[8] Rapaczynski, *Nature and Politics,* 76–77.

right with the rule of law) but, through his theory of labor, enlarges it. Each person's fence—the law as it applies to that person—encloses not simply his life but also whatever "he hath mixed his *labour* with."[9]

From both Hobbes and Locke then emerges the conception of privacy as a sphere. "This view . . . of a private sphere surrounding [man] that cannot be entered (first by other individuals and eventually by the state) without his consent, became the standard view of freedom in the liberal tradition."[10] Indeed, one finds even in J. S. Mill's account of liberty the notion of "self-regarding" spheres, dictated not by natural but by constituted rights derived from the greatest happiness principle.[11] And some contemporary theorists following in the liberal tradition conceive privacy as a sphere.[12]

Because a sphere takes up space, it must compete with whatever else takes up space—the state, or public sphere. In the liberal account, what is not private is that which intrudes. The effect of the imagery is to pit the private and the public against one another.[13] Aristotle would point out that the imagery works against the aim of liberalism insofar as it suggests that the private cannot expand without cost to the public. He would also say that liberalism compounds this general and abstract difficulty by encouraging morally inadequate conduct in each sphere. Hobbes, for example, allows subjects to do anything not forbidden by the sovereign. This would not seem so radical were it not for Hobbes's belief that human beings are fundamentally irrational, keeping obligations only out of fear of human or divine retribution for breaking them.[14]

[9] John Locke, *Second Treatise of Government,* ed. C. B. Macpherson (Indianapolis: Hackett, 1980), secs. 17, 27, 93, 123–24, 137–38, 171; see also Rapaczynski, *Nature and Politics,* 189.

[10] Ian Shapiro, *The Evolution of Rights in Liberal Theory* (Cambridge: Cambridge University Press, 1986), 277; see also 278.

[11] John Stuart Mill, *On Liberty,* ed. Gertrude Himmelfarb (New York: Penguin, 1982), 151, 141, and Mill, *Utilitarianism, with Critical Essays,* ed. Samuel Gorovitz (Indianapolis: Bobbs-Merrill, 1971), 18.

[12] For example, Robert Nozick, *Anarchy, State, and Utopia* (New York: Basic Books, 1974), and John Rawls, *A Theory of Justice* (Cambridge: Harvard University Press, 1971). See also Shapiro, *Rights,* 278–79.

[13] Thus, Arendt's account of Aristotle's political philosophy reflects the influence of the liberal tradition; see again, *Human Condition,* 27, for example.

[14] *Leviathan,* XXVI.174. On insatiable desires, see Rapaczynski, *Nature and Politics,* 32, 34, 42, 64; on keeping obligations, see 23 n. 15, 72–75, 88–90, 99, 104–5. I find Rapaczynski's positivist interpretation of Hobbes more persuasive than the prudentialist one.

Furthermore, Hobbes allows the sovereign to forbid anything—including what Aristotle would consider virtuous—either expressly or by imprinting on the "clean paper" of "common people's minds" whatsoever he deems necessary or beneficial to the security of the state.[15] The moral conduct of subjects, deriving from their own or the sovereign's will, must then be either arbitrary or in accordance with necessity.

Locke, in contrast, gives the responsibility of defining morality not to the sovereign or to the individual but to the majority. He appears to give this responsibility to the individual in indicating that moral conduct derives from a dialectic between the individual's reason and practical sense experience. The moral principles to which this dialectic gives rise are, however, those that most rational agents find acceptable. Locke differs from Kant, then, in allowing reason (in the service of morality) to accommodate natural preferences. But he differs from Aristotle in allowing reason to accommodate "normal" preferences.[16]

Locke says, in effect, that the standards of the private should derive from the public. He opens the private to corruption by the multitude. Aristotle argues, in contrast, that the standards of the private should emanate from wisdom, an attribute of few. Wisdom is not denaturalized Kantian reason but knowledge that distinguishes between natural preferences that are consistent with living nobly and those that are not. For Aristotle, then, privacy does not permit ordinary vices but requires extraordinary virtues. It does not sanction a right to do as one pleases or even mandate morally acceptable conduct (what is appropriate in public) but urges doing as one ought.[17] In sum, in Aristotle's view human

---

[15] *Leviathan*, XXX.221; see also XVIII.116–17, XXVI.174, XLVI.446.

[16] Aristotle would commend Locke for naturalizing rationality but would find that he overcompensates for the inadequacy of Kant's theory by leaving morality to the rational capacities and life experiences of the majority. This abbreviated account of Lockean morality and the comparison between Locke and Kant derive from Rapaczynski, *Nature and Politics*, 156–76, especially 166–67, 170.

[17] John Gray, in *Liberalism* (Minneapolis: University of Minnesota Press, 1986), 4, correctly finds in Aristotle a duty-based conception of natural right insofar as Aristotle connects virtue with choice making. But Gray maintains that this connection intimates a "rudimentary . . . conception of natural human rights," which is problematic. For, as Gray notes, these allegedly intimated rights are "very unequal" (to call them *human* rights is then misleading). Accordingly, "they coexist uneasily with Aristotle's . . . defence of natural slavery." In addition, they do not generate "a right to noninterference," because (as Gray does not note) not all virtue results from choice making (*NE* 1103a17, 1106a11–12, 1139a33–34, 1157b6–7, 31). If we under-

beings should conceive privacy not as a sphere that should (at best) accommodate common opinion but as activities that cultivate virtue and discount common opinion.

But what are the aspects of Aristotle's view of the private that make it worthy of consideration by contemporary liberal societies? First, the private is as important to Aristotle as it is to liberal thinkers. Aristotle agrees that the maintenance of the private is essential to the self-sufficiency and happiness of the individual and of the body politic. Accordingly, he would endorse the merging of liberal theory and classical economics. Second, Aristotle's conception of the private as harboring excellence justifies the public sector's expansion of the private, fostering the aims of liberalism. Third, privacy on Aristotle's account includes the freedom not to participate in political life which many liberal theories protect. Indeed, arguing that the best regime is an aristocracy, Aristotle advocates the political participation of, where possible, only the virtuous, whose numbers are normally small.[18] He would disagree, then, with communitarian critics who think that liberalism overemphasizes the private as such, encouraging preoccupation with the self and discouraging public-spiritedness.[19] Fourth, Aristotle's conception of the private allows for "limited moral pluralism," as does classical liberalism:[20] "To each man the activity in accordance with his own disposition is most choiceworthy" (*NE* 1176b26–27). Again, only the nature of the limits differ. Finally, Aristotle indicates that incorporating privacy into political society depends less

---

stand Aristotle's advocacy of independent, virtuous choice making not as "some conception of natural human rights" but as a part of his conception of privacy, then these difficulties disappear; in Aristotle's view, every human being has a right to privacy insofar as everyone—from children to the slavish to the philosophical—should be granted (by those who rule them) opportunities to cultivate the most virtue of which they are capable. But this right may sometimes require denying some persons (for example, children, law breakers) freedom to make choices, or it may circumscribe their choices; and it does not grant the eligible merely the freedom to choose, but also the resources and thus the encouragement or direction to choose virtuously.

[18] At least one scholar argues that Aristotle endorses monarchy even over aristocracy; see P. A. Vander Waerdt, "Kingship and Philosophy in Aristotle's Best Regime," *Phronesis* 30, no. 3 (1985), 249–73.

[19] Aristotle would thus be surprised to find some of these critics invoking him in their critiques of liberalism; see, for example, William A. Galston, *Justice and the Human Good* (Chicago: University of Chicago Press, 1980), and Alasdair MacIntyre, *After Virtue: A Study in Moral Theory* (Notre Dame: University of Notre Dame Press, 1981).

[20] See Shapiro, *Rights*, 275–76.

on political than on individual initiative, and so his political philosophy provides fewer political directives than insights into how to live. For all these reasons, liberal societies should find Aristotle's conception of the private eligible.

In sum, by way of its understanding of the public and the private, Aristotle's political philosophy indirectly illuminates the shortcomings of liberalism and provides insights into how liberal societies might mitigate or rectify their deficiencies. By assimilating Aristotle's teaching about the public and the private, in particular about the centrality of excellence to private activity, a liberal society can transform itself into a form of polity that promotes true freedom and approaches true aristocracy.

1

THE HOUSEHOLD:
A PRIVATE SOURCE
OF PUBLIC MORALITY

According to a widely accepted interpretation, one promoted unreservedly by Hannah Arendt, Aristotle depicts the private in the following ways: (1) as distinct and separate from the public; (2) as corresponding to the household; (3) as serving only individual and species survival; and, most notably, (4) as justifying "force and violence . . . because they are the only means to master necessity—for instance, by ruling over slaves." On this interpretation, Aristotle reveals "tremendous contempt" for the private by depicting it as a dark, despotic, and subhuman sphere in which freedom does not exist. "In ancient feeling the privative trait of privacy, indicated in the word itself, was all-important; it meant literally a state of being deprived of something, and even of the highest and most human of man's capacities."[1]

It follows in this widespread interpretation that Aristotle thinks that a "truly human" life awaits in the public sphere. One must earn this life by mustering the courage to leave the sheltered and predictable (if wretched) household.[2] One needs courage also to participate in the unpredictable world outside the household: the speeches, deeds, and political affairs of men. Moreover, in challenging men to initiate speech and action, the political realm calls

---

[1] Hannah Arendt, *The Human Condition* (Chicago: University of Chicago Press, 1958), 24–38, 45–46, 71–84. Arendt thus implies without resolving that the private on this account is both opposed to and the condition for freedom (see especially 27, 30–31).

[2] Arendt tries in this way to address the difficulty her interpretation creates: if the household is a miserable place, then why does it take courage to leave it?

on each "to distinguish himself from all others, to show through unique deeds or achievements that he was the best of all (*aien aristeuein*)." Freedom lies exclusively in the political realm because only through political speech and action can one excel and reveal one's individuality. On this account, Aristotle connects freedom with excellence and excellence with individuality, and he specifies agonistic political action as the means to all three. Accordingly, Arendt claims, "the 'good life,' as Aristotle called the life of the citizen, therefore was not merely better, more carefree or nobler than ordinary life, but of an altogether different quality."[3]

As I noted in the Introduction, I contest the view that Aristotle equates the private with the household. I argue that he conceives the private as activities, not as sites, and as activities not restricted to the household. An activity qualifies as private, if it cultivates virtue without accommodating or conforming to common opinion. Because in Aristotle's view the household can and should contain private activities, my interpretation acknowledges that he regards the household as a private place; that is, the private status of the household derives from its affording an opportunity to practice unqualified virtue.[4]

In the first three chapters of this book I consider the activities (and, to illuminate them, their agents) that Aristotle believes the household should contain and contest Arendt's interpretation of Aristotle's notion of the household. I do not dispute that Aristotle thinks the purpose of the household is to meet basic needs and foster the survival of the species, but I do dispute that he thinks fulfillment of this purpose requires force and violence. Chapters 1 and 2 show that he thinks the exercise of prudence on the part of household rulers can bring about the satisfaction of needs. Chapter 2 shows that in his view nature facilitates meeting needs without coercion by providing human beings who are inclined to do necessary tasks. Chapters 1 and 3 show that fostering species survival through marriage and child rearing does not require violence or despotism according to Aristotle. In these three chapters I also contest the view that Aristotle thinks the *only* purpose of the household is to meet individual and species needs. The household's other main purpose is to cultivate moderation and judgment in its members. Members may distinguish themselves by the way

---

[3] *Human Condition,* 31–49, 175–207; quotations from 41, 36–37.
[4] Whether household members take advantage of this invitation does not change the household's private status.

and the extent to which they exercise these virtues. Finally, these beginning chapters show that Aristotle does not perceive a "gulf" between the public and the private: ideally, human beings serve the public by exercising the uncompromised virtue acquired in the household both inside and outside the household. More precisely, my discussion shows that the household is, as Arendt says, distinct from the city, but not in the way she claims—and thus is not separate in the radical way she attributes to Aristotle.[5]

On the Relation between the Household and the City

Rejecting Arendt's interpretation that Aristotle conceives the household to be radically separate and opposed to the good life offered by the city points to the hypothesis that he conceives it to be like the city and thus to foster living well. But does rejecting her interpretation entail endorsing the claim that Aristotle conceives the household and the city to be virtually or essentially identical? How far does Aristotle go in assimilating the household and the city?

Does he go as far as Hegel, for example? According to Hegel, the family is "the first . . . ethical root of the state."[6] The state is prior to the family insofar as the purpose of the latter derives from the former:

> The philosophic proof of the concept of the state is the develop- ment of ethical life from its immediate phase through civil society, the phase of division, to the state, *which then reveals itself as the true ground of these phases.* . . . Actually, therefore, the state as such is not so much the result as the beginning. It is within the state that the family is first developed into civil society, and it is the Idea of the state itself which disrupts itself into these two moments.[7]

For Hegel, then, the family is theoretically a moment of the state, reflecting the state's rational foundations. The family maintains its distinctiveness only insofar as it is a particular instance of the uni-

---

[5] *Human Condition*, 28, 35.
[6] *Hegel's Philosophy of Right*, trans. T. M. Knox (London: Oxford University Press, 1967), sec. 255.
[7] Ibid., sec. 256, emphasis added.

versality of the state; that is, it "contains the moments of subjective particularity and objective universality in a substantial unity."[8]

On the one hand, some of Aristotle's claims seem to support such an understanding of the household, implying that the aims of the household and the city are the same and even that the household should serve the city rather than itself. First, in being "partnerships," the household and the city each "aim at some good" (*Pol* 1252a4). Moreover, the aim of the city, being "the most authoritative good of all" (1252a5–6), must subsume the good at which the household aims. Second, since "the household as a whole is a part of the city" and "the virtue of the part must have regard to that of the whole" (1260b13–15), one might infer that every aspect of the household should reflect the moral standards set forth by the regime. For example, parents should raise good citizens (1260b15–16, 19–20). Third, Aristotle seems to imply similarly, and in a part of the *Politics* concerning the best regime, that individuals should serve the city: "One ought not to think that a citizen belongs to himself, but that all belong to the city, for each is a part of the city" (1337a27–29). Thus again, one may infer that the household should generate good citizens. Notably, the source of one of Hegel's claims is found in Aristotle: "The city is prior by nature to the household and to each of us" (1253a19, 25–26), suggesting perhaps that the household should adapt its purposes to those of the city. Indeed, this view seems to be strengthened by Aristotle's explanation that the city stands to the individual as the body to the hand: a person cannot exist, or at least live well, without the city (1253a18–19). Perhaps Aristotle thinks, as Harry V. Jaffa infers, that "the *polis* . . . [is] the only community adequate for the fulfillment of man's specifically human potentiality," in which case all lesser communities must exist for the sake of it.[9]

On the other hand, not all these statements from Aristotle unequivocally support a Hegelian interpretation of his conception of the household as a phase of political goodness, its purpose virtually one with the city's. Most of them support equally the view that the household's purpose is different from but in accordance with the city's. Furthermore, other passages work against in-

---

[8] Ibid., sec. 255; see also sec. 181.

[9] Jaffa, "Aristotle," in *History of Political Philosophy*, 2d ed., ed. Leo Strauss and Joseph Cropsey (Chicago: University of Chicago Press, 1972), 74.

terpreting Aristotle's household as mirroring the ethical life of the city. First, the *Politics* opens by challenging the assumption that a household differs from a city only in size (1252a9–13). Aristotle shows, for example, that a household is more diverse than a city in that it can accommodate several forms of rule at once (1253b9–10, 1259a37–39, b1, 10–11). Second, he indicates that within a regime citizen virtue must be the same insofar as it derives from the regime (*Pol* 1276b30–31), yet he says that a city must be made up "of human beings differing in kind" (*Pol* 1261a22–24). The context—a critique of Plato's alleged proposals for communism—indicates that Aristotle is advocating moral as well as occupational pluralism (1261a16–22, 30–37).[10] Moral diversity must then derive from private sources.[11] Indeed, in contrasting the good man (*agathos*) and the good citizen (*spoudaios*) (*Pol* III.4), Aristotle indicates that their respective goodnesses derive from different sources and intimates that the good man's goodness derives in part from the household. According to Aristotle, human beings become "good and excellent [*agathoi kai spoudaioi*]" through "nature, habit, and reason [*phusis ethos logos*]" (*Pol* 1332a38–40; *NE* 1103a23–26, 1143b6–7, 1144b4–14). Men become good citizens (*spoudaioi*) by being ruled in the ways of the regime and discharging a particular function within the regime (*Pol* 1276b30–1277a1).[12] Thus, civic virtue is *incomplete* insofar as it derives from only habituation and listening (not nature); furthermore, it must always be *defective* except in the best regime insofar as it derives from and sustains the particular standards of a regime rather than deriving from and sustaining the good life (*Pol* 1277a1–5, 22–23).[13] But should we infer that good human beings can exist in regimes inferior to the best—in democ-

---

[10] More precisely, his statements are prescriptive in being descriptive.

[11] But in the same context he adds, "yet the good of each thing is surely what preserves it" (1261b9), indicating that the (private) parts of a city must cultivate not simply diversity but virtue.

[12] See also Robert Develin, "The Good Man and the Good Citizen in Aristotle's 'Politics,'" *Phronesis* 18, no. 1 (1973), 71, 78.

[13] As Develin explains, "we have indications that *agathos* implies some inherent, if cultivated, quality, while with *spoudaios* the accent is on effectiveness in action, often intimating 'the right man for the job', being used when no ethical aspect is to be stressed" (ibid., 77). Furthermore, in the best regime the *spoudaios* citizen is also a good man because he "works for the benefit of the *koinōnia* which is the state: the *politeia* is the point of reference for his *aretē*. This contributes to the end of the state, which is to produce *agathoi* men. (The state promotes the realisation of the potential)" (79). For Develin's philological analysis of *agathos* and *spoudaios* supporting these claims, see 73–79.

racies, oligarchies, polities, and even tyrannies? To the extent that unqualified virtue derives from nature, the answer is yes, since regimes cannot determine natural ability. But because natural ability alone does not make someone virtuous (NE 1144b4–30), the possibility of good human beings in defective regimes depends on there being in the regimes a source of habituation and education other than the regime. By Book III of the *Politics*, where Aristotle contrasts the good man and the good citizen, he has already indicated such a source of habituation and education, for by then he has noted or discussed domestic forms of rule (*politikē, basilikē, despotikē, gamikē, patrikē, oikonomikē*). But he affirms the possibility of the household's cultivating, not simply virtue that differs from civic virtue, but unqualified virtue, when he notes in Book III the possibility of a regime being constituted of (unqualifiedly) good men (1277a4–5). A reader of Aristotle must infer that the goodness of good men may derive from the household for the following reasons.

First, insofar as goodness comes from nature, and insofar as a human being's parents are a medium for nature, a good human being's goodness comes in this indirect sense from the household. Second, the best regime must be constituted of excellent parts, since a whole cannot be excellent without its parts being so (*Pol* 1332a32–34). Moreover, if such a part is truly excellent, then it must be excellent also in itself or apart. To maintain the possibility of an excellent city is then to maintain the possibility of excellent human beings and excellent households existing in defective regimes.[14] The possibility of excellent human beings in inferior regimes indicates that the household may be a source of their goodness—since it is among the private sources of habituation and education in a regime. It must be inferred as well that even in the best regime virtue must come from private as well as public sources, for otherwise it would be incomplete. Laws and public institutions, even of the best sort, cannot make one fully human.[15]

---

[14] Indeed, virtuous households are more likely to arise than virtuous cities, since a household requires far fewer good human beings to qualify as good than a city requires to qualify as good.

[15] Richard Bodéüs emphatically denies this interpretation of Aristotle's ethics, arguing that Aristotle essentially endorses Plato's (alleged) views; see *Le philosophe et la cité: Recherches sur les rapports entre morale et politique dans la pensée d'Aristote* (Paris: Société d'Édition "Les Belles Lettres," 1982), and my Appendix, "Premises of Interpretation," pp. 212–21.

Able to contain private activities, the household is a potential source of freedom; it may contribute to a fully human life.[16] In that human beings are obliged to strive to be fully human (*NE* 1098a16–17), they are obliged to the private rather than the public when the public falls short of goodness. But human beings ideally ought to uphold both public and private standards, since the whole human good does not lie in either but springs from their interaction.

We again see a contrast with Hegel's view, which describes the ethical "as the inter-penetration of the substantive and the particular." There is a difference between arguing that I can be wholly free only by making a dual commitment, to the public and the private, and arguing that "my obligation to what is substantive is at the same time the embodiment of my particular freedom." For Hegel, one is good or free only if the objective universality of the state is implicit in one's particular interests; it is as if for him the legitimacy of the private derives from the public because the public embodies the universal.[17] For Aristotle, in contrast, the public and the private (ideally) make distinctive contributions to the ethical; the private does not have to promote what the public promotes for its contribution to help actualize the ethical or be legitimate.

In summary, Aristotle is not arguing either that the household must be bad and distinct from the public (Arendt) or that it must be good and therefore a reflection of political goodness (Hegel). He is arguing that households may and should be a source of virtue, and that the sort of virtue they are capable of fostering differs from and may either be in tension with (if the regime is inferior) or complement (if the regime is good) civic virtue. In ordinary regimes, a good household distances itself from the regime, for in this way it can retain its standards (serving itself). In the best regime, a good household is in dynamic harmony with the regime, cultivating

---

16 See also E. Barker, *The Political Thought of Plato and Aristotle* (New York: Dover, 1959), 399–400. M. I. Finley observes that "it is often overlooked that Aristotle defined man as being not only a *"zoön politikon*, a *polis*-being, but also a *zoön oikonomikon*, a household-being" (*The Ancient Economy*, 2d ed. [Berkeley: University of California Press, 1985], 152). Contrast Jaffa's earlier noted interpretation: "The distinction between mere life, on the one hand, the consequence of procreation and self-preservation, and the good life, is apparent from the difference between the household and the *polis* . . . except as he lives in a *polis* a man cannot live a fully human existence, he cannot function as a man" ("Aristotle," 74).

17 *Hegel's Philosophy of Right*, secs. 261, 264, 265, 267, 270.

virtue that enhances civic virtue (serving the regime in serving itself).

THE HOUSEHOLD'S CONTRIBUTION
TO VIRTUE

In the remainder of this chapter I support the two main claims put forth in the previous section. In this section I show that, according to Aristotle, the household has the potential to cultivate uncompromised virtue, or, as I put it henceforth, the *ideal* household cultivates such virtue. The subsequent sections indicate the activities peculiar to the household which enable it to promote virtue that surpasses the virtue most regimes cultivate. These discussions serve to make clear that ordinary regimes need households because they are a source of unadulterated virtue that may filter into the regime. They also take up my second claim: that Aristotle's ideal household promotes an aspect of unadulterated virtue which a regime cannot promote. Thus, even Aristotle's best regime needs households. Promoting complete virtue requires promoting its public and private dimensions.

Aristotle indicates in several places that unqualified virtue characterizes the household properly understood. Explaining the nature of the universe in the *Metaphysics*, he writes: "Everything is ordered together to one end; but the arrangement is like that in a household, where the free persons are least allowed to act at random, and have all or most of their actions preordained for them, whereas the slavish and the animals have little common responsibility and act for the most part at random" (1075a19–23). The good household is a source of virtue because its parts assume an "orderly arrangement," as do the parts of the universe (1075a11–14). Aristotle thus implies that the orderly arrangement characterizing the household derives not from the requirements of political or other circumstances but from the requirements of virtue itself; it is preordained in this sense. Corroborating and making more precise this claim, he states at the beginning of the *Politics* that "what makes a household" ("and a city") is "partnership in" "perception of good and bad and just and unjust and the other moral qualities" (1253a15–18); that is, the household embodies moral standards.

Since the "good life" depends on "education [*paideia*] and virtue [*aretē*] above all" (*Pol* 1283a24–26), the household must assume a role in securing the good life. A human being must be not only educated but morally virtuous to live well. Education by the laws and institutions of a regime is indispensable for citizens, particularly from the point of view of the regime; all citizens being instructed similarly in the ways of the regime establishes and sustains the regime (*Pol* 1337a11–27). But each citizen should also receive a private education, which is superior to public education in not being uniform but tailoring itself to the needs and abilities of individuals (*NE* 1180b7–13). Moreover, if the regime should fail to cultivate habits in individuals (so as, for example, to prepare them to undertake occupations), then it devolves on "each man to help his children and friends toward virtue" (*NE* 1180a30–32). Thus, depending on the nature of the regime, a household may have both to instill the best moral standards in its members and to render them fit for practical life outside the household.

THE MEANS TO VIRTUE: RULE

How may a household instill virtue? According to Aristotle, through some sort of rule. Since nature adapts human beings to receive moral virtue (*NE* 1103a25), human beings should use a means according to nature to instill it. Rule is such a means. It is natural in the sense of inevitable and in that it confers benefits on or improves both the ruler and the ruled (*Pol* 1254a21–22).[18] We can infer its inevitability, for something must hold together parts that appear to be wholes (1254a28–31). We can also infer its desirability in that it facilitates a number of things becoming one—or their partnership—and "all partnerships aim at some good" (1254a4). Moreover, we can observe all around us the advantages ruling and being ruled confer: infants become adults because their parents rule them; a body becomes healthy because a soul rules it; a human being lives well because his intellect rules his appetite; even sounds form music because harmony rules them (1254b4–9, 1254a32–33). As human experience makes clear, the benefits rule confers on the ruler, on the one hand, and on the ruled, on the

---

[18] Rule is natural in the second sense in moving both ruler and ruled toward completion, toward what is best (*Pol* 1252b32–1253a1).

other, vary: the patient benefits more from the doctor's practice than does the doctor; children benefit more from parental care than do parents; masters benefit more from mastery than do slaves (*Pol* 1278b32–1279a8). Nonetheless, both ruler and ruled always benefit in some way—intentionally, accidentally, or indirectly—because they share some common task or purpose (*Pol* 1254a27–28).

That ruling and being ruled are according to nature does not mean that either is easy. What is according to nature appears to be divine insofar as it appears to be in the best state possible; but it is not "sent by the gods," or the same as fortune, because it requires effort on our part (*NE* 1099b9–24). Indeed, Aristotle observes, "in general, it is difficult to live together and be partners in any human activity" (*Pol* 1263a15–16). This observation seems to move Aristotle's notion of the household toward Arendt's interpretation—that the household is a place of toil yielding no real satisfaction. According to Aristotle, however, things brought into being through effort—nature's or man's—are the greatest and noblest of all things (*NE* 1099b22–24). They thus yield much pleasure, for "actions in accordance with virtue are by nature always pleasant" (1099a13–14). Furthermore, the difficulty of living together decreases to the extent that the parties recognize their common aim, a life as complete and self-sufficient as possible (*Pol* 1280b33–35, 1260b13, 1254a27–28).

THE AIM OF HOUSEHOLD RULE: VIRTUOUS INDIVIDUALS

In that the best household's aim is to instill unqualified moral virtue through some sort of rule, its aim appears to be indistinguishable from that of the best regime. Moreover, the aims of the best household and the best regime are alike in that they both seek to acknowledge the distinctiveness of individual human beings; according to Aristotle, diversity more than sameness gives rise to unity (*Pol* 1261a29–30, 22–24). Both the household and the city should promote similarity in the sense of virtue, but neither should promote homogeneity (1263b31–32). "Habits" deriving from household activities and "laws" from the regime can together make the city "one and common through education" (1263b36–40) without sacrificing diversity.[19] Nonetheless, as noted earlier, household activities are better suited to individualized instruction and thus to acknowledgment of individuality than is public education. Cities, then, should rely more on households than on laws and public institutions to maintain diversified excellence. The question is, *what* should household rule instill to achieve this diversity?

According to Aristotle, instilling moderation and judgment makes human beings virtuous without eradicating any distinctiveness other than a lack of virtue. The man and the woman of the household may exercise both moderation and judgment as well as "show who they really and inexchangeably are" by selecting and remaining with each other, managing the household, and caring for their children.[20] Likewise, children and servants may also acquire and demonstrate moderation, judgment or understanding, and distinctiveness by the ways they conduct themselves and respond to the heads of the household. Indeed, the extent to which members of the household practice moderation and judgment is itself expressive of distinctiveness.

TEACHING MODERATION

All household members must learn to be moderate toward things and each other. The various forms of household rule can teach members moderation by revealing to them the natural ends of their natural desires (*Pol* 1257b19–34). For example, household management (rule over the material conditions of a household) teaches that specific things must fulfill specific needs and desires: food satiates hunger, a bed satisfies the need for sleep; money itself cannot satisfy such needs.[21] Thus, household management teaches

[19] Philosophy too should help to effect this and may arise in the household (see Chapter 3, "An Intellectual Being: A Philosopher?" pp. 61–65) or in the city (see Chapter 6, "Leisure: Education in Reason?" pp. 155–60).

[20] Arendt indicates that Aristotle reserves the public realm for individuality (*Human Condition*, 41).

[21] This appears to be an elementary teaching, but according to Aristotle some heads of households fail to learn it; supposing that it is the function of household management to increase property, they strive to preserve or increase their money indefinitely. "The cause of this state is that they are serious about living, but not about living well" (*Pol* 1257b38–1258a1).

human beings to check their desire for money—itself an un-natural, because unfulfillable, desire.[22] The various household re-lationships also teach moderation in various ways. Forming a household entails the exercise of moderation in that it requires limiting oneself to one out of many sexual partners and compan-ions.[23] Parenthood teaches both the parents and the children mod-eration. Since children's reasoning powers are not developed, par-ents must find the mean between arguments and force which is effective for teaching their children (*Pol* 1260a13–14, b6–7, 1332b10–11; *NE* 1179b23–29). It is because children are potentially reasoning and reasonable beings—or "free persons"—that one ought to rule them in "kingly fashion" (*Pol* 1259a39–b1, 1253b4, 1285b32). And children, who are not inclined to be moderate, must learn to be so if they are to live well (*NE* 1179b24–34). Finally, as the next chapter shows, ruling slaves teaches both the masters and the slaves moderation.

Aristotle's characterization of the ideal household as requiring the exercise of moderation contrasts with the general contempo-rary liberal view according to which what goes on in the household is entirely a matter for the (undefined) discretion of household members. Indeed, activities are private according to Aristotle only when the actors heed the limits established by nature.

The moderation learned in the household not only helps to sus-tain the household but facilitates all human engagement.[24] Moder-ation is both the result of and fosters seeing what is required for living together. It is thus neither a strictly private nor a strictly

---

[22] The unlimited desire for money is created by money itself precisely because one can accumulate it without end. As William J. Booth explains, "mon-ey . . . permits men to disregard specific uses and removes the spatial impediment to accumulation: in short, by destroying the limits set by the household around property, it unleashes a desire, no longer tied to a narrow use, but in principle unlimited and provides that desire with a way past the natural barriers of the home" ("Politics and the Household: A Commentary on Aristotle's *Politics* Book One," *History of Political Thought* 2, no. 2 [1981], 223).

[23] Although Aristotle does not address directly the issue of sexual fidelity, he does criticize Plato's alleged proposal for the communism of women on the ground that "what belongs in common to the most people gets the least care" (*Pol* 1261b33–34). Since women constitute half of the free persons in a city (1260b19) and it matters that they are excellent (1260b16–18), they should be accorded care and thus not considered common property. For the same reason, women should not consider men common property. See also Chapter 3, note 24, pp. 52–53.

[24] Even philosophy, which is not in itself moderate, presupposes moderation.

public virtue, and so it—not courage—might be said to be in Aristotle's eyes the political virtue par excellence.[25]

TEACHING JUDGMENT

In addition to moderation, the good household teaches judgment (*Pol* 1253a15–18). Forming a household requires judgment in that it requires choosing a good partner. Raising children involves judgment as something to be taught. Ruling servants involves judgment in trying to compensate for the servants' lack of it. What is pertinent to this inquiry, however, are the ways judgment required by the household differs from that required by the regime. One significant difference involves natural affection; another, the end each aims to realize.

According to Aristotle, the end of the city is justice, which all take to be "some sort of equality"—that is, equal things for equal persons (*Pol* 1282b14–21). But this definition encompasses both natural justice, the fundamental principle of which is proportionality or desert, and conventional justice, the fundamental principle of which is arithmetical equality (*NE* 1134a26–28, b18–19).[26] The regime that is "by nature"—realizes natural justice—is best (*NE* 1135a5). But since realizing natural justice in a regime presupposes many deserving human beings and the ability to detect them—that is, requires fortune and virtue to achieve (*Pol* 1331b21–22, 1277a1–5)—cities should aim first to realize conventional justice.

Should the household also then seek conventional or ordinary justice? In two places, Aristotle says that it should not. "Political justice seems to consist in equality and parity," "but there does not seem to be any justice between a son and his father, or a servant and his master—any more than one can speak of justice between my foot and me, or my hand, and so on for each of my limbs. For a son is, as it were, a part of his father" (*MM* 1194b23, 5–15). As he

---

[25] Arendt seems to acknowledge that Aristotle counts moderation among the political virtues, but she indicates that she thinks it is "helpless to offset" the inherent unpredictability of human interaction (*Human Condition*, 191; see also 192–99).

[26] It encompasses both since it does not specify "equality in what sort of things and inequality in what sort of things" (*Pol* 1282b21–22).

explains in the *Nicomachean Ethics*, "there can be no injustice in the unqualified sense toward what is one's own, and a chattel or a child until it reaches a certain age . . . is, as it were, a part of oneself, and no one decides to harm himself. Hence there can be no injustice toward them, and therefore nothing unjust or just in the political sense. . . . what is just in households . . . is different from what is politically just" (1134b10–17).

By proceeding immediately to discuss natural justice, Aristotle suggests that it characterizes the household. The household appears to be even a paragon of natural justice in that inequalities within it are evident and determine who rules and who is ruled. And, as Arlene W. Saxonhouse explains, "the family, because its differences in *eidē* are observable, demonstrates a unity in diversity which perhaps becomes impossible in political life. In the *polis* obvious differences in *eidē* are absent. . . . The family with its definition of differences . . . attains a certainty in nature not available to the city."[27] Or, at least, not available to most cities. In other words, it appears that the household, being a model of natural justice, is a kind of model for the best regime. Aristotle would apparently like the natural superiority holding together the (best) household to hold together the (best) city. Indeed, he may insist on the preservation of households (in all regimes) because they have the potential to exemplify perfect unity or justice and by their examples point the city toward a higher justice.[28]

Aiming to realize natural, not conventional, justice, the good household ruler does not treat all members equally or give each a turn at ruling; rather, it is incumbent on this ruler to detect the virtues of each member and treat him or her accordingly, giving guidance or instruction when needed and freedom to make choices when deserved. The household is a compound of "unlike persons"—man, woman, servants, and children—who, moreover, have multiple functions or obligations—as husband and father, wife and household manager, son or daughter and future citizen (*Pol* 1277a5–8, 1253a4–14). There are thus not only manly virtues,

---

[27] "Family, Polity, and Unity: Aristotle on Socrates' Community of Wives," *Polity* 15, no. 2 (1982), 212–13.

[28] All regimes have the foundation to become best regimes in that they base themselves on the principle of rule, or acknowledge the political necessity of inequality. But, instead of imposing a fabricated inequality on top of a fabricated equality, which most regimes do by means of the rotational distribution of offices to all, they should assign authority on the basis of virtue.

womanly virtues, servile virtues (1277b20–23), and presumably even youthful virtues but also virtues attached to being a husband, father, wife, and child. A household thrives when each member performs his or her function, or upholds his or her obligations, in accordance with the virtues proper to doing so (*NE* 1098a14–15).

The variety of virtues indicates the variety of judgment in the household. Most notably, the judgment of those ruling differs from that of those being ruled, as becomes clear when we take into account the deliberative capacities of each kind of member and Aristotle's distinctions among intellectual virtues in the *Nicomachean Ethics*. One acquires prudence by repeatedly putting into effect good judgments about at least one's own affairs, if not the affairs of others (*NE* 1141b12–21, 29–1142a10). Lacking experience, the young cannot have prudence (1142a15–16). Lacking good judgment, or the ability to detect through deliberation what action to perform, and how and when to perform it, the slavish, who lack the ability to deliberate, cannot have prudence either (*NE* 1143a29–31, *Pol* 1260a12). The nonslavish adults of the household, however, having both experience and the ability to deliberate (*Pol* 1260a10–13), may have prudence. In fact, household management requires that they do (*NE* 1141b31–32). Nonetheless, the prudence of the man and the woman apparently differ. Although it is the responsibility of both to manage the household, the man should acquire possessions and the woman should oversee their use and consumption (*Pol* 1277b24–25).[29] It follows that the man should acquire the household servants (*Pol* 1255b37–39), since they are animate possessions (1253b32), and that the woman should command them, since their function is to assist in the use of other possessions (1253b32–33, 1254a2). Moreover, Aristotle indicates in several ways that the man, at least more than the woman, should guide their children; for example, "the man rules the child" (*Pol* 1260a10).[30] In addition, Aristotle assigns marital rule to both the

---

[29] Acquisition is the only part of meeting needs that justifies the use of strength or force. Although the natural modes of acquisition Aristotle assigns to household management (farming, raising animals, hunting, and fishing) alter or destroy nature, they are "by nature just" because plants and most of the lower animals are "for the sake of human beings" (*Pol* 1256b15–27); see also *The Politics of Aristotle*, vol. 2, ed. W. L. Newman (New York: Arno Press, 1973), 174–75, note on 1256b20. Moreover, although household management subsumes acquisition, the latter must occur outside the household proper.

[30] Chapter 3, "An Educated Being: A Parent?" pp. 57–59, provides more examples and support for this claim.

husband and the wife; that is, spouses rule each other (*Pol* 1253b9–10, 1259a39–b1, 4–10).[31] Since the man and the woman each rule over others, at least in part for the good of those others (*Pol* 1278b32–1279a8), each has complete moral virtue, which Aristotle calls justice and prudence (*NE* 1130a2–14, 1145a1–2; *Pol* 1260a17–18, 1277b25–26).[32] But because each rules over different persons, they again exercise prudence differently (*Pol* 1260a10–12, 20–24, 1277b20–23).

In contrast to the judgment of the free adult members of the household, the judgment of children and servants is lacking. Children have only the potential for judgment and prudence; servants can only follow judgment and comply with prudence (*Pol* 1260a12–14, 1254b22–23).

Variety of judgment appears naturally in the household; even more, in the good household, those who rule acknowledge it. Good household rulers do not command their spouse, children, and servants in the same way (*NE* 1134b15–16). By way of presenting the household, then, Aristotle suggests that private judgment differs from the judgment required by most regimes in that it acknowledges differences in kinds of, and aptitude for, virtue among human beings. Moreover, in trying to promote the virtues peculiar to each member, household rulers promote individuality.

In addition to promoting individuality, private differs from public judgment in not having law to aid it (*Pol* 1282b1–6). Both political and household rulers must employ "knowledge and choice" (*Pol* 1332a31–32) to bring about, respectively, the city's and the household's excellence. But, whereas political rulers may refer to legal knowledge, household rulers must rely only on their understanding of moral virtue. Private judgment may thus be even more difficult to acquire than public judgment. In any case, as the estate manager Ischomachus explains to Socrates, acquiring private judgment is difficult: "To acquire these powers a man needs education; he must be possessed of great natural gifts; above all, he must become very great [divine, *to megiston dē theion genesthai*]. For I reckon this gift is not altogether human, but divine—this power to

---

31 In Chapter 3, "A Pairing Being: A Wife," pp. 52–55, I discuss this relationship.
32 Justice implies prudence in that it means being able to effect what is good for others, and it differs from prudence in that it means effecting only what is good for others—not for oneself.

win willing obedience: it is manifestly a gift of the gods to the true votaries of prudence."[33] Insofar as ruling and being ruled in the household require judgment, they prepare free or able members for life as citizens (in any regime), since a citizen is one who "shares in judgment [*kriseōs*]" (*Pol* 1275a22–23). But, insofar as ruling in the household requires acknowledging natural differences and encouraging natural potential—that is, requires prudence (*phronēsis*) or justice (*dikaiosunē*)—it prepares one to live in the best regime or to contribute to its making. By ruling a household well, one comes to understand the meaning, benefits, and wisdom of natural justice.[34]

AFFECTION

Although one may become moderate and prudent by way of household activities, men and women do not live together out of a desire to be virtuous. Not least among the reasons they live together, indeed listed first in one place by Aristotle, is *philia*, friendship or affection (*NE* 1162a16–24). The friendship that arises between a man and a woman seems to be natural, Aristotle says, by which he means here instinctive (*kata phusin huparchein*). It is not merely that men and women are sexually attracted to one another or inclined by nature to couple, but rather that they are inclined by nature to form couples, to be friends.[35] Men and women are not, then, habituated, or, as contemporary jargon would put it, socialized, to pair. Moreover, their staying together or establishing households is not the consequence of acculturation either; for establishing a household is a means, not only to keep alive their natural affection for one another (*NE* 1157b5–13), but to satisfy

[33] Xenophon, *Oeconomicus* (Loeb Classical Library, 1923), 524–25.
[34] Aristotle may then be recommending having a family as a qualification for citizenship. During his time, adult males were considered citizens and could vote once registered, but they were not expected to speak at assemblies or to hold office until they were married, with a household; see Stephen R. L. Clark, "Aristotle's Woman," *History of Political Thought* 3, no. 2 (1982), 189. In Sparta, Lycurgus made having a family a legal qualification for citizenship; see Plutarch's *Lycurgus, Apophthegmata of the Lacedaemonians*, noted and cited by Numa Denis Fustel de Coulanges in *The Ancient City: A Study on the Religion, Laws, and Institutions of Greece and Rome* (Baltimore: Johns Hopkins University Press, 1980), 42.
[35] Although, to the extent that friendship involves attraction or being pleased with one another (*Pol* 1157a1–2), they are mutually attracted.

other natural desires: the desire to have children and the desire for assistance (*charin . . . tōn eis ton bion; eparkousin*) (*NE* 1162a20–23, *Pol* 1252a26–30). That it is entirely natural for human beings to establish households does not mean, as we see here, that they establish them exclusively for reasons of utility or necessity. Friendship, children, and assistance, though they may be useful, are more than necessary to survival (*NE* 1155a28–29, 1169b22, 1097b8–11, 1099b2–4, 1163b1–5). The desire to live with a man or a woman turns out to be in fact an indirect desire to live well. Hence Aristotle says that the friendship between a man and a woman who live together "seems to be one of utility and pleasure combined" (*NE* 1162a24–25, 1099a13–14).

That households are natural also does not mean that human beings establish them simply by instinct, without exercising judgment or choice. Nature, after all, includes human nature, and thus the ability to discriminate. Marriage is the work or result of friendship, and "friendship is the [intentional] choice of living together" (*Pol* 1280b36–39). At the same time, friendship in general is a need, and the sort in question is, as noted, instinctive (*NE* 1155a5, 1162a16). Aristotle's meaning must then be that, although a human being cannot live well without a mate, one can choose who that mate is to be. Human beings will continue to form households, but not, at least if they do so according to nature, without some discrimination.[36]

But, one might object, does Aristotle not, in stating at the beginning of the *Politics* that the city is the most important form of association, suggest that it, not the household, is the primary satisfier of the natural human inclination for friendship or association?

---

[36] To put the point in modern terms, one cannot live well unless one has self-respect, self-respect depends on having things of one's own that one esteems, and the surest way to have things one esteems is to choose them oneself. This is not to say, and this Aristotle would stress, that what one chooses is necessarily worthy of esteem—of being chosen—but rather that, in order for things and relationships to contribute to self-respect and thus to living well, they must be chosen. As Martha Craven Nussbaum explains, in Aristotle's view "the *choice* of the good must come from within and not by dictation from without. All reflective men might choose the same good life; but what makes each of them a *good man* is that he is the one who chooses it. And what is more, it will not count as a *good life* for him unless it is a life chosen by his own active practical reason: prohairesis enters centrally into the specification of the good life itself" ("Shame, Separateness, and Political Unity: Aristotle's Criticism of Plato," in *Essays on Aristotle's Ethics*, ed. Amélie Oksenberg Rorty [Berkeley: University of California Press, 1980], 423).

In fact, he indicates that this is not the function of the political partnership: it "must be regarded . . . as being for the sake of noble actions, not for the sake of living together" (*Pol* 1281a2–4). A household, being founded in affection, provides a kind of sociality that the city does not. The sociality public activity provides is ordinarily impartial, since citizens seek justice and think only impartiality—or law—can secure it (*Pol* 1287b4–5). That the companionship the household provides is affectionate and partial does not mean in Aristotle's view that it contravenes justice or nobility or the good life. In fact, "the truest form of justice is thought to be a friendly quality" (*NE* 1155a28). Aristotle wants us to see that partiality or intimate affection is a part of the good life and facilitated by privacy.

The human desire for affection is then a component of the human desire for privacy. Human beings seek affection not from many but from a few, and they want to know that those few are their own. This desire for persons we can call our own is, to recall, natural; "for there are two things above all which make human beings care for things and feel affection, the sense of ownership and the sense of preciousness" (*Pol* 1262b22–23).[37] We feel affection for what is ours and want to make ours what is dear to us, what we esteem. The household in particular enables us to show and sustain affection for a few and to define those few as our own. It is unique in satisfying our desire for a *private* social life. The desire for marriage and the social life that accompanies it is connected with the good life, then, because it satisfies not merely a desire for social life but also a desire for privacy.

Friendship and Justice in the Household

Characterizing the household as a place of inequality and affection, Aristotle seems to be contradicting his claim in the *Nicomachean Ethics* that persons who are separated by some wide gap

---

[37] Ownership is then only a necessary, not sufficient, condition for securing affection; the thing or person loved has also to be worth caring about, or precious. On this account, the desire to improve or make worthy what is one's own—be it property, a husband, or a child—seems to be a natural extension of affection for what is one's own. In Chapter 7, "True Friendship," pp. 174–80, I also discuss the conditionality of affection.

in virtue cannot be friends (1158b33–35, 1159a5). And if household members cannot be friends, then the household cannot be a model for the best regime, for "friendship seems to hold cities together, and legislators seem to concern themselves seriously with friendship more than with justice" (1155a22–24).

But, although it is true that family members are not ordinarily complete and enduring friends in the way that those who are "equal and similar" in virtue can be (*NE* 1159b2–4), they can be friends of a lesser sort:

There is a different kind of friendship which involves superiority of one party over the other, for example, that of a father toward his son, and in general that of an older person toward a younger, that of a man toward a woman, and of any sort of ruler toward the one he rules. These friendships also differ from each other. For friendship of parents to children is not the same as that of rulers to ruled; nor is friendship of father to son the same as that of son to father, or of man to woman as that of woman to man. Each of them has a different virtue and function, and there are different causes of love. Hence the ways of loving are different, and so are the friendships. (1158b11–19)

Moreover, Aristotle opens the possibility that family members can be complete friends if the party of lesser virtue loves the party of greater virtue to such an extent as to compensate for the inferiority: "This above all is the way for unequals . . . to be friends, since this is the way for them to be equalized" (1159b1–2).

As to the claim that the ideal household is a model for the best regime, it should be recalled that it is claimed to be such in that it exemplifies the principle of just rule: to each according to his or her virtue. It is not claimed that the best household is a microcosm or reflection of the best regime. The two cannot mirror one another because their constellations of virtue differ: the household is constituted of unequals; the best regime of equals and unequals. Unlike household members (and lesser friends), friends who are equal in virtue do not request assistance or benefits from one another, for their friendship is not based on lack or utility (*NE* 1159b10–15). On the contrary, they seek to confer benefits and to outdo each other in justness, temperance, and all the other virtues (*NE* 1169b11–13, 1168b25–31, 1169a11–12, 32–b1, 1107a6–7).[38] Aristotle seems then to lead us to the conclusion that the household exemplifies true justice but falls short of yielding true friendship. Yet he qualifies that conclusion by indicating that the free adult members may have complete moral virtue and thus the capacity for true friendship with each other, and by suggesting that love itself may compensate for some lack of virtue, enabling an inferior member to approach true friendship with a superior member. Aristotle may be telling us that true friendship is bound less by circumstance than by individual virtue.

Why then do *legislators* try to bring about friendship more than justice? In the best regime, legislators want to bring about true friendship more than true justice because true friendship inspires greater virtue than true justice. In a regime that rewards and punishes according to virtue, a good man exercises virtue in order to merit an honorable occupation or office and avoids vice in order to avoid disgrace. But he would "throw away both wealth and honors and in general the goods that are objects of competition . . . on the condition that [his] friends would gain more" (*NE* 1169a20–21, 26–27, 29–b1).[39] True friendship may even cause a man to sacrifice his life; indeed, Aristotle implies that having friends makes men willing to die for their country (1169a18–20). Further, "it is nobler to do well by friends than by strangers" (1169b12–13), and, to recall, the political partnership is for the sake of living nobly. Finally, among intellectually gifted good men, true friendship leads to the activity of philosophy (*NE* 1172a1–6), the supreme activity. By these statements Aristotle prompts the thought that the private has more power to elicit excellence than the public. Good legislators, then, are concerned to facilitate privacy and thus true friendship with laws and education.

In ordinary regimes, legislators want to bring about friendship more than justice because justice is a condition sought to remedy faction (*NE* 1155a22–26, 1134a30–33), which must be minimized for

---

[38] One can outdo another in temperance, for "there is no excess . . . of temperance . . . since the intermediate is a sort of extreme [in achieving the good]" (*NE* 1107a22–23). True friendship does and does not demand a kind of excess.

[39] Contrast Arendt's depiction of Aristotle's (and the ancient Greeks') conception of the good life as agonistic (*Human Condition*, 36–37, 41).

regimes to last. Ordinary regimes aim at political friendship, in other words, because it is a state of affairs in which citizens agree on the fundamental constitutional arrangements of the regime and thus on how to resolve conflict.[40] Hence Aristotle says that "when men are friends they have no need of justice" (*NE* 1155a26–27). At the same time, he indicates that even ordinary legislators should seek to bring about true friendship, for they too should be concerned with eliciting the most virtue possible from their citizens. Legislators everywhere are then obliged to facilitate privacy.

By depicting the household as a place that may, through its activities, cultivate virtue independently of the regime, Aristotle reveals the unwisdom of Plato's alleged proposal to abolish households. Indeed, it is clear that we should understand Aristotle's portrait of the household in Book I of the *Politics* as (among other things) a supplement to his explicit critique in Book II of the proposals advanced in the *Republic*. Had Aristotle meant to convey, as Arendt contends, that household activities oppose virtue, this would have sit poorly with his denunciation of the *Republic*'s proposal for communism. Why indeed preserve dark and despotic households if a class of individuals can collectively provide for the city?

Aristotle's account of the household is, nonetheless, more than a plea for preserving households. It serves as a portal into the private. He places it at the beginning of the *Politics* both because it signals the importance of the private and because human beings first experience the private in the household. Indeed, Aristotle hints that only by experiencing household life may one progress to the many other forms of private activity that constitute part of the good life (*NE* 1142a9–10).

We have, however, yet to uncover the full range of virtuous activities Aristotle's ideal household offers. In the next two chapters I thus consider mastery, serving, and the activities of women in the household.

---

[40] See Chapter 7, "Concord: Friendship among Citizens," pp. 184–87.

2

MASTERY AND SLAVERY

The claim that Aristotle thinks household activities ought to educate members in virtue appears to be problematic in view of the
fact that he includes mastery and slavery among those activities.
Neither commanding physical work nor doing it for another seems
to be edifying. As I noted in Chapter 1, Arendt argues that mastery
in Aristotle's view requires even force and violence. Moreover,
according to her, Aristotle believes that human beings "are *entitled*
to violence toward others" because "violence is the prepolitical act
of liberating oneself from the necessity of life for the freedom of
world."[1] Thus Arendt implies that Aristotle justifies not only the
physical subjection but the moral and spiritual degradation of
slaves.[2] "The slave's degradation was a blow of fate and a fate
worse than death, because it carried with it a metamorphosis of
man into something akin to a tame animal"; life as well as the good
life requires demoting some human beings to a nonhuman status.[3]

---

[1] *The Human Condition* (Chicago: University of Chicago Press, 1958), 31, emphasis
added; see also 32, 81–84, 119, 121. According to Mary P. Nichols, Aristotle depicts
slavery as violent, but also as unjust; see "The Good Life, Slavery, and Acquisition:
Aristotle's Introduction to Politics," *Interpretation: A Journal of Political Philosophy* 2,
no. 2 (1983), 171, 176.
[2] Put otherwise, the slave is subjected by both physical necessity and human
beings (*Human Condition*, 31).
[3] Ibid., 83–84. Arendt does not make clear everywhere in her account of slavery
in *Human Condition* whether she is describing the ancient practice of slavery or
Greek philosophers' conceptions of slavery. Indeed, her discussion as a whole implies that the philosophical account was meant to be a justification of the historical
practice and otherwise followed Greek public opinion.

Other scholars point out that Aristotle's theory of slavery is inconsistent because it indicates that slaves are both human and subhuman: Aristotle declares that slaves are human to signify their usefulness, but he does not technically classify them as human to justify their enslavement. According to these scholars, Aristotle's justification of natural slavery is, either intentionally or unintentionally, unconvincing because it fails to prove the existence of natural slaves.[4]

In this chapter I challenge both Arendt's rendition of Aristotle's view of the nature of slavery and the charge that Aristotle fails to show the naturalness of slaves and thus the justness of slavery. I argue that, according to him, the ideal or natural master-slave relationship is (1) private and domestic; (2) between human beings who are naturally unequal; (3) physically advantageous to both parties; and (4) edifying to both parties.

SLAVERY: A NONPUBLIC, DOMESTIC PRACTICE

I establish in this chapter that mastery and slavery are, according to Aristotle, private in the sense of being activities that cultivate unpoliticized virtue in their agents. But it should also be made clear that the slavery Aristotle is justifying is private in the more narrow and usual sense: he thinks that slaves, or at least most slaves, should be owned by individual households, not by the community. In the best regime, land-owning citizens would own "private hands," while the regime would own hands to work on the common farm land (*Pol* 1330a30–31, 1278a11–13); but the territory owned privately would be twice the size of the common farm land (1330a9–15), which could mean that there should be more privately owned than publicly owned slaves. This possibility, plus the fact that Aristotle's treatment of household slavery in Book I

---

[4] See, for example, E. Barker, *The Political Thought of Plato and Aristotle* (New York: Dover, 1959), 367–68, 372; W. D. Ross, *Aristotle: A Complete Exposition of His Works and Thought* (New York: Meridian, 1959), 235; R. G. Mulgan, *Aristotle's Political Theory: An Introduction for Students of Political Theory* (Oxford: Clarendon, 1977), 40–44; Nichols, "Good Life," 171, 175–76. Barker argues that Aristotle is aware of and compensates for (but does not resolve) the inconsistencies in his account; Nichols, unlike the others, contends that Aristotle fails intentionally to demonstrate the existence of natural slaves.

surpasses in length and detail all mention of public slavery in the *Politics*, indicates that he is a partisan more of private than public ownership of slaves.

Furthermore, since Aristotle observes that people take less care of what is owned by many (*Pol* 1261b33–34), it may be inferred that he thinks it would be more advantageous to the slave to be privately rather than publicly owned,[5] and more advantageous to the master to have fewer slaves (fewer slaves would be less inclined to slight their duties "on the grounds that someone else is taking thought for them"; 1261b35–36). Masters would also benefit from private ownership in that their servants would be able to render them a wider range of services (for example, constant cooking and child care) than they would be able to if they were housed and supervised by the city.

Finally, as I show below, by characterizing slaves not only as private but as domestics (as opposed to field hands), sharing in the life of the family, Aristotle gives us reason to think that each household should have at most a few slaves.

These points suggest that Aristotle's ideal system of slavery does not presuppose nature providing more slaves than free persons or, in other words, does not presuppose an unlikely ratio of slavish to free natures.

NATURAL SLAVES, ANIMALS, AND THE SLAVISH

Aristotle's definition of the natural slave also suggests, perhaps, that a sufficiency of slaves may exist: natural slaves differ from free persons in being able to participate in reason (*koinōnōn logou*) only by perceiving it; they do not have, in the sense of 'have charge of' or have completely, reason (*Pol* 1254b22–23). More precisely, not having the deliberative element (*to bouleutikon*), they cannot deliberate (*Pol* 1260a12). Aristotle explains what he means by passive reason in Book VI of the *Nicomachean Ethics*, where he identifies the intellectual virtues. Among these virtues is a naturally endowed faculty (1143b6–7) that he calls understanding (*sunesis*), the func-

[5] By receiving more or better food, clothing, and housing, a private slave in effect receives more pay (*Oec* 1344b4; note 15 below explains the composition of Book I of the *Oeconomica*).

tion of which is "to judge what someone else says" (1143a12, 14–15). Apparently, then, the person who has understanding can comprehend speech and can furthermore distinguish between speech in the service of good and that in the service of evil. It would, then, be "odd" if slaves did not have moral virtues of some sort, given that they "are human beings and participate in reason" (*Pol* 1259b21–28). What distinguishes natural slaves from free persons, however, is that, having only understanding, they cannot reason on their own and thus cannot conceive or define what is good and bad.[6]

But is this in fact Aristotle's definition of the natural slave? He declares also that "those who are as different [from other men] as the soul from the body or man from beast—and they are in this state if their work is the use of the body, and if this is the best that can come from them—are slaves by nature" (*Pol* 1254b16–19). It should be noticed, however, that Aristotle qualifies or softens the first set of implied comparisons (master = soul, slave = body) with another (man, beast), presenting two inexact threefold comparisons (master = soul = man, slave = body = beast). Thus it is clear at least that he does not mean to suggest that a master is pure soul. And since it is possible that he thinks animals have the capacity to perceive some kind of reason (*Pol* 1254b23–24), one cannot with certainty interpret him to mean that a slave is simply a body.[7] If the spirit of the statement is that 'a master and a slave are as far apart as a soul and a body or, more precisely, as a man and an animal,' then he could be claiming that there are human beings who, like animals, are less than fully rational but have souls or a kind of moral disposition.[8]

---

[6] See note 29.

[7] At 1254b23–24 there is a problem with the text. If one reads *logō* with Alois Dreizehnter, the translation is "The other animals do not obey reason, though perceiving it, but their feelings." If one reads *logou* with H. Rackham and Carnes Lord, the translation is "The other animals, not perceiving reason, obey their feelings." The manuscript with *logou* belongs to the family of the best manuscripts, though Lord says that the more usual translation is produced by Dreizehnter's reading, which I follow; see *Aristotle: The Politics*, trans. Carnes Lord (Chicago: University of Chicago Press, 1984), 26, 248 n. 16.

[8] On this reading, Aristotle does not create the difficulty that many scholars contend he creates. They correctly point out that he says that a slave is a human being and defines a human being as a rational and political (that is, social) animal. But, claiming that he defines a natural slave as simply a body or (at *Pol* 1254b23) as someone who does not possess reason at all, they wrongly insist that he means that natural slavery rests on a distinction of kind rather than of degree. They imply that

Aristotle's claims that animals have a kind of prudence (*NE* 1141a27–28) and even a divine element (*ti theion*) (*PA* 641a19, *GA* 737a10) suggest even more strongly that he does not intend, in comparing slaves to animals, to degrade slaves as much as to show their different nature.[9] As one scholar notes, animals and human beings represent a continuum according to Aristotle: "Taken as a whole, the animal world is found to present a graduated scale of perfection rising to man as its culminating point."[10] What is more, Aristotle implies that on a moral (not structural and functional) spectrum some animals surpass some human beings. Noble animals, sensing moral qualities, are more virtuous than vulgar human beings and are in this way comparable to natural slaves.

By characterizing the natural slave as having and being able to detect moral qualities, Aristotle seems to be implying a distinction between the natural slave (*phusei doulos*) (*Pol* 1254b21) and the vulgar or slavish (*andrapodon*) (*Met* 1075a21, *Pol* 1277a37). The slavish cannot be very responsible and do not respond to admonition (*Met* 1075a22, *Pol* 1260b6–7); by contrast, those who have understanding can recognize what is prudent (*NE* 1143a6–7, 14–15) and so obey it (*Oec* 1344a26).[11] Apparently, then, consistent with the plan of the

---

Aristotle cannot mean that a slave is someone who has partial reason, which is inconceivable, contravenes logic: "That reason should be present even in an imperfect form means a potentiality of reason in its fulness" (Barker, *Political Thought*, 365). Why? One would not claim that a deformed arm has the potential to be a complete arm. The comparison is indeed apt, for just as a deformed arm may perform some of the functions of a complete arm, imperfect reason may perceive some of what complete reason perceives. Both an imperfect arm and imperfect reason have a potential, but it is their own, not that of their complete counterparts. The *eidos* of a species is not the same as the *telos* of an individual member of it; "everything is defined by its work and its capacity (*tē dunamei*)" (*Pol* 1253a23), and capacity is determined less by the species or genus than by the parents or immediate ancestors (*GA* 767b30–768a3). The difference between superior and inferior members of a species is not that the superior can and the inferior cannot actualize a common *telos*, but that "all inferior things reach their end [or perfection; *to telos*] more quickly" (*GA* 775a20–23). If Aristotle means that the natural slave has undeveloped rather than stunted reason, then why does he distinguish between the slave's reason and the child's, which he says is undeveloped (*ateles*) (*Pol* 1260a12–14)? He of course recognizes the difference between being not yet mature and being maimed (see, for example, *DA* 425a10–11).
    [9] This is not to say that Aristotle never uses 'animal' in the negative sense (connoting amorality or immorality).
    [10] John Leofric Stocks, *Aristotelianism* (Boston: Marshall Jones, 1925), 64; see also 65–77; on Aristotle's conception of the ordered beauty and unity of nature generally, see 62–80.
    [11] See also *Politics*, trans. Lord, 248 n. 16.

Politics, Aristotle is discussing ideal slaves and the ideal sort of slavery.[12]

THE MASTER-SLAVE RELATIONSHIP

The finding that natural slaves are morally sensitive and comprehending casts doubt on the claim that Aristotle thinks masters should control them with force and violence. This doubt becomes more reasonable on consideration of other points of the section of the *Politics* (I.4–7) dealing especially with slavery.[13] In chapter 4 he designates a slave as a "possession" belonging wholly to the master (1254a9–13), but in Book II he observes that human beings care most for what is their own (1261b34, 1262b22–23); thus masters look after their slaves. Following up on chapter 5's suggestion that the slave perceives and obeys reason not force, he expounds in chapter 6 that the status of the natural slave derives from ill birth rather than from being captured in war. Similarly, in chapter 7 he explains that mastery (*despoteia*) is not the same as "expertise in acquiring slaves," which is "like a certain kind of expertise in war or hunting" (1255b37–39). Moreover, he characterizes a natural master-slave relationship as mutually affectionate (1255b12–14, 1260a39–40): one can be friends with a slave at least insofar as the latter is a human being, meaning, apparently, to the extent that the slave is morally virtuous (*NE* 1161b5–8).

The Duties of a Master

If not with force and violence, how should masters rule slaves? According to Aristotle, they should do so by including servants in the home, training them, and teaching them moral virtue to the

---

[12] See the Appendix, "The Composition of the *Politics*," pp. 221–26.

[13] In chapter 3 Aristotle introduces the subject of slavery with a passage that points toward my thesis and works against Arendt's (1253b14–22): "Let us speak first about master and slave, so that we may see . . . whether we cannot acquire something in the way of knowledge about these things *that is better than current conceptions.*" He proceeds to give two examples of such conceptions. The first is that there is no difference among types of rule, which he has already denied at 1252a7–9. The second popular view holds that mastery is contrary to nature: "In their view the distinction of master and slave is due to law or convention; there is no natural difference between them: the relation of master and slave is based on force, and being so based has no warrant in justice." It is clear here that he disagrees with both conceptions.

extent possible. To carry out these duties, a master should have the proper disposition toward each slave: she should regard a slave as part of herself, realize that she and the slave share the common goal of maximizing the self-sufficiency of the household, and recognize that therefore ruling badly would disserve them both (*Pol* 1255b9–11, 1254a27–28, 1252b31–1253a1).[14] A master should thus rule over a servant with justice (*NE* 1134b10–12, 1138b7–8). Xenophon, whose views on household management were shown, probably by Theophrastus, to agree largely with Aristotle's, conveys similarly that one should treat servants fairly in order to elicit their cooperation.[15] Xenophon's chief interlocutor in the *Oeconomicus*, Ischomachus, whom the interlocutor Socrates deems to be the greatest estate manager in all of Athens, convinces Socrates that the treatment of servants can make the difference between their continually wanting to run away and their staying at their posts and working.[16] Offering specific advice, Ischomachus recommends that one allow all but the most difficult servants to have families, for this increases their loyalty (*Oec* 1344b17). At the same time, a master should make servants feel a part of the master's family by sharing with them joys and troubles; this too wins their loyalty.[17] The master should share also her things in order to en-

---

[14] Aristotle indicates that the free woman of a household should manage its property (*Pol* 1277b24–25, 1264b1–3). Because he also gives the free male of the household authority over the children and reciprocal authority over his wife (see Chapter 3, "An Educated Being: A Parent?" and "A Pairing Being: A Wife"), he seems to mean when he says that the household should be "run by one alone" (*Pol* 1255b19) not that the male should manage everything but that he should be the sole delegator of authority.

[15] The first book of the Aristotelian *Oeconomica* was largely derived from Xenophon's *Oeconomicus* and Aristotle's *Politics*, probably by Aristotle's successor as head of the Peripatetic school; see the Introduction to Aristotle's *Oeconomica* (Loeb Classical Library, 1935), by G. Cyril Armstrong, 323.

[16] Xenophon, *Oeconomicus* (Loeb Classical Library, 1923), 380–83, 412–13. Xenophon apparently puts his own views into the mouths of both Socrates and Ischomachus in this dialogue; see E. C. Marchant's Introduction, ibid., xxiv.

[17] Ibid., 440–43. Barker makes a similar point to the one I am implying: "The slavery which Aristotle contemplates is one which has lost half its sting. It is a slavery in which the slave is admitted into the life of the family, and in which he becomes imbued with the tone and character of the family in which he lives. . . . He is a member of this lesser association, sharing in its full moral life, as a real 'part' . . . and not as a mere 'condition'" (*Political Thought*, 370). See also Abram N. Shulsky, "The 'Infrastructure' of Aristotle's Politics," (Ph.D. diss., University of Chicago, 1972), 41. Aristotle argues that natural slaves should be domestic servants in part because he thinks that masters should regard them as more than living tools. Ross contends that Aristotle conceives the slave as a domestic and only as a living tool (*Aristotle*, 233, 235).

dear her servant to her. Sharing, rather than exchanging, property is fitting in fact among all household members (*Pol* 1257a20–22). Ischomachus notes that, although servants do not own anything in the household, they may use it with the master's consent; and in the limited sense of tending to the household's property, they have a share in it.[18]

The master should also teach skills to her servants or, ideally, pay others to do so (*Pol* 1255b24–27), in order to promote the well-being of both the household and the servants. Ischomachus charges his wife with the responsibility of teaching weaving, baking, housekeeping, and serving to the servants.[19] Seeing that the servants learn skills is important also because, when skilled, servants may easily be commanded by a master or an overseer, freeing the master for politics and philosophy (1255b33–37).[20]

What the master cannot delegate is her duty to instill in servants the self-restraint and fortitude they need to do their work (*Pol* 1260a15–17, 35–36, b3–4).[21] Simply using or commanding servants is not edifying, but leading them in moral matters apparently is (*Pol* 1255b22–23, 31–36, 1325a25–27, 1260b3–5).[22] Indeed, Xenophon implies, Ischomachus acquired his gentlemanliness not by participating in the Athenian democracy but by such household activities as guiding "the servants into the path of justice with the aid of maxims drawn from the laws of Draco and Solon."[23]

Perhaps with servile virtues (*Pol* 1260a23–24) slaves can understand what it means to be loyal, honest, and conscientious with respect to their tasks, but they cannot generalize these concepts.[24] Thus, Ischomachus teaches his servants honesty by appealing to

---

[18] Xenophon, *Oeconomicus*, 444–45.

[19] Ibid., 426–27, 450–51; Ischomachus indicates that both he and his wife select and teach the servants moral virtue, but he charges her with overseeing them and the household generally (389, 414–27, 442–45); Xenophon and Aristotle seem to agree that the free woman should manage the household.

[20] For Aristotle's views on women as citizens and philosophers, see Chapter 3, "A Speaking Being: A Citizen?" pp. 59–61, and "An Intellectual Being: A Philosopher?" pp. 61–65.

[21] See also *The Politics of Aristotle*, trans. Ernest Barker (Oxford: Clarendon, 1968), 37 n. 4, and Barker, *Political Thought*, 369–70.

[22] The servants' need for personal and moral guidance may also account in part for the fact that "in household service many attendants sometimes do a worse job than fewer" (*Pol* 1261b36–38).

[23] *Oeconomicus*, 410–13, 476–77; see also 442–43.

[24] Or, as Barker says, "[the slave], like the other members of the household, shares in its moral life according to his place and in his degree" (*Political Thought*, 370).

their self-interest and aims "to make [them] upright in the matters that pass through their hands."[25] In sum, the primary aim of mastery on this account is to maximize the moral virtue of slaves.[26]

Slaves: Unequal Natures, Unequal Treatment

Treating servants well, even teaching them skills and virtue, does not guarantee their cooperation. Some human beings, though nature intends for them to be ruled by others, "refuse to obey that intention." Against these, Aristotle claims, nature justifies using the art of war (*Pol* 1256b24–26). Since it is always advantageous for superior to rule inferior, a slavish person unwilling to be ruled by someone more capable fails to perceive his or her own good and what is reasonable, just, and noble (*Pol* 1325b10–12). Such a person is more slavish than other slaves (*Oec* 1344a26), for a *natural* slave "is capable of belonging to another" (*Pol* 1254b20–21).[27] In short, being variously disposed to being ruled means that slaves are variously able to understand what is reasonable. Ischomachus recognizes this, pointing out to Socrates the differences among servants: some are discreet, useful, honest, loyal, temperate in eating and wine drinking and sleeping, modest with men, ambitious, attentive to their duties, possessing good memories, obliging, eager for the improvement of the master's estate (or, what is the same, "covetous of gain in a moderate degree"); but others are rogues prone to mischief, drunkards, sluggards, desperately in love, worthless, incorrigibly greedy, and persistently dishonest.[28]

Both Aristotle and Xenophon conclude therefore that masters should treat slaves variously (*Oec* 1344a29–30, 35–b11). Masters should distribute work according to ability and disposition, for example, giving the trustworthy more responsibility, such as child care (*Pol* 1277a37–38, *Oec* 1344a26). Yet a master should approach all slaves in the same way: trying initially, with patience or tem-

---

[25] *Oeconomicus,* 476–77.

[26] See also Barker, *Political Thought,* 368–70. Household management is concerned with instilling virtue more in the free household members than in the slaves (*Pol* 1259b18–21), but evidently because the slaves have less capacity for it.

[27] It is misleading, then, to say as Ross and Mulgan do that Aristotle divides the human race in two (*Aristotle,* 235; *Political Theory,* 43). There are in fact two reasons slaves differ in their dispositions. Each is born, like every living thing, with a unique "internal principle." And the circumstances in which they live either enhance or impede the exercise of their virtues. Thus, "the same completion is not reached from every principle" (*Ph* 199b17–18).

[28] Xenophon, *Oeconomicus,* 426–29, 440–43, 466–69, 474–77.

perance, to reason with or encourage a slave before resorting to command or force.[29] Indeed, one should treat a slave more like a free adult than like a child (*Pol* 1260b5–7, 1256b26).[30] In fact, "it is better to hold out freedom as a reward for all slaves" (*Pol* 1330a32–33); masters should provide an incentive for all slaves to work well (*Oec* 1344b15–16) and thus better themselves. Freedom should be conditional on their meeting the standards of conduct and performance that nonslaves meet.[31]

Ischomachus and his wife seem to be exemplary masters from Aristotle's point of view. They treat their servants according to merit: "I don't choose to put the deserving on a level with the worthless," Ischomachus explains. In addition, he understands that the two most effective ways to elicit cooperation from servants are speech and reward: to some servants, a master need only say why "it is good for them to obey"; others, however, respond only

[29] As W. W. Fortenbaugh explains, "Aristotle not only recognises the capacity of slaves to perceive reason. He also honours it and protests against withholding reasoned admonition and reason in general (1260b5–7). . . . Reason influences emotions and makes slaves more tractable. Hence a master should not punish a slave without offering a reason which prevents anger by justifying the punishment inflicted (*Rhet.* 1380b16–20). But offering a reason may be more than pragmatic and self-serving. It may also be giving a slave his due. For offering a reason involves acknowledging that slaves can follow reasoned admonition and judge for themselves whether or not a particular course of action is appropriate. . . . Slaves cannot put together reasoned arguments and cannot offer their master reasoned advice. But they can perceive their masters' [sic] reasons and can decide to follow them. To this extent they can partake of reason, so that Aristotle is on firm moral as well as psychological ground when he protests against refusing slaves reasoned admonition. To offer reasoned explanation is to respect a slave's cognitive capacity and to allow him to partake of reason as best he can"; see "Aristotle on Slaves and Women," in *Ethics and Politics*, vol. 2, *Articles on Aristotle*, ed. Jonathan Barnes, Malcolm Schofield, and Richard Sorabji (London: Gerald Duckworth, 1977), 137. Fortenbaugh's interpretation differs from mine in that he does not identify *sunesis* as the slave's capacity and suggests that Aristotle intends his argument to be merely theoretical (ibid., 136–37).

[30] This suggests that, although (nonslavish) children have a greater potential for reasoning than slaves, they cannot understand reasoning as well as slaves. Hence natural slaves are capable of caring for children. At the same time, Aristotle warns that children may acquire vulgar habits from anything vulgar they hear or see (*Pol* 1336a41, b2–3), thereby recommending that the best slaves or fully rational adults such as the parents care for the children.

[31] This condition would allow those persons who might be mistakenly enslaved—because they were born from slavish parents—to win their freedom. (Nature does not prevent either slavish parents from bearing nonslavish offspring or nonslavish parents from bearing slavish offspring; *Pol* 1255b1–4.) Aristotle's provision for emancipation is not then an admission that all slaves, as such, can attain full reason (Barker, *Political Thought*, 365) but a recognition of the injustice that may result from nature's irregularity and a corrective to that injustice.

to the prospect of getting something they want. What motivates servants varies, "some natures being hungry for praise as others for meat and drink." One who seeks his approval, Ischomachus treats "like a free man by making him rich; and . . . as a gentleman." Finally, Ischomachus implies that he and his wife resort to punishment to make servants obey only when the servants are careless, and then they apparently only rebuke them or give them the inferior clothes and shoes when distributing such articles among their servants.[32]

Aristotle and Xenophon are saying, in contemporary terms, that "the relationship between master and natural servant . . . results in despotic rule in inverse proportion to the possession of reasoned speech by the ruled. Only if reasoned speech is wholly absent is the rule perfectly despotic."[33] They both present the use of force or punishment as a last resort or an exception to the way one should generally rule servants. Mastery seems primarily to be the art of rewarding—knowing when, how, whom, and with what to reward (NE 1107a6, 1138b20–25, 1141b27–28).[34] It therefore requires justice (dikaiosunē) or prudence (phronēsis)—the knowledge of and ability to effect what is good for another human being (NE 1130a3–4, 1142b16, 21, 1143b21–22).[35]

THE NATURAL AND PRIVATE STATUS OF SLAVERY

One can discern four respects in which Aristotle believes slavery to be natural. Most obvious, slavery enables those who are more virtuous than slaves to attain moral and intellectual excellence, their natural end, by freeing them from necessary tasks (Pol 1253b24–25, 1254b25–26, 1255a19–21, b35–37; NE 1179a9–11). Slavery is in this respect a condition of virtue or freedom, as Arendt's account also observes.[36] Second, slavery is natural because slaves

---

[32] Xenophon, Oeconomicus, 444–45, 472–77; see also 468–69.

[33] John F. Wilson, "Power, Rule and Politics: The Aristotelian View," Polity 13, no. 1 (1980), 89.

[34] For Xenophon, see Oeconomicus, 474–75.

[35] As Stephen R. L. Clark puts it, "the oikonomos, the head of the household exercising his good sense in its management, is a model for the phronomos [sic] no less than the statesman" (Aristotle's Man [Oxford: Clarendon, 1975], 210).

[36] Human Condition, 30–31, 83 n. 9.

are natural: some human beings can rule themselves only indirectly, by subjecting themselves to morally and intellectually superior human beings;[37] others, wholly lacking in moral virtue, require superiors to take the initiative in showing them what is best for them.[38] Aristotle is thus consistent, saying that both the practice of slavery and slaves are natural. Third, slavery is natural in that it helps a slave realize his potential or natural end as a human being. A slave, being alive, has of course a natural end for which he exists: "It is absurd to suppose that purpose is not present because we do not observe the agent deliberating" (Ph 199b27). As a slave, he learns skills and develops his inclination to belong to another into loyalty, honesty, and friendship. Indeed, he becomes less slavish. For slaves, then, slavery is not a condition for living a full life, it is that life. Fourth, mastery, what effects slavery, is natural in that it edifies a master. By caring for, befriending, training, and morally guiding a slave, a master exercises justice, temperance, and prudence. Strengthening the virtues of the free, mastery thereby facilitates their engagement in politics and philosophy. The benefits politics and philosophy yield are thus attributable in two indirect respects to the practice of slavery.

Whereas slavery ideally realizes a slave's potential, mastery does not maximize, but only enhances, a master's virtue. Nature itself qualifies the virtue mastery confers: ruling over inferiors, whether in private or in public, does not exercise all the virtues of a free person. What distinguishes mastery from forms of public rule and indeed defines it as private is that it creates, by bringing about the satisfaction of needs, opportunity to exercise all virtues or achieve excellence.

One scholar suggests that Aristotle, by claiming that "slavery makes politics and philosophy possible," may be implying a hope that "politics and philosophy can relieve man of his unnatural slavery to nature."[39] Those who are free to engage in politics and

---

[37] Barker makes the same point at Political Thought, 370.

[38] Some natural slaves identify themselves by voluntarily putting themselves in the service, and under the tutelage, of their superiors. As for the rest, their identification is made possible by their showing themselves to be unable to care for themselves. The naturally slavish cannot be identified by their appearance, including their race, because "matter does not produce difference" (Met 1058b3–7, Pol 1254b27–34).

[39] Nichols, "Good Life," 176.

philosophy because of slavery may come to see a way for everyone to live the good life—a way to bring into being a world without slavery or unjust domination, or, in another scholar's words, a world characterized by "political relationships" rather than "political rule."[40] This speculation, however, attributes too much optimism to Aristotle and does not account for the inclusion of slaves in the best regime (*Pol* 1328b19–20, 1329a35–36, 1330a25–30, 1334a2). We should conclude that Aristotle thinks there could be, with the help of politics and philosophy, not a regime without slavery but a regime with the right kind of slavery—a sort of private sponsorship and form of rule. For, although politics and philosophy may relieve us of our slavery to nature, they cannot alter the natural human hierarchy. Forms of rule, both public and private, remain indispensable.

---

[40] Wilson, "Power, Rule and Politics," 96. "Political relationships," in contrast to "political rule," rest "neither on power or force, nor on command, but on discussion and persuasion" and can form only if "moral and intellectual virtue . . . are developed in due measure in each of [a political community's] members."

3

WOMEN, THE PUBLIC, AND THE PRIVATE

Understanding Aristotle's vision of the public and the private requires deciphering his views on women. On the one hand, he observes that women constitute half of a city's free persons (*Pol* 1260b19, 1269b16–18, 1299a20–22);[1] on the other, he mentions them otherwise in his political philosophy only in connection with the household. That women in his view are both free and live in the household does not, as we have seen, present a contradiction—in fact, it serves to support my claim that he believes one may live a free life in the household; but that Aristotle makes a point of observing that women are "half of the city" and yet seemingly advocates their engaging only in household activities—not a half share of a city's activities—does make one doubt the consistency of his views on women. Or, assuming the consistency of his views, this apparent difficulty makes one wonder what other activities he thinks women should undertake, what kind of life they should lead. In answering this question, I aim to show that the appropriate kind of life is one that helps bring about harmony between the public and the private.

In trying to discern the life Aristotle advocates for women, it is helpful to consider what he thinks of them—of their distinctiveness from men and of their capabilities. In recent years,

---

[1] W. L. Newman observes that at 1299a22 "it is implied that women and children are citizens, which is of course not strictly the case"; *The Politics of Aristotle*, vol. 4 (New York: Arno Press, 1973), 257.

scholars, some in the context of advancing feminist theories, have charged that Aristotle disparages women. One group, for example, Maryanne Cline Horowitz, Eva C. Keuls, G. E. R. Lloyd, Nicole Loraux, and Susan Moller Okin, maintain that Aristotle's biological writings are misogynistic because they portray the female as inferior to the male.[2] Another group, for example, Stephen R. L. Clark, Jean Bethke Elshtain, and Okin, argue that Aristotle, by relegating women to the household, regards them as suited only to necessary, not political or intellectual, activity.[3] This latter group accuse Aristotle not only of trapping women in the household, but, like Arendt, of depicting the household as unable to provide fulfilling activities. Hence, they conclude that Aristotle regards women as unfulfilled and unfulfillable: indicating that women should be locked inside, he evidently thinks that they are unfit to experience the freedom of the world.[4] Whether this interpretation is accurate remains to be considered.

THE FEMALE: A BIOLOGICALLY INFERIOR BEING?

An inquiry into Aristotle's views on women should begin perhaps by considering the following questions: (1) what, according to

[2] Horowitz "Aristotle and Woman," *Journal of the History of Biology* 9, no. 2 (1976), 183–213; Keuls, *The Reign of the Phallus: Sexual Politics in Ancient Athens* (New York: Harper & Row, 1985); Lloyd, *Science, Folklore and Ideology: Studies in the Life Sciences in Ancient Greece* (Cambridge: Cambridge University Press, 1983); Loraux, *Les enfants d'Athena: Idées athéniennes sur la citoyenneté et la division des sexes* (Paris: François Maspero, 1981); Okin, *Women in Western Political Thought* (Princeton: Princeton University Press, 1979). For a response to Horowitz and to the charge of sexism in Aristotle's biology, see Johannes Morsink, "Was Aristotle's Biology Sexist?" *Journal of the History of Biology* 12, no. 1 (1979), 83–112.

[3] Clark, *Aristotle's Man: Speculations upon Aristotelian Anthropology* (Oxford: Clarendon, 1975), and "Aristotle's Woman," *History of Political Thought* 3, no. 2 (1982); Elshtain, *Public Man, Private Woman: Women in Social and Political Thought* (Princeton: Princeton University Press, 1981), and "Aristotle, the Public-Private Split, and the Case of the Suffragists," in *The Family in Political Thought*, ed. Jean Bethke Elshtain (Amherst: University of Massachusetts Press, 1982).

[4] Arendt admits, however, that according to this ancient conception of the household *both* the male and the female functions—"the labor of man to provide nourishment, and the labor of the woman in giving birth"—"were subject to the same urgency of life." On her interpretation, life outside the household is worthy only of man, not of woman, but the man must earn it by mastering necessity. Arendt is correct to point out that in Aristotle's view no human being can escape necessity; see *The Human Condition* (Chicago: University of Chicago Press, 1958), 30–31, 48 n. 38.

Aristotle, are the biological ways females differ from males? (2) does he think that these biological differences are marks of inferiority? and (3) in the case of human beings, does he indicate that these differences bear on their moral and intellectual abilities and thus on their potential as political actors and thinkers? In this section I address the first two questions; I answer the third question in the course of examining what Aristotle says about women in his political works.

Three Definitions of Gender

According to Aristotle, male and female differ in three significant biological respects. In explaining the first, Aristotle comes remarkably close to the modern chromosomal theory of sex differentiation. He says that the principle (*archē*) of an animal—which is situated in the heart—determines its sex (*GA* 766a31–b4); gender is thus determined before the appearance of sexual parts.[5] The possession of male or female parts is, nonetheless, the second significant respect in which male and female differ: "A creature, however, really is male or female only from the time it has got [such] parts" (*GA* 766b5–6). Thus, Aristotle approached saying that a male-coded embryo and a female-coded embryo appear to be the same until seven weeks after conception. Third, male and female differ in their reproductive functions: "By a 'male' animal we mean one which generates in another, by 'female' one which generates in itself" (*GA* 716a14–15). It is clear, then, that Aristotle regards sexual parts and reproductive functions as merely manifestations, not causes, of maleness and femaleness. At the same time, by noting the undetectability of the male and female principles, Aristotle leaves open the possibility of their ambiguity.

---

[5] According to Joseph Needham, *A History of Embryology*, 2d ed. (New York: Abelard-Schuman, 1959), it was in fact Aristotle who "pushed back the origin of sex-determination to the very beginning of embryonic development" (54). For more on this topic, see Konrad Blersch, *Wesen und Entstehung des Sexus im Denken der Antike* (Stuttgart: Verlag von W. Kohlhammer, 1937), as recommended by Needham, and Erna Lesky, *Die Zeugungs und Vererbungs Lehren der Antike und ihr Nachwirken* (Wiesbaden: Franz Steiner Verlag, 1950). Needham claims further that "the depth of Aristotle's insight into the generation of animals has not been surpassed by any subsequent embryologist" (42). For a discussion of some of Aristotle's claims in this field that are "substantially modern" (48) and were profoundly influential, see especially 37–60.

Form and Matter: Contributions to Procreation

Though manifestations, reproductive functions are nonetheless notable features of gender. Aside from the one generating outside and the other inside itself, the most striking difference between male and female apparatuses is that during procreation the male provides the form, the principle of movement, or the soul, whereas the female provides the matter, material, or body (*GA* 729a10–12, b14–21, 735a9, 737a28–30, 738b20–27, 740b25, 765b9–15). It appears that the male provides an offspring's being and the female merely nourishment for it. And is this not proof, as Keuls claims, that "Aristotle was one of the fiercest misogynists of all times, obsessed with the need to prove that women play no genetic part in reproduction"?[6] No, it is not; the context of these statements reveals that they do not debase the female. It explains that the male provides sentient soul—only a part of the soul (*GA* 736b14–27). Moreover, the sentient part of the soul endows living beings (only) with sense perception—without it they would be lifeless limbs (*GA* 741a13–14). The male, then, through his semen, provides that part of the soul that "cannot be separated from the body" (*DA* 413a3–5). The semen also contains the rational part of the soul, but this part is generated not from the male himself but from "outside," and is thus "partly separable" from physical matter (*GA* 736b30–39, 737a8–12). "Reason alone enters in, as an additional factor, from outside, and alone is divine; because bodily activity has nothing to do with its activity" (*GA* 736b27–29).[7] A physical substance cannot alone yield a nonphysical entity.[8]

---

[6] *Reign of the Phallus*, 405.

[7] Semen supplies reason in its potential state. At what point during gestation it becomes actualized Aristotle does not say; see *Aristotle: Generation of Animals*, trans. A. L. Peck (Loeb Classical Library, 1963), 169 n. a; W. D. Ross, *Aristotle: A Complete Exposition of His Works and Thought* (New York: Meridian Books, 1959), 121. We can, however, infer at least that Aristotle does not think reason becomes actualized from the moment of conception, since in the *Politics* he indicates that abortions should be legal as long as they are "induced before perception and life arises" (1335b24–26). Despite this ambiguity, according to Needham, Aristotle's "description of the entry of the various souls into the embryo was afterwards made the basis for the legal rulings concerning abortion." Yet, Needham claims that Aristotle "did not think, however, that [the different sorts of souls] were in-breathed from any source external to the embryo." He admits that Aristotle includes a final cause in his theory of causation but gives nonetheless the contrived explanation that "Aristotle alone was unharmed by Aristotelianism. . . . He himself knew how to change rapidly from metaphysician into physicist and back again, how to bow politely to the final cause and press on with the dissection" (*History of Embryology*, 40, 49–50, 56, 59).

[8] See also John Leofric Stocks, *Aristotelianism* (Boston: Marshall Jones, 1925), 80.

In response to those who consider Aristotle's science and its implications misogynistic, it is true that Aristotle maintains that the man contributes something more important to reproduction than the woman; both sense perception ("a sort of knowledge") and reason contribute more to living well than does having a body (GA 731a32–34, 736b30–32, 732a4–10). Indeed, since the mental faculties constitute the essence of a human being, in Aristotle's view a child could be said to be more the essence of his or her father than of his or her mother.[9] But if arrogating the procreative function to the male, Aristotle seems hardly to intend the repression of the female;[10] if it carries any social or political implications, the finding that the man is more the source of a child than the woman suggests that he ought to be the more important parent.[11] If Aristotle indeed

[9] There is debate as to whether the ancient Greeks commonly supposed that the male parent makes the more important contribution to reproduction and to heredity and as to whether Aristotle thought so. According to Lloyd, the supposition prevailed before Aristotle, who then provided "massive support" for it (Science, 86). As evidence for its prevalence, Lloyd mentions Aeschylus's Eumenides, in which Apollo defends Orestes against the charge of matricide by arguing that he was really the offspring of his father, Agamemnon, not of Clytemnestra: "She who is called the child's mother is not its begetter, but the nurse of the newly sown conception. / The begetter is the male." Apollo then notes Athena as proof that "there can be a father without a mother" (658–64; trans. Hugh-Lloyd Jones [Englewood Cliffs: Prentice Hall, 1970]). According to Alan H. Sommerstein, however, this was not a widespread view. Sommerstein claims that the Athenian public would have recognized and perhaps ridiculed the view as "the speculative theory of an advanced philosopher," even if they would not have associated it in particular with Anaxagoras (to whom Aristotle ascribes it at GA 763b31–33), for they regarded the mother-child bond as closer than the bond between father and child; see Aeschylus, Eumenides, ed. Alan H. Sommerstein (Cambridge: Cambridge University Press, 1989), 206–8. Needham argues that "the denial of physiological maternity" may have originated among the Egyptians, that it prevailed a century before Aristotle (he also cites Eumenides), and that Aristotle's own beliefs "are in striking contrast" to it (History of Embryology, 43–44). My aim is not to adjudicate the historical claims but merely to make clear that the doctrine of physiological paternity was at least not unheard of in Aristotle's time and to point out that Aristotle seems neither to endorse it unequivocally nor dispute it entirely. It is true that he disagrees on some points with Anaxagoras, as well as with Empedocles and Democritus (GA 763b31ff.), but his findings nonetheless expand on their work (see Generation of Animals, trans. Peck, xvi). He does suggest that a mother provides genetic input to her offspring (contrary to Keuls, Reign of the Phallus, 145, and Lloyd, Science, 95–96, but see 96 n. 140)—thus siding with the majority of the Presocratics (see Eumenides, ed. Sommerstein, 208; Lloyd, Science, 86–111). But he distinguishes himself from them by claiming that the female does not contribute the same kind and amount of seed as does the male (see Lloyd, Science, 91–97). He thus manages to synthesize the two main scientific views of procreation.

[10] Keuls, Reign of the Phallus, 145.

[11] Working against this suggestion is Aristotle's claim that male animals do not trouble over their young (GA 759b7–8) and that females, especially human females, are "more considerate in rearing the young" and "more compassionate" than males

understands nature to be conferring the responsibility of raising children more on the father than on the mother, then Aristotle's biology could be understood to intend—if one assumes that child rearing is a burden—the repression of the male. Indeed, it is ironic that Keuls thinks it chauvinistic for Aristotle to claim that a father is more a father than a mother is a mother.[12]

In addition, by saying that "the menstrual discharge is semen, though . . . it lacks one constituent, and one only, the principle of soul" (GA 737a28–30), Aristotle clearly means that woman's matter—not the woman herself—lacks soul, and then again only sentient soul.[13] Like males, she receives the principle of soul when conceived. A female results when the matter holds sway over the form (GA 766b15–17), but form still infuses the matter.[14] Moreover, the principle of soul she receives is not wholly from her father but in part from outside. Finally, Aristotle gives no indication as to whether males and females receive equal or unequal measures or kinds of rational soul from outside; presumably, the amount or kind received varies from individual to individual regardless of gender.[15] We cannot then attribute to Aristotle, as Okin contends, a "basic assumption that the male is always and in every way superior to the female."[16] Indeed, Aristotle says, it must be

(HA 608b2, 8–9). But Aristotle's political works indicate that human child rearing ought to go beyond comforting and that fathers should contribute (NE 1162a4–7; see also note 44, below). Furthermore, Aristotle notes in his biological works exceptions to the general rule that females tend their young (e.g., HA 621a20ff.); and since ancient Greek literature traditionally compared women to bees, it is most noteworthy that Aristotle points out that the worker bees not the queen bees tend to the offspring (GA 759b7–8; see also note 49, below). Thus, Aristotle may be confident that female animals tend the young (Lloyd, Science, 99) while believing nonetheless that raising children is or ought to be a different enterprise. What is natural to most other animals may not be natural to us (see Clark, "Aristotle's Woman," 189).

[12] Reign of the Phallus, 145, 405–6.

[13] It is in this respect only that "the female is so to speak a deformed [or maimed] male" (GA 737a27–28, a remark that is frequently taken out of context). Thus, contrary to Lloyd's assertion that Aristotle understood the relationship between male and female as an example of that between form and matter (Science, 86), the female is simply the inferior reproductive partner.

[14] See also Stocks, Aristotelianism, 79; Ross, Aristotle, 122; Clark, Aristotle's Man, 210, and "Aristotle's Woman," 181. By the same token, even if a male results, nutritive soul—the female element—is still necessarily present.

[15] Although Aristotle uses nous at GA 736b27, the context suggests that he means all forms of reason or intellectual virtue. On the various forms, see NE VI; on Aristotle's three different usages of nous, see Terence Irwin's glossary in his translation of the Nicomachean Ethics (Indianapolis: Hackett, 1985), 429.

[16] Okin, Women, 82; see also 86; Lloyd, Science, 104–5.

"granted that the female possesses the same soul [as the male]" (*GA* 741a7–8). Both receive nutritive soul from the mother and sentient soul from the father, and both may or may not receive soul from outside.

Women: A Different Species?

The preceding observations undermine Loraux's and Lloyd's contention that Aristotle shared and promoted the (allegedly) prevailing ancient Athenian view that women are a different species from men.[17] According to Loraux, this view had its genesis in Greek myths. These myths, following the Hesiodic formula, told that all women were born of, or descended from, one woman. Women were not only self-reproducing but also unlike men in that they were introduced into the world rather than being already there. Loraux's evidence that the ancient Greeks regarded women as a different species is that Aristotle presents as a contemporary belief the 'rule' that daughters resemble their mothers. Loraux contends, moreover, that although Aristotle refutes the possibility of female auto-reproduction, he too portrays women as being as different from men as birds are from fish.[18] With respect to Loraux's first point, Aristotle says in fact that females take after their mothers more than they do their fathers (*GA* 767b3–4), that some take after only their fathers (*GA* 767a37–b1), and that some take after neither parent (*GA* 767b4–5). The 'rule' allows for some resemblance between fathers and daughters and admits of—perhaps many—exceptions. Moreover, Aristotle makes no reference to common opinion (*GA* 767a36–b6). Second, his account of the developing embryo suggests that male and female human beings are much more alike than are birds and fish. His calling male and female "contraries" (*GA* 724b8–10, 766a22) and claiming that they have different natures (the female is, for example, "passive," "weaker and colder"; *GA* 729b13–16, 775a14, 30–35) seems to support Loraux's claim. Aristotle explains in the *Metaphysics*, however, that women differ from men not as footed from winged animals but as white from black swans (1058a31–37). Male and female of the same species differ merely physically; their "essence" and "for-

---

[17] Lloyd cites Loraux (*Science*, 94–95).
[18] Loraux, *Enfants d'Athena*, 76–78, 80–81, 91–92. "The first woman of the *Theogony* is not the 'mother of humanity,' but the 'mother' of women" (78).

mula" are not contrary (1058b8–10, 21–24). Again, "matter does not produce difference" (1058b7).[19] Thus, Aristotle declares, "woman does not differ in species from man" (1058a29–31).

Our Androgynous Natures

"Although male and female are indeed said in referring to the whole animal, it is not male or female in respect of the whole of itself, but only in respect of a particular faculty and a particular part" (*GA* 716a28–31). Apart from their sexual characteristics, human beings are neither male nor female; they are, more precisely, androgynous: "Things are alive in virtue of having in them a share of the male and of the female" (*GA* 732a11–12). It is not surprising, then, that "a boy actually resembles a woman in physique, and a woman is so to speak an infertile male" (*GA* 728a17–18); or that mutilating "just one part [of males] results in . . . close approximation to the appearance of the female" (*GA* 766a26–29, 716b5–11). If Aristotle's biology is misogynistic, then it must also be misanthropic.

Ultimately, then, Aristotle reconciles his apparently inconsistent claims that male and female souls are basically the same, that they are opposite, and that they are both mixed. 'Male' and 'female' are opposite principles, the one being of movement, the other of material cause (*GA* 715a5–7).[20] But as *archai* they are abstractions; neither can exist without the other. They are compelled to unite. The result is necessarily a combination of male and female (*GA* 766b5–6). Nonetheless, male *or* female parts emerge (*GA* 766a37–b1), since "mixing is the coming to be one of what is mixed as they are changed."[21] In addition, 'male' and 'female' are qualities that generally attach to human beings having, respectively, male and female sexual parts. In sum, Aristotle seems to be claiming that, although there are male and female qualities, actual men and actual women manifest various combinations of these qualities. In-

---

[19] It is not then evident why "[Aristotle's] statement that women have fewer teeth than men (*Hist. An.* 501b)" is "the nadir" of his "misogyny parading as science" (Keuls, *Reign of the Phallus*, 145). Keuls, not Aristotle, seems to think that this is a statement about woman's inferiority.

[20] See also *Generation of Animals,* trans. Peck, xlv.

[21] This is Clark's paraphrase of *On Generation and Corruption* 328b22; he refers the reader to *De Sensu* 447a12; cf. III.3.11. As Clark explains, "the metaphysics of form and matter perverts, but does not quite obliterate the theory of mixture" (*Aristotle's Man,* 208).

deed, Aristotle seems even to imply, paradoxically, that deviations from the norm are the norm (*GA* 767b10–12, *Pol* 1259b1–3).

THE HOUSEHOLD: A WOMAN'S DOMAIN

Aristotle's biological findings about the sexes inform his political understanding of men and women. Of most political relevance are his observations that men and women have both male and female qualities, and that men generally exhibit male, and women female, qualities. The latter is the *reason* (not given by Clark) that "Aristotle himself would commission men and women for the male and female roles."[22] What are these roles? Speaking generally, Aristotle regards the household, as some feminist scholars are quick to point out, as woman's domain, and the domain outside the household as man's. Left unqualified, this generalization is misleading. But it is helpful at this point because it indicates that Aristotle's political understanding of men and women concerns the household. Since we know that household activities cultivate moral virtue, we have grounds for speculating about the capabilities and duties of women. More specifically, though Aristotle writes about woman largely with reference to her household tasks, he gives us reason to think that he believes her to be fit for life outside the household.

A PAIRING BEING: A WIFE

To recall from Chapter 1, according to Aristotle a man and a woman form a household for many reasons: natural affection, reproduction, assistance. The ideal union not only realizes these aims but makes each partner more virtuous. Between two decent human beings, this happens naturally, for each imitates what in the other he or she approves of, corrects the other, and engages in virtuous activities (*NE* 1172a10–13).[23] Pairing with another good human being is a means to self-perfection.[24] This view is not the

[22] Ibid., 211.
[23] See also ibid.
[24] We can be reasonably certain that Aristotle recommends either lifelong monogamy or (serial) monogamy for both sexes. He says that "love is ideally a sort of excess of friendship, and that can only be felt towards one person" (*NE* 1171a11–12).

same as that of Aristotle's contemporaries and predecessors for whom marriage was a religious act and union, the aim of which was to perpetuate the domestic worship. But it resembles that view in holding marriage in highest esteem. In this respect, Aristotle's view comes closer to that of an earlier age than to that of his own, if Fustel de Coulanges is right about the nuance between them: "In ancient times, instead of designating marriage by its particular name, *gamos*, they designated it simply by the word *telos*, which signifies sacred ceremony, as if marriage had been, in those ancient times, the ceremony sacred above all others."[25]

In contrast to that view, however, the sacredness of marriage according to Aristotle coincides with its pleasurableness. For his contemporaries and ancestors, "marriage . . . was obligatory. Its aim was not pleasure; its principal object was not the union of two beings who were pleased with each other, and who wished to go united through the pleasures and the trials of life."[26] Insofar as pleasure and virtue are inseparable in Aristotle's view (*NE* 1175b27–28, 1176a15–19), the aim of marriage is pleasure. Through proper pleasure, the best marriage yields happiness.

One might, however, doubt that Aristotle means to convey that marriage should give pleasure and happiness to the woman. For, according to him, a husband should rule a wife (*Pol* 1259a39, 1260a10) and a human being cannot be happy without exercising reason or speech (*logos*) to the extent he or she is able (*NE* 1097b22–25, 1098a3–8). The "political rule" that should obtain between a husband and a wife cannot be the usual sort whereby "the ruler and the ruled interchange in turn," because husband and wife are not equals (*Pol* 1259a39–b10). But if they are not equal and should not take turns ruling, then why does Aristotle say that their proper relationship is political? Perhaps, as Arlene W. Saxonhouse proposes, Aristotle means that just as political order requires citizens who are equal to make some among them superior—by distributing power, titles, and honors—so the household requires that

---

Furthermore, friendship requires association; indeed "there is nothing so characteristic of friends as living together," and "one cannot live with many people and divide oneself up among them" (*NE* 1157b6–19, 1171a3). See also Chapter 1, note 23, p. 20.

[25] Numa Denis Fustel de Coulanges, *The Ancient City: A Study on the Religion, Laws, and Institutions of Greece and Rome* (Baltimore: Johns Hopkins University Press, 1980), 32–45, quoting 36.

[26] Ibid., 43.

someone acquire the accoutrements and power to rule. Conventions more than nature or virtue may sustain the husband's rule.[27]

This interpretation is correct to suggest that Aristotle does not regard the difference between men and women as radical. As Saxonhouse notes, he says that nature only tends to make males fitter to lead than females (*Pol* 1259b1–3). One might note further that males are constituted without this superiority not seldom but sometimes (*pote*); and, in addition to these males, two other classes of males—the young and the old—are less likely to hold sway (*kratein*) over females (*GA* 767b11–12). Moreover, Aristotle does not speculate on the extent of the usual gap between male and female leadership capabilities. Nonetheless, he maintains their *natural* inequality in this area in particular (*Pol* 1259b1–2, 1260a10–12). Thus, we cannot account for Aristotle's considering the marital relationship political on the grounds that he deems the inequality characterizing it to be mostly superficial or conventional.

Furthermore, it is not evident that a central or defining presupposition of political rule is equality (for example, "intellect rules appetite with political and kingly rule"; *Pol* 1254b5–6). Of additional importance to Aristotle's definition of political rule is, as noted, the notion of reciprocity or alternation between ruler and ruled (*Pol* 1261a30–31, 1277b9–10, 1279a8–10; *NE* 1132b33–34). Thus another problem arises: if the husband stands always as ruler to his wife (naturally or conventionally), then in what sense can political rule obtain between them?

To see that Aristotle is not contradicting himself one must first appreciate that equality may be proportional or arithmetic (*NE* 1134a26–28),[28] allowing marital rule to be not only political but "aristocratic" (*NE* 1160b32–33, 1161a22–25).[29] Second, as Mary P. Nichols points out, "[Aristotle's] concept of political rule does not necessitate that rulers and subjects exchange positions. To rule and

---

[27] "Family, Polity, and Unity: Aristotle on Socrates' Community of Wives," *Polity* 15, no. 2 (1982), 205–6. R. G. Mulgan also proposes this interpretation but does not think that Aristotle is committed to it since he presents the household as arising out of natural differences; see *Aristotle's Political Theory: An Introduction for Students of Political Theory* (Oxford: Clarendon, 1977), 46–47.

[28] See also Mulgan, *Aristotle's Political Theory*, 37, and Mary P. Nichols, *Socrates and the Political Community: An Ancient Debate* (Albany: State University of New York Press, 1987), 159, which cites Mulgan.

[29] According to Saxonhouse, the accounts of the marital relationship in the *Politics* and in the *Nicomachean Ethics* are somewhat different ("Family, Polity, and Unity," 206 n. 5).

be ruled in turn may mean that rulers recognize their subjects' independence. Thus, while [a ruler] rules them, *he is also ruled by them*—his rule is only partial, or 'in part.' He is limited by his subjects' desires and opinions, which he must take into account in his choices and actions."[30] Or, as Clark says, the man "should rule as would one destined to take his turn as subject."[31]

The husband-wife relationship is reciprocal and approaches equality also in that each partner compensates for (*NE* 1160b33–35, 1162a22–24) and corrects the other's deficiencies.[32] Each equally needs the other to achieve wholeness. What is required for a union to be satisfactory, then, is not necessarily the leadership of the male but the couple's "mutual help and comfort."[33]

Useful for understanding Aristotle's conception of marriage is Hegel's. As Aristotle believes, Hegel points out that it is the difference between the sexes and among individuals not of the same blood lines that makes a union between a man and a woman both possible and ethical; for only a union of differences can give rise to separate wholenesses and only separate wholenesses emerging from a mixture of differences can unite. In the best marriage each individual freely surrenders "immediate exclusive individuality" for inclusive individuality.[34] Ideally, according to Aristotle, it seems, marriage should effect a dynamic equilibrium between male and female virtues not only in a household but within a husband and a wife themselves.

An Ethical Being: A Household Manager

For the sake of survival, marriage leads to the acquisition of a house and domestic servants (*Pol* 1252a30–34, b9–14). The husband should rule the household only insofar as delegating the task

---

[30] *Socrates*, 159, emphasis added. Nichols is, however, describing Aristotle's view of the relationship between a statesman and his subjects.

[31] "Aristotle's Woman," 184. Clark, however, takes Aristotle to mean that only in some matters would a husband listen to a wife: their rule is "in part" insofar as "they share the rule of the household, not by turns but by role-division."

[32] See also Xenophon, *Oeconomicus*, trans. E. C. Marchant (Loeb Classical Library, 1923), 422–23.

[33] Clark, *Aristotle's Man*, 209; see also Xenophon, *Oeconomicus*, 418–19.

[34] See *Hegel's Philosophy of Right*, trans. T. M. Knox (London: Oxford University Press, 1967), secs. 161–68.

to his wife (*Pol* 1255b19, 1260a10, 1277b24–25; *NE* 1160b34–35), which is the just treatment she is due (*NE* 1134b16). He warrants the title of household manager along with her, however, because he supplies provisions (*Pol* 1277b24–25). This division of labor is natural (*NE* 1162a20–24). Thus, Aristotle would regard Xenophon's Ischomachus as exemplary, for he takes responsibility for the household's "incomings" and directs his wife "to remain indoors and send out those servants whose work is outside, and superintend those who are to work indoors, and to receive the incomings, and distribute so much of them as must be spent, and watch over so much as is to be kept in store, and take care that the sum laid by for a year be not spent in a month."[35]

Evidently, along with Xenophon, Aristotle thinks that women tend to have the virtue of thrift, which is not stinginess but the ability to use property "with moderation and liberally" (*Pol* 1265a32–37).[36] This ability is choiceworthy, as is the character it presupposes (*Pol* 1265a35–38; *NE* 1120a2–3, 1121b3–10). But Aristotle also evidently thinks that wives can and ought to acquire prudence and justice, for superintending servants well requires, to recall from Chapter 2, instilling as much virtue as possible in them by reward, admonishment, and if necessary punishment. Having only the deliberative element (*to bouleutikon*) without authority (*akuron*) (*Pol* 1260a12–13), perhaps the female (*to thēlu*) alone would have difficulty ruling servants, but as a wife she acquires authority.[37] And over time, through experience, she develops her deliberative capacity into prudence (*phronēsis*) (*NE* 1141b8–10, 1142a14–

[35] Xenophon, *Oeconomicus*, 388–89, 424–25; see also 420–23, 444–45.
[36] See also Clark, *Aristotle's Man*, 210, and "Aristotle's Woman," 182.
[37] Thus I propose a variation of the view that a woman's deliberative capacity lacks authority because it would not prevail, would even be scorned, in the society of men. Another interpretation of Aristotle's claim is that a woman's emotions often overrule her reason. W. W. Fortenbaugh dismisses the first view (while noting that it would be "true enough") and proposes the second in "Aristotle on Slaves and Women," in *Ethics and Politics*, vol. 2, *Articles on Aristotle*, ed. Jonathan Barnes, Malcolm Schofield, and Richard Sorabji (London: Gerald Duckworth, 1977), 138–39. Saxonhouse, citing Fortenbaugh, notes both views but commits to neither; she points out, however, that *kuros* does not mean "is superior to" but "has authority over" ("Family, Polity, and Unity" 208). See also Horowitz, "Aristotle and Woman," 207–12, which gives evidence that Aristotle uses the adjective *akuros* "both as a political term implying lack of legitimate power or authority and as a biological and medical term implying inadequacy of capacity" (207). Thus, Horowitz concludes, a woman has no right to deliberate *because* her deliberative faculty is impotent (207, 211).

16, b28–33). Having temperance, justice, and prudence, Aristotle's ideal woman, like Ischomachus's wife, not only "is quite capable of looking after the house by herself," but perhaps, as Ischomachus says of all masters, can be made fit to be a king (*Pol* 1277a14–15, b16–18).[38]

AN EDUCATED BEING: A PARENT?

Assigning his wife the duties of overseeing their household property and directing their servants, the husband should not charge her also with the full responsibility of raising their children. Aristotle gives at least three reasons why the father should assume in fact the greater share of child rearing.[39] The first is the husband's obligation to treat his wife justly (*NE* 1134b16). Second, a child needs a leader (*ton hēgoumenon*) (*Pol* 1260a31–33), and "the male is by nature fitter to lead [*hēgemonikōteron*] than the female" (*Pol* 1259b2). Third, and similarly, raising children is difficult; directing servants to do things (which they know how to do) (*Pol* 1255b31–35) is easier than minding and teaching (generally intemperate and uncooperative) children (*NE* 1162a4–7, 1179b32–34; *Pol* 1260b6–7).[40]

Accordingly, when Aristotle explicitly mentions the parent-child relationship in the *Politics* he uses *patrikē* (paternal rule) to characterize it (1253b10, 1259a38),[41] and in the *Nicomachean Ethics* he refers to rule over children in the household as *patrikē* (1180a19).

---

[38] For Xenophon, see *Oeconomicus*, 414–15, 472–73. Although ruling over nonfree persons does not provide the experience required to be a good (political) ruler (*Pol* 1277b7–9, 13–16), the experience of being ruled as a free person does (*Pol* 1277b9–13). Moreover, as shown, the wife does in part rule her husband. The suggestion that in Aristotle's view women might be capable of ruling does not deny that he thinks they will usually not rule as well as men.

[39] See also E. Barker, *The Political Thought of Plato and Aristotle* (New York: Dover, 1959), 398, which states similarly that "there are times when Aristotle seems almost ready to think that the father may suffice for the moral instruction of his children."

[40] Indeed, the task is so difficult it requires help from the regime (*NE* 1180a14–22; *Pol* 1337a11–12, 22–27).

[41] There is dispute among translators over whether the term at 1253b10 should read *patrikē* (paternal rule) or *teknopoietikē* (parental [rule]). I follow Dreizehnter's reading because, (1) when enumerating the roles of household members at 1253b6–7, Aristotle lists "master, slave, husband, wife, father, and children"—"mother" does not appear; and (2) Aristotle himself seems to confirm this reading by using *patrikē* (undisputably) at 1259a38 when again discussing household relationships.

Moreover, he states that "rule over the children is kingly; for the male parent is ruler on the basis of both affection and of seniority" (*Pol* 1259b10–12).[42] Listing the types of rule in the household, he states that "the man rules the child" (*Pol* 1260a10). He connects "children" and "male parent" or "father" (*Pol* 1259b16–17, 1260b9) and couples the phrase "rule over children" with "and wife" (*Pol* 1259a39, 1278b37–38). One argument he gives against elderly men becoming fathers is that they are not able to give their children paternal assistance (*tōn paterōn boētheia*) (*Pol* 1334b40–1335a1).[43] Finally, the discussion of the parent-child relationship in the *Nicomachean Ethics* (1161b16–1162a9), in which Aristotle uses—by contrast—the term "parents" (*goneis*), is mostly about the love between parents and children.[44] Thus, Aristotle supports in his political works a possible social implication of his finding that the male is physiologically the more important reproductive partner.[45]

Yet Aristotle points out that children are a "common good" (*koinon agathon*) (*NE* 1162a28); husband and wife seem to be, as Ischomachus says, "partners [*koinōnous*] in their children."[46] In one place Aristotle says that household management includes giving "serious attention . . . to the virtue of free persons" (*Pol* 1259b18, 21, 1259a39–40).[47] If a woman is to instill in her children the virtue befitting a free person, then she herself must be educated. In fact, "both children and women must necessarily be educated looking to the regime" (*Pol* 1260b15–16). But the reason for educating women is the excellence of the *city* (1260b16–18). A woman's excellence can contribute directly to that of the city only if she is active in one of the two ways most befitting a free person (*Pol* 1255b36–37, 1260b18–19). Otherwise, her education can indirectly serve the city through her education of her children, the future partners (cit-

---

[42] According to Aristotle, a father should be twenty years older than the mother of their children (*Pol* 1335a28–29, 33–34).

[43] See *Politics*, vol. 3, ed. Newman, 459, note on 1334b40.

[44] This interpretation may account for the assertion that "a father"—not a mother—"may disown a son" (*NE* 1163b19). On this interpretation, a child, as a kind of student of the father, and not so much of the mother, is more likely to disappoint the father than the mother; also, mothers tend to love their children more than fathers do (*NE* 1161b26–27, 1168a25–26).

[45] Aristotle seems then to be criticizing the general practice in ancient Greece of a male youth being "socialized not through identification with his father, but through the erastes relationship" (Clark, "Aristotle's Woman," 186).

[46] Xenophon, *Oeconomicus*, 422–23.

[47] This is another reason the husband warrants the title of household manager.

izens, homemakers, and parents) of the regime (1260b19–20).[48] Apparently, then, the ideal way of life for a woman resembles the way of life of the "king" bee (*GA* III.10).[49]

A Speaking Being: A Citizen?

Aristotle's portrait of woman as wife, household manager, and mother maintains that a woman may have not only temperance, generosity, justice, and prudence but also the capacity for speech. She rules her husband in turn by voicing her opinions—about, perhaps, his deficiencies in virtue, the servants he has acquired, or his child rearing; she directs her servants, explains to the best, and admonishes the worst; and she helps to teach her children. In fact, Aristotle indicates, a household cannot thrive, perhaps even exist, without speech (*logos*) (*Pol* 1253a18), by which he means not simply communication but the ability to perceive and to explain or make known (*dēloun*) the good, the bad, the just, and the unjust (1253a14–15). What is more, the city cannot thrive without speech that improves human beings.

Contrary to the claims of Okin and Elshtain, then, Aristotle affirms that women can and should engage in political speech. Aristotle states at the beginning of the *Politics* that free women and natural slaves do not have the same natural constitution (1252a34–b1); having the ability to deliberate (*to bouleutikon*) and not simply to understand (*sunesis*), women have the capacity for their own judgments, not merely right opinion. They are clearly not "methodologically and politically struck dumb by being shunted into a sphere Aristotle declares devoid of *significant* speech if not speechless."[50]

[48] See also Saxonhouse, "Family, Polity, and Unity," 209.

[49] By describing queen bees as kings (*basileis*), Aristotle may be reacting against what Loraux and Keuls identify as a Greek misogynistic literary convention of portraying a good woman as an industrious bee (*la femme abeille*) (*Enfants d'Athena*, 82, 108–17; *Reign of the Phallus*, 230–31). Aristotle in fact explains at length that the kingly queen bees are ladies of leisure: "The bees attend upon the kings—because the bees are generated from the kings"; "they allow the leaders to do no work," including that of raising the young (*GA* 760b16–20, 759b7–8).

[50] Elshtain, *Public Man*, 49; see also 47 and 50. See also Okin, *Women*, 91; Okin gives *Politics* 1277b as a reference, meaning apparently lines 28–29, in which Aristotle says that true or right opinion is a virtue of the ruled—among which, as has been shown, women are not always or strictly speaking.

If Aristotle finds in women all the makings of citizens, then why does he fail to say so explicitly? According to Loraux, the Hesiodic genre of myths imbued the Greeks, including Aristotle, with images of women that served to justify their political exclusion. Not only are women a different species from men, but they are a plague disrupting their world: by seducing men, women once made and continue to make men sexual, and thus more distinct from the gods and separate from each other.[51] In fact, Aristotle points out that separateness is politically salutary (*Pol* 1261a16–24) and that the right degree of fraternity is likely to come about among men who have wives (1262b1–2). More to the point, however, Aristotle is reluctant to propose that women be eligible for citizenship for prudential and philosophical, not psychological, reasons. First, by including such a provision in his best regime he might risk not having its other provisions taken seriously. Second, making the proposal explicit might give the appearance of contradicting his claim that women should perform domestic duties. According to Okin, Aristotle's critique of Plato in Book II of the *Politics* conspicuously virtually ignores Plato's proposal for women's equality because Aristotle has already (in Book I) established women's domestic role. By contrast, Saxonhouse suggests that Aristotle's inattention to the proposal indicates his basic endorsement of it.[52] In fact, both explanations are correct. Aristotle's defense of the household (and therewith of the roles of all its members) neither presupposes the innate inferiority of women nor intends their political subordination. Arguing that women should uphold certain domestic responsibilities implies their political exclusion as much or as little as arguing that men should uphold certain domestic responsibilities implies their political exclusion.

Plato avoids the appearance of contradiction merely by proposing women's equality in the *Republic* and their domesticity in the *Laws;* but he in fact avoids contradiction by revealing in the *Laws* a stronger commitment than in the *Republic* to the natural potential of women. The *Laws* shows that reinstating the private and the role of women in it does not undermine their worth.[53] Aristotle follows

[51] Loraux, *Enfants d'Athena*, 76–81.

[52] Okin, *Women*, 85–86; Saxonhouse, "Family, Polity, and Unity," 209.

[53] See Okin, "Philosopher Queens and Private Wives: Plato on Women in the Family," in Elshtain, ed., *The Family in Political Thought*, 43, 49. Contrary to Okin's view, I do not think that the changed role of women in the *Laws* is a "significant

up by hinting that women might perform both domestic and political roles.

An Intellectual Being: A Philosopher?

Women have moral virtue, but are they fit for the highest intellectual activity—theoretical speculation? If so, should they undertake it?

Femaleness Revisited

According to Aristotle, to grasp the first principles and proceed to their origin (*NE* 1141a18–19, b2–3), one needs intuitive reason (*nous*) (*NE* 1141a7–8, 19–20) (bestowed, to recall, from outside) as well as moral virtue (mainly so as not to be distracted by appetites and desires) (*NE* 1170a2–4, 1178a1–b7). Evidently, then, at least some women could philosophize. What a woman thinks lacks only the validation that comes from recognition or citizenship (*Pol* 1260a13). And, as Aristotle observes, "virtue and intuitive reason, the sources of excellent activities, do not depend on the possession of power" (*NE* 1176b18–19). In fact, the possession of power, honor, or reputation would seem to distract a human being from contemplation, which is a self-sufficient and thus solitary activity (*NE* 1177a27–34, *Pol* 1325a16–17) sustained only by reason itself (*NE* 1177a20–21). By contrast, one must cultivate recognition. By assigning citizenship only to men, then, Aristotle reduces their opportunity, and increases women's, to contemplate.

But if, as seems to be the case, men and women have, as far as any human being can figure, the same chance of receiving and developing a constitution fit for theoretical speculation, then what justifies the assignation of politics to men? The answer lies in Aristotle's understanding of the differences between male and female natures. The male is, to recall once more, by nature better at leading than the female. This suggests that men are more likely than women to covet honor, which results from and facilitates leadership. According to Aristotle, the ambitious attempt noble actions

---

casualty of [its] 'realism' " (ibid., 43), but rather that the role of the guardian women in the *Republic*, deprived as they are of privacy, is a significant casualty of ideology, the dangers of which the whole of the *Republic* intends to point out and the *Laws* intends to highlight by rectifying.

(though they are not capable of them), advertise their good luck (expecting to be honored for it), and are ostentatious (*NE* 1125a28–32). By contrast, those with proper pride (*megalopsuchia*) attempt few deeds, do not speak about themselves, and are independent (*NE* 1124b25, 1125a5–6, 1124b31–1125a1). Does Aristotle mean to remind us, by this juxtaposition of natures, of the active male and the passive female natures? If so, if he thinks that women tend to need others less, or need fewer others, than men, if he thinks that women tend to be morally self-sufficient, then he seems to envision a connection between female and philosophical natures.[54]

Put another way, a female virtue seems to be, not the capacity to resist stoically the lure of the public, but an absence of desire— indeed a disinclination—to participate; abstention from public participation does not pain the female nature (*NE* 1104b4–9, 1102b27–28). As Aristotle says of the virtuous person, "such a person wishes to spend time with himself, for he does so with pleasure" (*NE* 1166a23–24).[55]

Other differences Aristotle detects between male and female natures further suggest a connection between contemplation and femaleness: the female's natural (that is, civilized) manner of life is sedentary and she is physically weaker than the male (*GA* 729b12, 775a30–35, 14, 19–20; *Rh* 1361a2–3); she is also more apt to learn, less simple, more retentive in memory, more wakeful, and more difficult to rouse to action, and she needs less food; by contrast, males are more spirited, wilder, more simple, more ready to help,

---

[54] There is, however, debate on whether *megalopsuchia* is a virtue proper to the philosopher. For arguments that it is, see R.-A. Gauthier, *Magnanimité: L'idéal de la grandeur dans la philosophie païenne et dans la théologie chrétienne* (Paris: Librairie Philosophique J. Vrin, 1951), 56–117. For opposing arguments, see D. A. Rees, "'Magnanimity' in the Eudemian and Nicomachean Ethics," in *Untersuchungen zur Eudemischen Ethik*, ed. Paul Moraux and Dieter Harlfinger (Berlin: Walter de Gruyter, 1971), 231–43, as recommended by Carnes Lord in *Education and Culture in the Political Thought of Aristotle* (Ithaca: Cornell University Press, 1982), 201 n. 25; Lord agrees with Rees.

[55] Saxonhouse, "Eros and the Female in Greek Political Thought," *Political Theory* 12, no. 1 (1984), suggests that Plato and Aristotle associate philosophy and the female by associating "eros . . . with creativity and the feminine" (22, 24). She points out that "the beautiful itself," like a child, is in their view engendered; the language associated with philosophy is that of reproduction. The female is "erotic, desirous of giving birth, pregnant with life, and loves what she has created" (24). Thus, Socrates is androgynous; see 13, 17, 19, 21, 25, and also Clark, "Aristotle's Woman," 187, 190. Although this view may hold for Plato, Aristotle links philosophy not with the feminine principles of creativity and birth but with privacy.

and more courageous (*HA* 608a21–28, 33–b18).[56] Moreover, though Aristotle in another passage lists self-control (*sōphrosunē*) among the moral excellences of both the man and the woman, he identifies (again) courage as a male virtue but industry (*philergia*) as a female one. Women at their best, however, do not love all work, only unservile or liberal work (*aneu aneleutherias*), work becoming a lady (or a gentleman) (*Rh* 1361a3–7).[57] Thus, although the peculiarly male virtues of strength, fitness, and courage serve the community, a community is not fully happy unless it secures the female virtues as well (*Rh* 1361a1–3, 7–11).

Finally, suggesting once again that female and philosophical virtues intersect, Aristotle repeats Sophocles' declaration that "silence is a woman's crown" (*Pol* 1260a30).[58]

In short, although Aristotle nowhere implies that one gender is more likely than the other to receive intuitive reason, he suggests that, if possessed, it is facilitated more by a female than by a male nature. The inclination to privacy, quietude, or a "passive" way of life is both a female and a philosophical one. The female nature does not, unlike the male nature, resist the quiet life essential for thought. Aristotle is not, then, as Clark contends, "disposed to regard femaleness as a privative rather than a positive attribute"; femaleness is positive because it prefers privacy.[59]

The Woman's Role Revisited

Some women may be capable of philosophy, and female nature may even be conducive to it, but ought women to philosophize? To find out, one might consider whether the social arrangement Aristotle recommends encourages women to philosophize. First, not only do household activities cultivate the moral virtues needed for

---

[56] On the other hand, Aristotle includes in this passage adjectives that depict the female as more emotional, cunning, and deceitful than the male; at least the first would tend to work against her contemplating, but perhaps no more and maybe less than would the male's more restless nature.

[57] See John Henry Freese's note on *aneleutheria*, in *Aristotle: The "Art" of Rhetoric* (Loeb Classical Library, 1926), 50 n. a.

[58] For a different explanation of this quotation, see Saxonhouse, "Family, Polity, and Unity," 209; for relevant commentary, see Fortenbaugh, "Aristotle on Slaves and Women," 138–39.

[59] *Aristotle's Man*, 207. That Aristotle thinks also that women may be suited for political life does not undermine this contention; it underscores his view that men and women manifest combinations of maleness and femaleness, are drawn variously to publicity and to privacy.

philosophy, they seem also to do so better than political activities in that the latter are more diverse, demanding, and so distracting. Moreover, the philosopher does not need many other human beings (*NE* 1178a20–28, b1–7). Second, it is good for a household to have servants because it is barbaric to treat women like natural slaves (*Pol* 1252b5–6, 1252a34–b1); women should have time to satisfy their desire to work in a way befitting a free person.[60] Furthermore, having the assistance of both her husband and the regime's educational programs (*Pol* 1337a11–12, 22–27) in raising her children, the silence that so becomes a woman and fosters philosophy could be hers. Thus, in addition to her private nature, life in a well-constituted household, like a queen bee's, facilitates a woman's intellectual activity.[61]

One might point out, however, that according to Aristotle philosophical inquiry must begin with opinions, which a woman in the household does not have access to. This problem might suggest, on the one hand, that women ought to be citizens. On the other hand, Aristotle says that philosophy should begin with reputable opinions (*Top* 100a29–30). These *may* be found among citizens but *are* found among the wise (*Top* 100b21–28) and therefore (ideally) in the liberal arts,[62] which can be voluntarily pursued in private. Thus, Aristotle hints how women should be educated—a question he raises by declaring that they should be educated (*Pol* 1260b15–16), but one he does not explicitly answer. The possibility that some women should undertake theoretical activity also helps explain Aristotle's view that they are half of the free persons of a city; as only wives, household managers, and parents, women would contribute only indirectly and partially their share of the noble actions for which the political partnership exists (*Pol* 1281a2–8).

Aristotle leaves no doubt that men would contribute their share

---

60 To recall from Chapter 2, Aristotle's main justification for natural slavery is to provide free persons (the man and the woman) with the opportunity for politics and philosophy (*Pol* 1255b35–37). It is perhaps no accident that the first mention of philosophy in the *Politics* occurs in a discussion of the household.

61 That Aristotle recommends that women not exert their minds when pregnant (*Pol* 1335b16–18) indicates at least that he assumes they can exert them, and perhaps that he thinks they should when not pregnant—which in a good regime, with laws limiting childbirth (*Pol* 1265b6–7, 1335b22–23), would be most of their lives.

62 See Chapter 6, "Leisure: Education in Reason?" and "Leisure: Public and Private Good," pp. 155–64.

to the best regime, but he leaves some doubt that their contributions would be philosophical; after all, they spend their youth as soldiers, their middle years as public officials, their late middle years as fathers, and their last years as priests (*Pol* 1331b4–5, 1329a2–17, 1332b35–42, 1335a28–34, b34–37). On the other hand, Aristotle seems to suggest that legislators should promote the best way of life by allowing a choice between serving the city in the capacity of either office holder or philosopher (*Pol* 1324a29–35, 1325b14–21, 27–32).[63] In short, he leaves open the possibility that the best regime would include male philosophers for the same reason he leaves open the possibility that it would include female citizens; not even if all human beings were either purely female or purely male could it be established a priori who should philosophize and who should govern.

FEMINIST CLAIMS REVISITED

According to Elshtain and Okin, Aristotle derived his view of the role of women in society from his own culture and sought to justify the status quo. This accounts for his depiction of woman as subsumed and defined by the household. As Okin puts it, "Aristotle's assumption that woman is defined by her reproductive function and her other duties within the household permeates everything he has to say about her." In Aristotle's view, she continues, "women's work is clearly regarded as in no way compatible with the life

---

[63] I agree with P. A. Vander Waerdt that Aristotle regards politics as unleisured but disagree with him that Aristotle thinks all citizens in the best regime would be released from politics by the permanent rule of a king; see "Kingship and Philosophy in Aristotle's Best Regime," *Phronesis* 30, no. 3 (1985), 249–73. Aristotle makes clear that in the best regime citizens in their later prime would rule, implying that nature makes this arrangement fair: "Nature has provided the distinction [between rulers and ruled] by making that which is the same by type have a younger and an older element, of which it is proper of the former to be ruled and the latter to rule. No one chafes at being ruled on the basis of age or considers himself superior, particularly when he is going to recover his contribution when he attains the age to come. In one sense, therefore, it must be asserted that the same persons rule and are ruled, but in another sense different persons" (*Pol* 1332b36–42, 1333a2–3). The only way to reconcile this with Aristotle's advocacy of the philosophical life is to infer that ruling extends to making philosophical contributions to the regime. For other arguments against Vander Waerdt's thesis, see Chapter 5, "Political Laws: Offices and Entitlement," pp. 119–31.

of excellence."[64] Elshtain and Okin agree that Aristotle, by absorb-
ing woman completely within the household, "precludes the possibility for female self-transformation over time" or provides for
"the obliteration of the woman's [personality]."[65] Their conclusions impute to Aristotle not only an uncritical mind but a belief in
a modern public-private dichotomy and a rigid determinism.

One should note, however, that there is no textual evidence for
the claim that Aristotle is simply trying to justify the status quo.[66]
He never holds up the Athenian household or women as models,
whereas often in the *Politics* he illustrates his points with historical
examples. Apparently he did not find laudable traditional practices
concerning women. It is not the case, then, as Elshtain implies,
that Aristotle's idealism permeates only half his political theory,
that his (alleged) "ideological justifications of a way of life" are
separable from his "logic of explanation (Aristotle on politics as a
form of action)." In her view, this implicit division allows and justifies disregarding particular dimensions of Aristotle's theory (such
as his views on women and slavery) "without so eroding the overall structure of the theory that one's favored alternatives are
dropped."[67] In fact, since Aristotle's idealism permeates the whole
of his political theory, since his object is not to defend the practices
of his culture but to propose better ones, it is, for the purpose of
understanding his political proposals, beside the point whether, as
Keuls claims, "Aristotle . . . like other Athenian men, had little
insight into the reality of the activities in the women's quarters."
Neither knowledge nor ignorance of the (alleged) fact "that the
typical women's part of the house was a sweatshop, and a labor
ethos was instilled in women from childhood on" would have

[64] Okin, *Women*, 86, 89; see also 73–96 and Elshtain, *Public Man*, 41–51, "Aristotle," 52–56. Among the difficulties with arguing that Aristotle believes "the female's
primary function is reproduction" (Okin, *Women*, 81) is that he recommends that
polities limit by law the number of children per couple and legalize abortion as a
means to compliance with the law (*Pol* 1265b6–7, 1335b22–25).

[65] Respectively, Elshtain, *Public Man*, 41 (see also "Aristotle," 55), and Okin,
Women, 94.

[66] Similarly, "it would be a mistake to think that Aristotle's view is simply the
creation of a prejudiced male" (Fortenbaugh, "Aristotle on Slaves and Women,"
139).

[67] *Public Man*, 51, 53.

prevented him from speculating about what a woman's way of life *ought* to be like.[68]

As noted at the outset of the chapter, the widespread feminist interpretation also assumes wrongly that Aristotle associates freedom with the public and unfreedom and the household with the private. In so assuming, Elshtain and Okin draw the wrong conclusions from Aristotle's teleological understanding of the world.[69] Simply, they see that in Aristotle's view nature assigns woman a domestic function and conclude that he thereby regards her as subhuman.

Furthermore, although Aristotle believes that nature gives every living being a purpose, potential, or developmental destination, one must keep in mind that he finds in every class exceptions and aberrations,[70] and that he believes a being's environment can either foster or impede the realization of its potential. Thus, no entire class and no individual being is completely determined; or rather, the real potential of any being is the end that being would reach in the best environment imaginable. To support her thesis, Okin, like Elshtain, must maintain that Aristotle is inconsistent, that "in spite of his expressed beliefs in the power of the environment to shape and alter the human character and abilities, he is no more interested in applying these beliefs to women than in applying them to slaves."[71] In this and the previous chapter I have sought to show just how consistently he does apply these beliefs.

A point of clarification is perhaps in order: by suggesting that women could be citizens and philosophers, Aristotle is not advocating matriarchy. He is not promoting maternal thinking as the basis for political consciousness (as some contemporary social fem-

---

[68] Keuls, *Reign of the Phallus,* 124. As Saxonhouse points out, "rather than see the philosophers as apologists for their societies, as spokesmen for a political order that suppressed and segregated women, we must see them as critics and analysts, discovering for the Athenians the foundations of their society and discoursing on the adequacy as well as the inadequacy of those foundations" ("Eros and the Female," 9; see also 24–25).

[69] An understanding that Okin calls Aristotle's "functionalism" (*Women,* 78) and Elshtain, more accurately, his "teleological determinism" (*Public Man,* 42; see also "Aristotle," 54). Elshtain makes explicit the mistaken assumption about the nature of the public and the private at *Public Man,* 45, 47, 49, and "Aristotle," 52, 53, 56, 65.

[70] See Lloyd, *Science,* 99.

[71] *Women,* 93.

inists, such as Elshtain, advocate); nor is he recommending the politicization of female consciousness (as other contemporary feminists, such as Mary Dietz, urge).[72] Nor is Aristotle suggesting, as Clark claims, "that dominance relationships of the kind embodied either in patriarchal or matriarchal culture can be seen as peripheral to the central concerns of human society."[73] For not only are both male and female virtues invaluable to the household and the city, so is their rule.[74] Moreover, Aristotle teaches us that both male and female virtues should rule within our souls; for our own well-being, we should try most of all to achieve within a dynamic equilibrium between the public and the private.

[72] For a discussion of the goals of feminism as understood by some contemporary feminist scholars, see Mary Dietz, "Citizenship with a Feminist Face: The Problem with Maternal Thinking," *Political Theory,* 13, no. 1 (1985), 19–37, especially 33–34.
[73] "Aristotle's Woman, 191.
[74] Clark, *Aristotle's Man,* 208, 211, and "Aristotle's Woman," 191, and Saxonhouse, "Eros and the Female," 23, 25, also make the first claim; John F. Wilson, "Power, Rule, and Politics: The Aristotelian View," *Polity* 12, no. 1 (1980), 96, also makes the second.

4

THE ECONOMY:
A PUBLIC PLACE
FOR PRIVATE ACTIVITY

Although it is generally true that pre–seventeenth century philosophers did not focus on economic questions, they were not, as
has been suggested, disinterested in them.[1] One finds, in Aristotle
in particular, not only his commonly known argument that an
individual cannot live virtuously without property, but the parallel
one that a city needs property too. One finds, not only these arguments, but the concept of a public economy. Aristotle is unlike
some modern political thinkers in that his economic proposals do
not provide the *key* to his philosophy and thus to his views on the
public and the private, but they do help to illuminate those views.

Before proceeding to the interpretive debate, we should address
a not insignificant methodological controversy: what material in
the Aristotelian corpus is legitimate and relevant to Aristotle's economic views? First of all, to stress, as M. I. Finley does, that Aristotle "wrote no *Economics*" is misleading.[2] As noted in Chapter 2, the
first book of the *Oeconomica* includes Aristotle's own writing, and
the remainder of the work draws on his thinking. Further, two of
the three books of the *Oeconomica* pertain to economic matters; the
first book on household management is useful especially in conjunction with Book I of the *Politics*, and the second book, although
comprising largely anecdotes, directly concerns public economy—

---

[1] See Robert L. Heilbroner, *The Worldly Philosophers: The Lives, Times, and Ideas of
Great Economic Thinkers*, 4th ed. (New York: Simon and Schuster, 1972), 36.
[2] *The Ancient Economy*, 2d ed. (Berkeley: University of California Press, 1985), 21.

the ways rulers collect taxes and manage a city's economic affairs.[3] As to the possible objection that *oikonomia* means household management, one must note, as Finley admits, that Aristotle could be using the word to mean public administration (*Pol* 1299a20–23, 1308b32; *Oec* 1345b7–1346a25).[4] Second, although Finley and others indicate that only Book V of the *Nicomachean Ethics* and Book I of the *Politics* should form the basis for a discussion of Aristotle's economic views, one finds throughout the *Politics*, not systematic treatments of economic questions, but passages that complete his conception of an economy.[5] One must be mindful, though, of his placement of economic proposals—whether in the books about ordinary regimes or in those about the ideal regime.

RIVAL INTERPRETATIONS

There are at least six overlapping interpretations of Aristotle's understanding of economics. One that has been shown in previous chapters to permeate Arendt's and feminist accounts of Aristotle holds that he understands economics to mean the business of fulfilling needs in the household: "According to ancient thought . . . the very term 'political economy' would have been a contradiction in terms: whatever was 'economic,' related to the life of the individual and the survival of the species, was a non-political, household affair by definition."[6] An economy may be defined as "an instituted process of interaction between man and his environment, which results in a continuous supply of want-satisfying material means."[7] As earlier chapters have revealed, there is no doubt

---

[3] In addition to the text itself, see G. Cyril Armstrong's "Introduction" to *Aristotle: Oeconomica* (Loeb Classical Library, 1935), 323–25.

[4] Finley, "Aristotle and Economic Analysis," in *Ethics and Politics*, vol. 2, *Articles on Aristotle*, ed. Jonathan Barnes, Malcolm Schofield, and Richard Sorabji (London: Gerald Duckworth, 1977), 150 n. 32; see also Finley, *Ancient Economy*, 20.

[5] Finley, "Aristotle and Economic Analysis," 142; Joseph A. Schumpeter, *History of Economic Analysis*, ed. Elizabeth Boody Schumpeter (New York: Oxford University Press, 1954), 60.

[6] Hannah Arendt, *The Human Condition* (Chicago: University of Chicago Press, 1958), 29; Ernest Barker makes the same point in *The Political Thought of Plato and Aristotle* (New York: Dover, 1959), 357, but contradicts it in his translation of *The Politics of Aristotle* (Oxford: Clarendon, 1946), 22 n. 1.

[7] Karl Polanyi, "The Economy as Instituted Process," in *Primitive, Archaic, and Modern Economies: Essays of Karl Polanyi*, ed. George Dalton (Boston: Beacon, 1968), 145.

that Aristotle establishes the importance of and explains how to institute this process in the household; but he also indicates the importance of establishing such a process in the city when he declares at the beginning of the *Politics* that the raison d'être of cities is self-sufficiency (1252b27–1253a1). Indeed, since Aristotle contends that both the household and the city aim to achieve self-sufficiency (the self-sufficiency that is possible for each) (*Pol* 1261b11–12, 1280b33–35, 40-1281a1), it would be odd for him to offer only a theory of domestic economy.

According to Ernest Barker and Eric A. Havelock, Aristotle understands economics in terms of moral relationships between human beings and to concern only indirectly (primarily through the master-slave relationship) the meeting of physical needs and wants. Havelock, however, departs from Barker (giving us a third interpretation), by arguing that Aristotle extends economics beyond the family to include "the regulation of moral and authoritarian relationships between persons"; "in the larger area of the state, economy is another name for politics."[8] On the one hand, then, it might be said that Havelock, unlike Arendt and Barker, sees that Aristotle has some kind of concept of public economy. On the other hand, given that Havelock's Aristotelian economy is a function of human goodness and not of the condition of scarcity, it is clearly not Havelock's intention to suggest that there is agreement between Aristotle and modern economists about the origin of economy.[9]

M. I. Finley, Robert L. Heilbroner, and Joseph A. Schumpeter argue that, although one finds in Aristotle's works commonsense descriptions of economic activities, one does not find either economic analysis or a concept of economy. They argue that Aristotle did not have a concept of public economy because the ancients did not abstract the elements of production. Without the "impersonal, dehumanized" conceptions of "land, labor, and capital," "the laws of supply and demand," "cost" and "value," they could not conceive "the market system." "Of course," Finley explains, "they farmed, traded, manufactured, mined, taxed, coined, deposited and loaned money, made profits or failed in their enterprises. And

---

[8] Havelock, *The Liberal Temper in Greek Politics* (London: Camelot, 1957), 343–44, 354. Barker, *Political Thought,* 357–59; for his supporting arguments, see 359–400.

[9] Havelock argues that Aristotle rejects all liberal ideas, including that of a *societas cupiditatis*—a political association aiming to satisfy private wants (*Liberal Temper*, 295–375).

they discussed these activities in their talk and their writing. What they did not do, however, was to combine these particular activities conceptually into a unit, in Parsonian terms into 'a differentiated sub-system of society'."[10]

Finley does not merely rely on this intellectual explanation; he also emphasizes that the ancients lacked a concept of economy because their division of the population, into money-handling, noncitizen "metics" on the one hand and land-owning citizens on the other, prevented the possibility of investing in land and manufacture. "Greek conditions of choice" precluded the ancients from envisioning an "investment model." It was because their economy was confined to producing, trading, and money-lending that they did not conceive a market system.[11]

According to Finley, Heilbroner, and Schumpeter, then, the question of whether Aristotle had a concept of public economy is necessarily over whether he conceived a capitalist system.[12] Karl Polanyi maintains that Aristotle presents a nonmarket, "sociological," concept of public economy—a "substantive" rather than a "formal" definition.[13] Polanyi essentially agrees with Finley that Aristotle could not have arrived at the concept of a "disembedded" economy because market mechanisms during his time were at most embryonic; economic functions were still largely "embedded" in noneconomic institutions and customs.[14] Nonetheless, living amid economic developments, Aristotle had the empirical basis for developing a concept of economy that was more than a concept of political or moral relations, as Havelock contends. According to Polanyi, Aristotle detected an economic dimension of human experience but found it expressed through "community, self-sufficiency, and justice"; in Aristotle's view, neither the fact of scarcity nor

[10] Finley, Ancient Economy, 21; see also 22, 182, and "Aristotle and Economic Analysis," 146–56; Heilbroner, Worldly Philosophers, 17–27, 36; Schumpeter, History of Economic Analysis, 9, 53–65; but see note 19 below.

[11] Finley, "Aristotle and Economic Analysis," 156–57; see also Heilbroner, Worldly Philosophers, 26.

[12] See especially Finley, Ancient Economy, 22–23. This point is implied by Schumpeter's account (History of Economic Analysis, especially 58).

[13] For Polanyi's discussion of the distinction, see "The Economy as Instituted Process," 139–48.

[14] "Aristotle Discovers the Economy," in Primitive, Archaic, and Modern Economies, ed. Dalton, especially 80–82, 84–86, 111; see also Heilbroner, Worldly Philosophers, 17–18, and Havelock, who, although he does not give a historical explanation, finds in Aristotle's texts a fundamental duality between liberal economic theory and agrarianism overcome by the latter (Liberal Temper, 353–65).

self-interest, but institutions or "the interests of the community," work to ensure the satisfaction of needs.[15] The economy arises out of and depends on the community; the community is logically prior to the economy.

Cornelius Castoriadis also argues that Aristotle conceives the economy as wholly conventional. He admits that Aristotle says that need is the source of economies, since it is an available measure of value, and he also admits that Aristotle regards individuals as the necessary judges of their needs. But Castoriadis contends (as Polanyi hints[16]) that Aristotle thinks *paideia*—the institutions of a regime—determines or creates needs. *Nomos* conditions human beings. Moreover, man is convention's creature because, according to Aristotle, his *physis/telos* compels him to make himself: man is not ontologically determined. Thus, there is no ontological ground of the city—of *nomos*. To be sure, according to Aristotle human beings must bring about their own virtue, or make themselves. But it is equally clear that nature supplies them with directives, or the ontological basis for virtue. In fact, Aristotle denies that "everything just is merely conventional" and claims that "only one form of government is by nature the best everywhere" (*NE* 1134b24–25, 1135a5). Contrary to Castoriadis's suggestion, the fact that man is a political animal does not override or make clear the meaning of his naturalness.[17] Men may only change natural justice and their natural appetites (*NE* 1134b18–1135a5, *Pol* 1253a31–37).

In other words, as Polanyi and Castoriadis indicate, Aristotle indeed has a concept of public economy and finds self-judged needs to be the impetus for and self-sufficiency to be the end of an economy. But in Aristotle's view, education or law cannot change the fact that nature manufactures needs and makes them felt only and unmistakably by individuals. Accordingly, law must acknowledge low nature by providing means to satisfy needs and by merely guiding rather than trying to supplant individual judgment. Indeed, Aristotle's fundamental observation that a whole cannot be sound unless its parts are supports the claim that the economy serves the whole by way of serving individuals.

In this chapter, I aim to show not only that Aristotle has a con-

---

15 "Aristotle Discovers the Economy," 96–100, 107.
16 Ibid., 99.
17 Cornelius Castoriadis, "From Marx to Aristotle, from Aristotle to Us," *Social Research* 45, no. 4 (1978), 713–15, 725–35.

cept of public economy but that it presents economic concepts that resemble modern ones. To borrow Polanyi's distinction, Aristotle's description of an ideal empirical economy, his substantive concept of economy, suggests elements of a formal concept of economy. My objective in this chapter is to identify the economic concepts that inform Aristotle's institutional vision of economy. It should become clear that Aristotle is not so much uncritically compounding the two meanings of "economic" as trying to develop the conceptual apparatus to account for and explain the features of a market economy. To support this thesis, however, I need not show that Aristotle abstracts land, labor, and capital, for there are other concepts of a market economy—self-love as the economy's animus and subsistence as its end, for example, but also division of labor, private property, distribution, freedom of trade, competition, currency, value, monopoly, population growth, and even natural justice.[18] Aristotle's use of some of these concepts—for example, those of money and private property—might appear in Schumpeter's terms as nothing more or not much more than commonsense requirements or fundamental facts of a *market;* not bearing or suggesting any superstructures, they cannot be said to embody discoveries and could be said to be commonplace.[19] But they still convey important insights: Aristotle's justification of private property presupposes the notion of incentive, and he distinguishes currency from capital.

It is not, in any case, mostly the degree of sophistication of Aristotle's concepts—some of which are and some of which are not more than commonsense definitions—that holds together the thesis that he not only describes but conceptualizes or analyzes market economy; it is rather that his treatment of these concepts re-

[18] These are some of Adam Smith's cardinal concepts, as summarized by D. P. O'Brien, *The Classical Economists* (Oxford: Clarendon, 1975), 30–36. Because Smith's ideas more than those of anyone else dominate classical economics, they are the basis for the notion of classical economics referred to in this chapter.

[19] Schumpeter, *History of Economic Analysis,* 9, 54. Schumpeter himself says that Aristotle's contribution to economics is pedestrian and commonsensical (only) from the contemporary standpoint and grants Aristotle at least "an analytic *intention*" with respect to "matters touching value, price, and money" (57, 64; see also 60–63). By "economic analysis" Schumpeter means "the intellectual efforts that men have made in order to *understand* economic phenomena or, which comes to the same thing, . . . the analytic or scientific aspects of economic thought" (3).

veals an appreciation of their connectedness.[20] His discussion of economic matters in both theoretical and practical terms suggests that he would be sympathetic to the later, modern displacement or disembedding of economics. That he witnessed economic activity becoming divorced, however tentatively, from traditional practices may have facilitated his attempt to express economic relations in conceptual terms, an attempt the impetus for which was his *not* finding such relations embedded in all human relationships. In any case, he tries to show that economics is not a dimension of all human experience by showing that it is a compartment of that experience.

Aristotle and Classical Economics

Among the fundamental ideas that are common to Aristotle and modern, especially classical, economics is that of natural law. As D. P. O'Brien explains, Adam Smith was influenced by four basic propositions common to any natural-law system: "that there is an underlying order in material phenomena; that this underlying order is discoverable either by reasoning from observed phenomena or from innate moral sense; that discovery of the underlying order leads to the formulation of natural laws which, if followed, lead to the best possible situation; and that positive legislation should reflect these natural laws."[21] It would appear that Smith's belief that natural right rests not on reason but on the mechanism of sentiment does not separate him from Aristotle as much as one might think[22]—a thought to which I have occasion to return.

[20] Polanyi and I agree on the conceptual unity of Aristotle's economic ideas. He writes: "We have . . . every reason to seek in his works for far more massive and significant formulations on economic matters than Aristotle has been credited with in the past. In fact, the *disjecta membra* of the *Ethics* and *Politics* convey a monumental unity of thought. Whenever Aristotle touched on a question of the economy he aimed at developing its relationship to society as a whole" ("Aristotle Discovers the Economy," 95–96).

[21] *Classical Economists*, 22; see also 24–32.

[22] See Joseph Cropsey, "Adam Smith," in *History of Political Philosophy*, 3d ed., ed. Leo Strauss and Joseph Cropsey (Chicago: University of Chicago Press, 1987), 639; O'Brien, *Classical Economists*, 31.

Another point is worthy of note: mainstream classical economics "was in essence not a model building phenomenon." David Ricardo's Corn Model "was not a very serious detour" in the development of classical economics and "attracted hardly any disciples."[23] That Aristotle built no Ricardian models, then, does not mean that his economic concepts can have no affinity with classical economics.

It has, however, been indicated that a formal concept of economy tries to explain the logic of "a definite situation of choice" rather than to describe an "instituted process."[24] Thus, the claim that Aristotle presents elements of a logical concept of economy must be supported by evidence that he is trying to simplify reality, generalize relations, or present an ideal type.[25] In fact, Aristotle makes several such attempts. For example, he does not describe agriculture and commerce, but he explains the concepts of natural and unnatural acquisition. He also presents the concept of self-sufficiency—an ideal that resembles Adam Smith's concept of the stationary state. The concepts of commensurability and of the just price simplify reality by revealing the logic of exchange. Aristotle's distinction between public administration and political rule is also part of his attempt to clarify or conceptualize things economic. He may not have conceived all the logical constructs necessary to complete an economic model or system, but in conceiving a few building blocks, and in suspecting others, he appreciated some of the ideas classical economics later systematized.

The attempt to ally Aristotle's political philosophy with classical economics still might appear misguided, since his portrait of the best regime promotes a fundamentally agrarian economy supported by public and private farmers (*Pol* 1278a11–13, 1330a9–13, 25–31). Fundamental agrarianism is not, however, pure agrarianism; self-sufficiency cannot be achieved, Aristotle teaches, without a profit-generating market. Furthermore, one must always bear

---

23 O'Brien, *Classical Economists*, 43.
24 Polanyi, "The Economy as Instituted Process," 140, 145.
25 See Finley, *Ancient Economy*, 182, which cites Max Weber. It should be noted, however, that in practice, even under a market system, the formal and substantive meanings of economic of course coincide, and that not even Weber, Parsons, Marshall, or Durkheim disentangled the two meanings (Polanyi, "The Economy as Instituted Process," 141). Aristotle may not have disentangled the two meanings any more than he did, not so much because he lacked empirical or intellectual resources, but because, as he declares, it is crude to spend much time discussing economic matters (*Pol* 1258b35).

in mind that Aristotle proposes both ideal and second-best measures. Agrarianism can be expected to prevail only among a certain sort of populace. Where virtue is not the norm, legislators should expect that money-making will attract most men; accordingly, if they are concerned to preserve the regime, they should legislate only to discourage, not to prohibit, money-making among citizens.

One might point out, however, that this sketch of the second-best economy nonetheless rejects the "invisible hand" theory and natural liberty doctrine that together are the essence of classical economics, a fact not hitherto observed. But two other observations are relevant here. First, Smith's harmony theory presupposes the desirability of order or reason. Second,

> liberty continued to mean for Smith what it had meant to Locke, to Aristotle, and to the long tradition of political philosophy: the condition of men under lawful governors who respect the persons and property of the governed, the latter having to consent to the arrangement in one way or another. . . . [The capitalist project] is animated by a search for methods of institutionally liberating every man's natural instinct of self-preservation in the interest of external, politically intelligible freedom and peaceful prosperous life for mankind as a whole.[26]

Thus, Aristotle's second-best regime and Smith's best seem to intersect.[27]

THE BEST ECONOMY

We should now consider evidence for the claim that Aristotle has a concept of public economy that both reveals an appreciation of some of the concepts of classical economics and highlights the failings of liberal economic theory and the dangers of a liberal economy.

---

[26] Cropsey, "Adam Smith," 652. See also Cropsey, *Polity and Economy: An Interpretation of the Principles of Adam Smith* (The Hague: Martinus Nijhoff, 1957), 24; O'Brien, *Classical Economists*, 32.

[27] For the claim that the first five chapters of Adam Smith's *Wealth of Nations* develop Aristotle's thoughts on economics, see Schumpeter, *History of Economic Analysis*, 60, 63.

The Division of Labor and Productivity

One fundamental concept Aristotle and classical economics share is the division of labor.[28] He recommends, not only that private slaves mainly provide services and public slaves mainly produce goods, but that different slaves among each group assume different tasks. For example, some public slaves should produce food, some artifacts; still others should transact business. Among those producing artifacts, some should make shoes and some, houses. Among those transacting business, some should transact domestic and others foreign business (*Pol* 1261a22–37, 1327b11–13, 1328b5–7, 20–21, 1329a35–37, 1331a32–35, b1–4). To surmise that Aristotle might have conceived and found appropriate further divisions of labor may not be unreasonable, but it is not necessary in order to show his recognition of the basic idea.[29] Still, Aristotle would almost certainly recommend that labor cease being divided before it becomes so injurious to the body as to make laborers useless (*Pol* 1337b12–14).

But is the rationale for such a division the one classical economics gives—namely, productivity? Aristotle indicates that it is indeed one rationale: a city cannot be excellent without its citizens being excellent, and they cannot be excellent if they are in want of sustenance and possessions (*Pol* 1332a32–34, 1329a17–19, 1330a2). The good life presupposes self-sufficiency (*Pol* 1252b27–1253a1, 1321b17–18). One might object, however, that self-sufficiency is not growth, which requires the production of surplus and investment, or capital.[30] On the one hand, this observation indeed seems to signal a crucial difference between Aristotelian and classical economics. Aristotle praises acquiring wealth "naturally" by agricultural means and bartering because such activities are limited: they arise from needs and end with the satisfaction of those needs.

---

[28] Schumpeter acknowledges that this is part of Aristotle's bequest to economic theory but denies that the knowledge that the division of labor increases productivity embodies a scientific discovery (*History of Economic Analysis*, 9, 60). My claim is not that it is such a discovery, only that division of labor is one of Aristotle's many concepts that together begin to resemble the concept of a market system.

[29] According to Adam Smith, the extent of division of labor is a function of the capital stock available to support it. Furthermore, Smith admits that division of labor in the agricultural sector—the sector that according to Aristotle should predominate—is necessarily limited by the seasonality of many tasks (O'Brien, *Classical Economists*, 209).

[30] Ibid., 34.

And he seems to denounce money-making precisely because it allows and encourages the production of (unnecessary) surplus or profit (*Pol* 1257a6–1258b33, *Oec* 1343a26–30). On the other hand, he also indicates that both individuals and cities should have more than necessities. "Self-sufficiency is having everything available and being in need of nothing"—but in need of nothing for living "at leisure in liberal fashion"; self-sufficiency is the mean between penury and luxury (*Pol* 1326b29–31, 36–39). One cannot be generous without having things to give away or loan; one cannot exercise moderation if one feels always in need (*Pol* 1263b11–14; *NE* 1120a5–6, 24–26, 34–b2, 1119a16–18, b15–17).[31] In fact, Aristotle lists wealth (*ploutos*), goods or money (*chrēmata*),[32] and profit (*kerdos*) among the pleasant things that, though they "admit of excess," "are worthy of choice in themselves" (*NE* 1147b23–25, 29–30, 1148a22–28, b2–5). Citizens should also have money to pay taxes (*Pol* 1283a17–19). A city too needs surplus. It needs surplus goods to trade for goods it cannot itself produce (*Pol* 1327a25–27).[33] In addition to surplus goods, a city needs "a certain abundance of money [*chrēmatōn tina euporian*]" to finance an army, a navy, and domestic projects and functions (*Pol* 1328b10–11, 1267a20–21, 1327a21–23; *Oec* 1345b19–27). In short, a city should accumulate wealth as long as it is intended for future *use* (*Pol* 1327a25–31, 1328a33–35, 1267a21–24, 1256b36–37), a view consistent with the spirit of the classical economic notion of investment.[34]

[31] Thus, the concept of "*property* as a right of disposing of definite objects" was not foreign to Aristotle, as Polanyi implies ("Aristotle Discovers the Economy," 90).

[32] *Chrēmata* "is an ambiguous word, often meaning money and always suggestive of it"; see *The Politics of Aristotle*, vol. 2, ed. W. L. Newman (New York: Arno Press, 1973), 187, note on 1257b7.

[33] "In order to procure supplies, it is imperative that a city should be able to import commodities which it does not itself produce, and to export, in return, the surplus of its own products" (*Pol* 1327a25–27). Regarding trade as a *means* to self-sufficiency, Aristotle is not, as Finley says, conceding that self-sufficiency is not in fact possible (*Ancient Economy*, 125). And contrary to Polanyi's claim ("Aristotle Discovers the Economy," 94, 98–99), Aristotle does have an economic concept of scarcity. Nature is niggardly from the point of view of civilization, and natural slaves cannot alone redress the condition of scarcity.

[34] As noted earlier, Aristotle's description of a self-sufficient regime calls to mind Adam Smith's description of a "stationary state": a state that "has attained its 'full complement of riches,' which full complement is a function of the nation's laws and institutions, and its soil, climate, and geographical situation" (Cropsey, *Polity and Economy*, 75–76; see also O'Brien, *Classical Economists*, 210–11). Smith divided surplus, which he called "stock," into three categories: "that for the immediate consumption of the holders of stock (food, clothes, housing, and furniture); circulating

Where Aristotle's notion of division of labor differs from the modern one is in not presupposing prosperity as its *main* rationale. Its main rationale is the diversity or inequality of individuals; nature makes each being to suit a purpose (*Pol* 1252b1–2, 1256b20–21). The fortunate consequence is not merely self-sufficiency but quality products (*Pol* 1261a35–39), and not only these but the edification rather than the stultification of all workers (*Pol* 1255a1–2, b12–13, 1278b32–36). The latter is the inevitable consequence of assuming equality when dividing labor, a consequence of liberal capitalism which Adam Smith hinted was on the order of a moral irregularity[35] and which Karl Marx declared to be much worse.

Distribution

If both citizens and cities need wealth, then how should they acquire it? According to Aristotle, a regime's territory should ideally be large enough and its population small enough so that each household may own two tracts of land (one near the city, the other near the border) from which household members can live liberally but moderately (*Pol* 1330a14–16, 1326b30–32).[36] Private domestic and field hands provide necessary labor (1330a25–31). Farming,

---

capital (. . . money, stocks of provisions, raw materials, stocks of finished goods); and fixed capital (machinery, productive buildings, land improvements, and useful or acquired abilities). According to Smith, fixed capital was of no use without the co-operation of circulating capital and, writing at the beginning of the Industrial Revolution, he placed relatively little emphasis upon it. Capital formation was produced by directing stock into categories 2 and 3. It was increased by parsimony and diminished by prodigality and misconduct" (O'Brien, *Classical Economists*, 207).

In Aristotle's view, to borrow Oakeshott's terms, economic players form not simply a transactional association but an enterprise association in that they share a substantive purpose—namely, the economic well-being of the city; this does not detract from the fact that they make decisions in response to continuously emergent situations and that therefore "these decisions are only contingently connected with the common purpose" (*On Human Conduct*, 114–15). Because, in a well-arranged regime, the marketing element in effect procures a substantive condition benefiting the whole, Aristotle can without contradiction denounce mere transactional association (*Pol* 1280b17–23, 29–31) while including a market in the best regime.

35 Cropsey, "Adam Smith," 647–51, and *Polity and Economy*, 77–79, 89–92; see also O'Brien, *Classical Economists*, 209–10.

36 On this interpretation of *Pol* 1326b30–32, see *Aristotle: The Politics*, trans. Carnes Lord (Chicago: University of Chicago Press, 1984), 266 n. 15. Eric Roll observes that the notion of incentive informs Aristotle's arguments for private property: people care for their own property more than communal property (*Pol* 1261b33–35, 1262b22–23, 1263a27–29) and are less likely to quarrel about property if it is distributed according to merit or industry (*Pol* 1267a39–41); see *A History of Economic Thought*, 4th ed. rev. (Homewood, Ill.: Richard D. Irwin, 1974), 31. As Schumpeter remarks, Aristotle's arguments for private property "read almost exactly like the arguments of middle-class liberals of the nineteenth century" (*History of Economic Analysis*, 59).

raising livestock, and raising other animals are the three "most proper" forms of livelihood because, productive only of limited things, they do not exacerbate acquisitiveness; they are the "most just" forms because they do not derive wealth from human beings (*Pol* 1257b33–1258a1, b1–2, 12–20; *Oec* 1343a28–29). Aristotle evidently agrees with Xenophon's Socrates that "[farming] seems to turn out the best citizens."[37]

But, as we know and as Aristotle has observed, a household is not as self-sufficient as a city (*Pol* 1261b11–12). Households may need the produce of other households; thus Aristotle says that citizens should share their private property (*Pol* 1329b41–1330a2). Sharing property is better than buying or selling it because it is a sign of and cultivates generosity, which is more noble than self-interest (*Pol* 1263a30–39, 1270a19–21; *NE* 1120b27–1121a7). But households also need their own artifacts and equipment—shoes, pots, harnesses—items citizens cannot expect their slaves to make because of their lack of expertise and their duties. Thus, need gives rise to a class of artisans (*Pol* 1291a1–2, 1328b6, 21) and a means for citizens to acquire their wares—that is, a market (*Pol* 1321b14–17, 1331b1–2).[38] This market should not apparently be restricted to barter and trade, as Barker and Ross imply, but should be open to commerce because, as noted earlier, a city needs taxpayers and other sources of revenue (*Pol* 1283a16–18, 1259a34–35; *Oec* II).[39] In short, paradoxically, human beings need the unnecessary sort of expertise in business (*Pol* 1258a14–16).[40] The need for commerce in

---

[37] *Oeconomicus*, trans. E. C. Marchant (Loeb Classical Library, 1923), 411–12.

[38] Such a class would be constituted of those who have more virtue than slaves but less virtue than citizens (*Pol* 1260a36–b2). Aristotle does not give a clear account of the virtues of the artisans as a human being; see *Aristotle: Politics*, trans. H. Rackham (Loeb Classical Library, 1932), 64 n. c. On the ambiguity, see *Politics*, vol. 2, ed. Newman, 222, note on 1260b1; for a different interpretation, see *Politics*, trans. Barker, 37 n. 2. Perhaps this only testifies to Aristotle's seeing not so much classes as gradations of virtue among human beings (see Chapter 2).

[39] Barker, *Political Thought*, 373–90, especially 375, 377, 389, 390; W. D. Ross, *Aristotle: A Complete Exposition of His Works and Thought* (New York: Meridian, 1959), 236.

[40] Roll observes that Aristotle's condemnation of usury is meant to set the ethical limits of commerce (*History of Economic Thought*, 33): it is wrong to accumulate money by selling money for the sake of accumulating money, but fine to accumulate money by selling goods for the sake of procuring other goods and services. It should be noted, however, that "Aristotle's long discussion of the two arts of money-making was not just an attempt to drive home an ethical distinction. . . . For the first time in the history of economic thought the dichotomy of money and real capital . . . is stated; but later economists stripped it of its ethical garb" (ibid., 33; see also 34, 35, and Schumpeter, *History of Economic Analysis*, 62).

all regimes, even in the best, accounts in part for Aristotle's inclusion of "an excursus on liberal economic theory" in his defense of agrarianism in Book I of the *Politics* (chaps. 8–11). The other reason for the excursus, which Havelock cites as the only reason, is Aristotle's desire to dethrone liberal economics.[41]

The Nature and Effect of Money-Making

Aristotle disagrees with the liberal view that, as Michael Oakeshott puts it, "productive enterprise" is "itself, internally, a want-satisfying activity."[42] Money-making intensifies rather than satisfies desire. It tends to become obsessive because money, unlike goods, can be accumulated without limit; it does not spoil or take up space, and the supply is limited virtually by how much others are willing to exchange (*Pol* I.9). Free enterprise does not yield freedom.[43] In fact, it can generate conflict: when men see others making a profit, they become angry out of envy or due to the perception that it "involves taking from others" (*Pol* 1258b1–2, 1302a38–b2). Finally, because money has only relative not absolute value (*Pol* 1257b10–14), its use habituates men to judge relatively. It is, then, the having rather than the acquiring of a certain amount of money that is pleasant and choiceworthy; having money fulfills the need to know that tomorrow's needs can be fulfilled easily (*NE* 1133b10–13)—knowledge that allows engagement in liberal pursuits today.[44]

Since a life focused on money discourages virtue, citizens should not engage in business (*Pol* 1328b39–41). Moreover, a regime cannot afford to lose its citizens—its soldiers, rulers, fathers, philosophers, and priests—to obsessive and incendiary pursuits. Since

---

[41] Havelock, *Liberal Temper*, 353–65.

[42] *On Human Conduct*, 293–94.

[43] See also William J. Booth, "Politics and the Household: A Commentary on Aristotle's *Politics* Book One," *History of Political Thought* 2, no. 2 (1981), 221, 223; Leo Strauss, *The City and Man* (Chicago: University of Chicago, 1964), 33.

[44] To appreciate Aristotle's point more precisely, one should also note that he is critical not of producing or making but of acquiring. He seems to rank action (*praxis*) above production (*poiēsis*) when he says that "life is action not production" (*Pol* 1254a7)—apparently because production is not activity for its own sake (*NE* 1140b6–7); see *Politics*, trans. Barker, 10 n. 2. Nonetheless, he includes in the category of *poiēsis* the making of an argument, a speech, and a poem—products he deems, in the *Topics, Rhetoric, Poetics,* and *Metaphysics,* important to living well; see John Herman Randall, Jr., *Aristotle* (New York: Columbia University Press, 1960), 272; Arendt, *Human Condition,* 301. In short, Aristotle appears hostile only to the 'homo faber mentality' central to classical economics, insofar as classical economics has corrupted *poiēsis* (see Arendt, *Human Condition,* 304, 306).

Aristotle recognizes the need for a market and merchants even in the best regime, we must therefore conclude that he thinks that noncitizens should transact business.[45] He would seem then to be recommending the sort of arrangement that existed during his time, according to which only outsiders—transient and resident aliens—carried out business; he might also agree with Xenophon, who, in a pamphlet on revenues, notes that metics are one of the best sources of revenue since they pay taxes and are not paid by the state.[46] Yet Aristotle notes two dangers of admitting "the seafaring mass" to the polis: overpopulation resulting in poverty, which in turn leads to unrest and crime (*Pol* 1265b6–12, 1327b7–8),[47] and democratization.[48] He reminds us that citizens are draftable and that, when the lowest class of citizens help to bring about a victory, the cause of democracy is strengthened because they thereafter have influence in the assembly (*Pol* 1304a17–24, *AC* 27.1).[49] It would be better, then, for public and private slaves—noncitizen members of the city (*Pol* 1326a16–21, b20–22), not immigrants—to transact business for citizens. Apparently, the main acquiring a free male householder should do is that of acquiring servants.

The Just Price versus the Natural Price

What principle should govern the allocation of goods within the market? Aristotle indicates that the principle of distributive justice is proportionate equality: "As builder is to shoemaker, so must the number of shoes be to a house" (*NE* 1133a22–23)—but what exactly does this mean? A compelling interpretation, which both Finley and Polanyi put forth, is that the producer's standing in or worth to the community ought to determine the value and so the price of his products.[50] Thus, not only should the builder's house command

---

[45] In a significant but unelaborated departure from his thesis that Aristotle has only an embedded concept of economy, one in which community, not gain, is the object, Polanyi states: "If exceptionally gainful retailing there must be for the sake of a convenient distribution of goods in the market-place, let it be done by noncitizens" ("Aristotle Discovers the Economy," 97).

[46] See Finley, "Aristotle and Economic Analysis," 156–58, and *Ancient Economy*, 65, 70–79, 162–64.

[47] As is well known, T. R. Malthus made the study of the economic ramifications of population size part of classical economics (O'Brien, *Classical Economists*, 56–66).

[48] Aristotle may be responding to Xenophon's proposal to allow metics to own residential property (see Finley, *Ancient Economy*, 163, and "Aristotle and Economic Analysis," 158).

[49] See also *Politics*, trans. Barker, 213 n. 2, 378, and *Politics*, trans. Lord, 260 n. 27.

[50] See Finley, "Aristotle and Economic Analysis," 142–48; Polanyi, "Aristotle Discovers the Economy," 97, 107–8.

more than the shoemaker's pair of shoes, but builder Ariston's house might command more than builder Aischron's. Another possible meaning is that the skills of each producer, abstracted from the talent brought to those skills and from social status, should determine price.[51] Thus, Ariston's and Aischron's houses should command the same price. According to Schumpeter, if this is Aristotle's meaning, then it appears that he "was groping for some labor-cost theory of price" or reaching for the notion of abstract labor as the basis for the commensurability of goods. But Schumpeter's speculative interpretation contravenes the spirit if not the letter of proportionate equality.[52] It seems that Aristotle indeed thinks that the worth of the producer should determine the price of his products; but it is important to say, as Finley and Polanyi do not, that Aristotle maintains that a community ought to base the worth of a producer and thus of his goods or services— not on his family name, wealth, or the fact that he is a human being—but on his talent or expertise and, insofar as these presuppose integrity or other moral qualities, his moral virtue (NE 1131a24–29). Put differently, because the caliber of a good or service reflects the excellence (or lack thereof) of the producer—who chooses what to produce (a cure, a lecture, a table) and is responsible for its quality (a fradulent cure, an organized lecture, a sturdy table)—the producer's excellence merits reward.

Aristotle means then that 'as builder X's excellence is to shoemaker Y's, so must the number of Y's shoes be to X's house.' Prices among houses and shoes should vary considerably; a pair of Mr. Reliable's durable shoes should command more than Mr. Cheapskate's shack. Likewise, not all products or services of a kind

[51] The view of Schumpeter, Spengler, and Soudek as reported by Finley, "Aristotle and Economic Analysis," 146.

[52] Schumpeter, History of Economic Analysis, 60–61 n. 1. Aristotle would no more think of the builder's labor as simply a multiple of the shoemaker's than he would think of the man's courage as simply a multiple of the woman's, or of the woman's intellect a multiple of the slave's. This is not because, as Marx explains and Finley agrees, Aristotle was blinded by his culture's prejudices and practices from seeing the homogeneity of human labor; it is the result rather of Aristotle's observing and reflecting on the differences among human beings and their achievements or products; see Finley, "Aristotle and Economic Analysis," 148; Harvey C. Mansfield, Jr., "Marx on Aristotle: Freedom, Money, and Politics," Review of Metaphysics 34, no. 2 (1980), 355–57, 363, 367. As Finley points out, Schumpeter's hypothesis is also rendered doubtful by the fact that "Aristotle does not once refer to labour costs or costs of production" ("Aristotle and Economic Analysis," 146; see also Ancient Economy, 81).

should command the same price: as author P is to author Q, so the price of author P's book should be to that of author Q's book; likewise, professor A's classes should command higher fees than professor F's; at the same time, perhaps carpenter Sam's services should command higher fees than professor F's.

But Aristotle also identifies need as the basis of price: money is merely "the exchangeable representation of need" (*NE* 1133a26–29). Different things cannot in fact become commensurate—an apple, a trinket, and a book seem to have different values apart from circumstances—but, for practical purposes, "they can become commensurate enough in relation to our needs" (1133b19–20).[53] On this account, price is necessarily determined by the buyer's estimate of his need and of the capacity of an item or service to fulfill it, and by the seller's estimate of his need(s) and of the capacity of an amount of money (its purchasing power) to fulfill them.

These two accounts of the just price are in one way compatible. Taken together, they indicate that price ought to reflect a judicious or true estimate of need; the price of an item or service ought to measure its contribution to virtue or noble living. Citizens ought to need the right products and services. Ideally, the market would be a place in which prudence and moderation were exercised and through which other virtues were facilitated: a preserve of private activity. But Aristotle is not, contrary to Polanyi's assertion, naive. This concept of the just price is an ideal, one that presumes that consumers consider their true or civilized needs. Demand *should* be a function of the requirements of virtue.[54] Still, Aristotle realizes that wants do not always reflect virtue or the interests of the community but nonetheless do set prices (*NE* 1133b1–3). The bargained, or "natural," price must prevail.[55]

[53] Even Marx credits Aristotle with the discovery of the commensurability of goods. But Marx argues that need cannot be the basis for commensurability because it is subjective or "partly arbitrary," whereas human labor is objective or "nonarbitrary." Aristotle would point out in response that only need could possibly render a toilet bowl commensurable with the most beautiful painting (see Mansfield, "Marx on Aristotle," 354–55, 360).

[54] As Roll says, "in Aristotle we see the first separation and reunion of the positive and the ethical approach to the economic process. . . . But the distinction between the forms which economic activity actually takes and the ethical precepts which should underlie it is clearly brought out" (*History of Economic Thought*, 35).

[55] Put broadly, the best regime is possible because "no miraculous or non-miraculous change in human nature is required for its actualization; it does not

But Aristotle recognizes not only the intractability but the salutariness of self-interest or neediness, especially in economic matters. First of all, neediness, whether in its correct or perverse form, makes human beings willing to engage in exchange or reciprocate, and only exchange can bring about self-sufficiency (*NE* 1133b6–10, 1133a2; *Pol* 1321b14–18). By contrast, Polanyi argues that Aristotle thinks self-interest precludes reciprocity: "The bargained price might yield a profit to one of the parties at the expense of the other, and thus undermine the coherence of the community instead of underpinning it."[56] Recall that Aristotle says commerce involves taking from others, but he also says "by their consent." This does not make commerce necessarily just, but it cannot be understood to have the power of undermining the community in the way that war does (*Oec* 1343a28–33). The unifying effect of self-interest tends to outweigh its divisive potential. Self-interest, by way of commerce, is salutary also in that it generates revenue for the city. Indeed, one wonders if behind Aristotle's recommendation to confine the market to one locale in the regime (*Pol* 1331b6–13) lies not only a concern for the virtue of the citizens but for the degree of competition in the market.

The Role of Government: Agoranomoi *and Treasurers*

As even Adam Smith observed, competition alone cannot optimize exchange.[57] It is not then without reason that Aristotle dis-

---

require the abolition or extirpation of that evil or imperfection which is essential to man and to human life"; see Leo Strauss, *Natural Right and History* (Chicago: University of Chicago, 1953), 139; contrast Polanyi, "Aristotle Discovers the Economy," 107. Technically, according to Adam Smith, the natural price is the "right norm" of market prices (Cropsey, *Polity and Economy,* 72; O'Brien, *Classical Economists,* 79, 80, 82). Schumpeter also thinks that Aristotle is arguing that competitive prices are the standards of commutative justice, but he rejects the claim that Aristotle believes goods and services have inherent objective, "metaphysical" values (*History of Economic Analysis,* 61–62).

In addition, as Finley points out against Polanyi, Aristotle "knew perfectly well that prices sometimes responded to variations in supply and demand"; the relative value of currency and the supply-demand-price mechanism did not escape him (see *Pol* 1259a5–36, 1308a36–38; *NE* 1133b13–14, as cited by Finley, "Aristotle and Economic Analysis," 149; see also Roll, *History of Economic Thought,* 35). Schumpeter, who decries the early theory of supply and demand as close to common sense, nonetheless admits that it is scientific (*History of Economic Analysis,* 9).

56 "Aristotle Discovers the Economy," 108; see also 97, 110–11.

57 O'Brien, *Classical Economists,* 31–33; see also Cropsey, "Adam Smith," 651, 652, and "Political Morality and Liberalism," in *Political Philosophy and the Issues of Politics* (Chicago: University of Chicago Press, 1977), 138. On the role classical economics in general assigns to government, see O'Brien, *Classical Economists,* 272–77; Oakeshott, *On Human Conduct,* 294–95.

cusses legal justice after he identifies want as the basis of exchange (*NE* V.6–7). In the *Politics* he recommends specifically that regimes establish the office of market manager (*agoranomos*) to make and enforce rules of fair practice (1321b12–14, 1299b16–17). Describing the Athenian arrangement, Aristotle writes:

> Market magistrates . . . are required by the laws to take responsibility for all goods that are on sale, to ensure that what is sold is in good condition and genuine. . . . measures magistrates . . . are responsible for all measures and weights, to ensure that the salesmen use honest standards. . . . corn-wardens . . . are responsible for seeing, first, that the unground corn is sold honestly in the market, and then that the millers sell the meal in accordance with the price which they paid for the barley-corn, and that the bread-sellers sell the loaves in accordance with the price which they paid for the wheat and that their loaves are of the prescribed weight. . . . port-superintendents . . . are bidden to take responsibility for trade and to compel the traders to convey to the city two thirds of the . . . [incoming] corn. (*AC* 51)

Such regulation is necessary in the markets of all regimes (*Pol* 1321b12, 1299b10–12), since not only slaves but also ordinary citizens are tempted to engage in corruption. But how regimes effect superintendence of the market may vary. A regime may decide to subsume the office of market manager under "a single office for orderliness" or charge a local board with overseeing the market (1299b14–20). Moreover, it may select *agoranomoi* in any of twelve ways (1300a30–31); the best way, however, is to appoint or elect from among persons with appropriate acumen or expertise (1299b25, 1300b4–5).[58] By any means, there should be greater supervision of the best regime's market, both because it is easier to control slaves than free persons and because the best regime should of course meet higher standards of conduct in all areas (1299b27–30, 1300a4–8).[59]

Regimes should also establish the office of treasurer (*tamias*), to collect funds and allocate them to various government agencies

[58] For a summary of the ways, see *Politics*, trans. Lord, 259 n. 58, and Harvey C. Mansfield, Jr., *Taming the Prince: The Ambivalence of Modern Executive Power* (New York: Free Press, 1989), 308 n. 27.

[59] Thus, apparently, Aristotle thinks that obedient slaves might conduct themselves better in the market than might less supervised ordinary citizens.

(*Pol* 1321b31–33). This office should tax most "the special products of the country"; at a rate only second to these, sales and services that are not "everyday transactions"; necessary goods and services should be taxed the least (*Oec* 1346a6–8). The tax office should also make sure that the regime's budget is balanced (*Pol* 1314b4–5, *Oec* 1348b23–30). This function is important enough that government may have to find innovative, even nobly deceitful, ways to collect funds, of which Book II of the *Oeconomica* provides dozens of examples.[60]

Every regime should have, then, at least these two exclusively "economic" offices (*ai oikonomikai*) (*Pol* 1299a23, 1259a35–36, 1256b36–37). These offices should not, however, carry with them the sort of power a general has (*Pol* 1300b9–12). Regimes should not have command economies;[61] regulations should not be many or strict (*Pol* 1264a29–32);[62] and government should tax only according to its current or anticipated needs. A well-managed city does not tax and spend unnecessarily (*Pol* 1314a40–b7).[63] In fact, because economic offices should not be powerful, they should not, technically, be called offices (*archas*) (*Pol* 1299a20–28).

Why should economic administration exert less power than political rule? Because of the nature of economic activity and the needs of regimes. It would be futile to try to limit much what is by nature limitless; circumscribing free enterprise beyond a certain

---

[60] For example, Mausolus, lord of Caria, told the people of Mylassa that their unfortified city was under threat of attack and solicited funds to build walls, but he kept the money without building them (*Oec* 1348a11–18).

[61] During the Peloponnesian War, before an expedition, generals arranged to have local markets along a prospective route set up or prepared for the arrival of their troops; also, both armies and navies brought along civilian retailers, whose job it was to wait on the men and sometimes to sell booty locally (Polanyi, "Aristotle Discovers the Economy," 103–4, which cites Xenophon's *Cyropaedia* VI.ii.38f and the Aristotelian *Oeconomica* II.23a). Thus, military leaders literally commanded economies. Aristotle may be making (at *Pol* 1300b9–12) an oblique reference to this practice.

[62] See *Politics*, vol. 4, ed. Newman, 268, note on 1300b11.

[63] Greek city-states normally levied taxes on an ad hoc basis, when they needed to finance a war or expedition, relieve famine, or the like. According to Finley, any form of direct uniform tax was considered tyrannical (*Ancient Economy*, 164, 175). The various temporary ways cities should raise revenue according to Aristotle may be found not only throughout Book II of the *Oeconomica* but in the *Politics* as well; for example, governments might establish temporary monopolies (1259a21–35). Aristotle thinks, however, contrary to the apparent practice of most ancient city-states, that government should act more prudently by always having sufficient funds to finance a war (*Pol* 1271b10–17, 1314b14–16).

extent makes it unfree. Furthermore, it may be that unregulated interests tend toward order. Aristotle would remind us as well that regimes need funds; regulations should keep economic activity orderly and as ethical as possible, they should not repress a source of revenue.

In sum, according to Aristotle, government has the tricky task of both overseeing and reaping the necessary benefits of the economy. Laws must be conducive to the preservation of a regime, but at the same time the regime should not exist for the sake of transacting business (*Pol* 1280a31–38, b17–35).[64]

THE SECOND-BEST ECONOMY

Regimes lacking ideal conditions—enough land for two tracts per household, a class of good men, and a class of natural inferiors to support them—must necessarily make more concessions to free enterprise. If there is not enough land and slaves for each citizen to live moderately, then some or all citizens must support themselves; wage labor and money-lending must complement agriculture and retailing as means of livelihood (*Pol* 1278a15–18, 1258b25, 1289b27–35, 1290b38–1291a6, b18–20). This is the situation that exists in democracies and oligarchies (1290a13–16, 1291b11–16).

Furthermore, the marketing element has to be greater in number and more vigorous than in the best regime, for the city has a greater need for revenue. Like the best regime, ordinary regimes have to support a militia (*Pol* 1291a7–8, b21) and provide common public services, but they also have to provide meals to their poor. The best regime too should provide common messes, but these should serve as political assemblies for the citizens (*Pol* 1330a3–8). How can ordinary regimes manage to feed their poor? Aristotle recommends the Cretan system: crops and animals for common meals are grown and raised on public land by farmers who rent the land for the privilege of keeping the surplus (*Pol* 1272a16–21). According to Aristotle, this form of welfare is the most just, for it ensures that the poor will not starve and yet does not enable them to live as they wish (*Pol* 1267b8–9); further, it does not require the middle and upper classes to support them without return (*NE*

[64] See also Strauss, *City and Man,* 32–33.

1132b31–34). If, however, there is not sufficient public land to support the poor, then a regime must resort to something like the Spartan system, according to which all citizens are taxed a fixed amount, the penalty for noncompliance being the revocation of the privilege to participate in government (*Pol* 1272a13–15).

Ordinary regimes also need more funds than does the best to finance public service, as Aristotle records was the practice in democratic Athens (*AC* 24.3). A regime should fine the wealthy (who prefer to attend to their business; *Oec* 1352a5–9) for failing to serve and use the fines—and presumably other revenue—to pay others to serve; this ensures that all do their duty (*Pol* 1297a38–41). But Aristotle endorses the exclusively Athenian practice of paying citizens for a range of duties not only for political but also apparently for economic reasons. He seems to have attributed the health of the Athenian economy, indicated by a virtual absence of demands for debt cancellations and land redistribution, to the distribution of public funds,[65] perhaps appreciating the general idea of supply-side economics? One suspects that he endorses pay for public service also because, unlike a welfare system, it effects reciprocity or justice.

Ordinary citizens can be counted on to generate through commerce the revenue needed for these public expenditures, for they desire lots of goods, luxuries, and profit, believing that an abundance of possessions and money brings happiness (*Pol* 1291a3–4, 1318b16–17, 1257b8–9, 20–23, 33–1258a2). The public, then, should take advantage of private acquisitiveness. At the same time, no government should encourage baseness; government should allow commerce but not endorse it as a way of life.[66] Accordingly, it should institute the best economic measures to the extent practicable: locate the market apart from the city and regulate it, prohibit officeholders from money-making, and encourage agrarian livelihoods (the latter it could achieve by taxing only or mostly manufactured goods rather than produce, and commercial rather than farm land).[67]

---

[65] See Finley, *Ancient Economy*, 173.

[66] See also Cropsey, "On the Relation of Political Science and Economics," in *Political Philosophy*, 39, and Abram N. Shulsky, "The 'Infrastructure' of Aristotle's *Politics*" (Ph.D. diss., University of Chicago, 1972), 226–27.

[67] The rationale for encouraging agriculture in ordinary cities differs from the rationale for an agriculturally based economy in the best regime. In the latter, farming as a livelihood keeps citizens from producing and consuming too much; in

A regime may in addition establish an upper limit on the amount of wealth any one citizen can accumulate—this being the greatest amount of wealth one can have without becoming so arrogant as to desire to rule continuously (*Pol* 1295b3–1296a2, 22–27). But if this limit is too low, the regime cannot benefit from the rich. Besides, any attempts to equalize property by law are ordinarily undone by common insatiable greed (*Pol* 1267a37–b5). Contrary to the claims of Phaleas and later of Marx, material conditions cannot alone eradicate or even substantially quell the limitless desire of human beings; citizens should receive education rather than equal property (*Pol* 1266a36–39, b28–31). Property matters per se should be left alone (*Pol* 1267b12–13).

It should be observed that the most acquisitive members of a society are the wealthiest only if they also have enough self-restraint (*engkrateia*) not to squander their acquisitions. The most virtuous, such as the citizens of the best regime, do not have to be constantly mindful of their consumption, for intellectual engagement displaces or transforms desire; the temperate man (*ho sōphrōn*) has no need for will (*NE* 1146a9–12, 1104b5–6).[68] In any case, the various classes in a society, albeit apparently defined by their wealth, may in fact be defined by their virtue.

If a regime allows its populace to exercise their varying degrees of acquisitiveness while nonetheless encouraging them to be moderate and generous, the following should result. Those of middling acquisitiveness will have a sufficient amount of property and will be willing to share it; those more acquisitive will, by way of their striving, provide revenue for the city;[69] those who are least ac-

---

other regimes, its primary advantage is to keep the people too busy for politics; they will happily elect—on the basis of wealth or capability—a few among them to rule (*Pol* 1318b9–1319a4). Encouraging farming is, then, a way to turn democracy into oligarchy or aristocracy.

[68] By way of a story about Thales of Miletus, Aristotle conveys the power of intellectual activity to supplant the desire to accumulate and consume: Thales figured out a way to make money easily and quickly, "thus showing how easy it is for philosophers to become wealthy if they so wish"; yet Thales was not rich, because, as he explained to those who reproached him for being poor, wealth is not what philosophers "are serious about" (*Pol* 1259a6–18). See also Shulsky, "Infrastructure," 181.

[69] One might also observe that the tension between an individual's desire to increase personal wealth and the good of the whole, "whatever political difficulties it might cause, has the advantage of keeping the ethical question concerning wealth in view; a reconciliation would run the risk of allowing that question to fade from view in so far as the individual's actions no longer raised political resistance against them" (Shulsky, "Infrastructure," 217).

quisitive will benefit from the voluntarism of the well-off. At least with respect to political stability, it is fortunate if those of middling wealth predominate (*Pol* IV.11–12). A regime can, however, achieve an overall middling amount of wealth, and thus stability, with a mixture of classes (*Pol* 1297a6–7). In any case, a regime's economy should be arranged so as to profit from the different natures of its populace (*Pol* 1296b10–12).[70]

On the Relation between Politics and Economics

How might Aristotle's teaching on economics be summarized— for a legislator, for example? First, only at the peril of their regime can legislators adopt the strategy of solving economic matters by addressing exclusively the moral constitution or relationships of their populace. The urgency and universality of neediness eventually impacts on such a regime either through starvation or insurrection or both; the "naturally private" will not let itself be ignored.[71] Furthermore, an exclusively educational approach to economic problems overlooks the fact that in a naturally ordered regime those who affect the economy the most have the least capacity for virtue. At best, they are likely to think in terms of what is good for the economy, not in terms of what is good for the whole; charity and moderation may be lost sight of. Thus, Aristotle concludes, the fundamental macroeconomic decisions should be made

[70] As Ross explains Aristotle's proposed economy, "it is the sort of arrangement under which rich men give to the public the freest admission that is practicable to their picture-galleries, their parks, and their moors. In so far as socialism means a better organisation of industry by the state, Aristotle would be in sympathy with it, for he has a far more positive view of the state's functions than the *laissez-faire* school of individualism. But in so far as it means the taking away from private industry of its rewards, the attempt to create an equality of possessions which the natural inequality of capacity and industry will constantly upset, he is an individualist, and no one has better expressed the common sense of individualism" (*Aristotle*, 238). But Ross's surrounding commentary describes rich men out of existence by denying men the means to get rich in Aristotle's regime.

[71] Strauss uses this phrase to refer to the body (*City and Man*, 32). According to Strauss, Aristotle maintains that the public safety or the mere preservation of society should be the highest law only in extreme situations—situations "in which the very existence or independence of society is at stake." At the same time, he admits that "it is not possible . . . to define precisely what constitutes an extreme situation in contradistinction to a normal situation" (*Natural Right and History*, 160–61).

by legislators. Education can address economic concerns most effectively if it takes the form of law. In short, an economy is, albeit indirectly, a function of the virtue of a regime's legislators.[72]

Legislators should not, at the other extreme, address economic matters exclusively, or mistake economic prosperity for political success. A populace continually engaged in commerce, trade, and war with a view to empire—preoccupied with acquiring—cannot be happy either individually or collectively. Thus, according to Aristotle, legislators must acknowledge that economic matters are also always moral or political ones.[73]

Not all political matters are economic, for the demands of distributive and commutative justice only partially meet those of political friendship.[74] But, on the plane of economics, there is a dialectic

---

[72] This returns us to the question, raised earlier in the discussion about Castoriadis's views, as to what Aristotle means by the naturalness of the city. Like Castoriadis, David Keyt maintains that "Aristotle's own principles" in effect show that "the political community is an artifact of the practical reason, not a product of nature"; "Three Fundamental Theorems in Aristotle's Politics," *Phronesis* 32, no. 1 (1987), 54; see also 59–60. The context of this chapter calls for the following brief response to Keyt. According to Aristotle, although the existence of the economy, like that of the city, is dependent on law, it is a product of nature, for human appetites are its internal source of motion, the presence of which, Keyt argues, defines natural existence according to Aristotle. Consider also Randall's explanation of *Ph* 199a11–15, which is consistent with my point and worth quoting at length (one may find it helpful to substitute "economy" where Randall writes "house"): "'Processes by nature' and 'processes by art' . . . are not two quite different kinds of process. 'By nature,' *physei*, a tree is made out of a seed; 'by art,' *apo technēs*, a man makes a house out of wood and bricks. 'But,' says Aristotle, 'if a house had been a thing made by nature'—if the wood and bricks had grown into a house—'it would have been made by nature in the same way as it is now made by art; and if the things made by nature were made also by art'—if men could make a tree—'they would come to be in the same way as they now do by nature.' There is in each case a necessary order of means and ends that would have to be followed. Both are processes whereby natural materials are made by a natural agent to realize the forms potential in those materials, made to realize their implicit ends. And while nature cannot make a house in any other way than houses are made, and hence must work through man as her agent in housebuilding . . . and while man cannot make a tree, and hence must leave the making of trees to nature, we do not have here two radically incompatible kinds of process, but rather a natural cooperation" (*Aristotle*, 274–75). On the natural/conventional nature of Aristotle's economy, see also Mansfield, "Marx on Aristotle," 357.

[73] See Cropsey, "Political Science and Economics," 39; Mansfield, "Marx on Aristotle," 357–58, 363, 366–67.

[74] By contrast, according to Arendt (whose own views derive from her interpretation of the Greeks), economics is "the enemy of politics" because it lacks the "open-endedness" of politics and "rarely produces great speech"; see George Kateb, *Hannah Arendt: Politics, Conscience, Evil* (Totowa, N.J.: Rowman & Allanheld, 1983), 117, 122.

at work between it and the political. The economic arrangements of a regime necessarily shape the moral virtues of the inhabitants: what, where, and how often they produce, acquire, and consume affects their potential for happiness. But so also does their moral constitution, as shaped by their education or training, bear on the economy; only the vantage point of the more human activities reveals the never wholly satisfying nature of the life process and its proper role in life.

On the level of practice, Aristotle's advocacy of the hegemony of the political aims to prevent what amounts to a perverted preoccupation with self-preservation from dominating the lives of citizens and rulers. Such domination would, as Aristotle seems to have foreseen, transform citizens into jobholders and rulers into managers.[75] Focused on the naturally private, no one would have the time or the inspiration to pursue or to encourage truly private activities.

On the philosophical level, Aristotle shows that the economic does not permeate human relationships. His strategy is to reveal the economic as a practically distinct part of life and a theoretically distinct part of political thinking. His recommendation that regimes physically contain the market may even be understood as a metaphor for his theoretical objective. Aristotle exposes economics ultimately in order to point out that the study that derives from preoccupation with the naturally private is only a part of the study of the public and the private.

---

[75] See Oakeshott, *On Human Conduct*, 143–47; Arendt, *Human Condition*, 45.

5

Preservative Law:
Ordering the Regime

Like the household and the economy, laws according to Aristotle ought to serve both a utilitarian function and, if possible, virtue. A city cannot be good or aspire to goodness unless it lasts, so the foremost aim of laws must be to preserve a city. In this chapter I discuss the sorts of laws or legal provisions that must be present in any city for it to last.

Preserving the Private

The central teaching in Aristotle's discussion of indispensable laws is that a city cannot last without securing order. Although that teaching may be obvious to all but proponents of anarchy, what securing order requires is not always accepted or understood. According to Aristotle, order requires cultivating habits in human beings, because not all human beings respond to argument, living as passion directs (*NE* 1179b23–1180a5). By embodying reason and either the promise of reward or the threat of punishment, laws have the power to cultivate habits, in effect judging for individuals. What is more, laws should cultivate not only public habits but private habits, habits that would seem not to bear on a city (*NE* 1180a2–4). Not always understood is the significance of Aristotle's advocacy of laws that embody reason. If the habits laws encourage are reasonable, then the thinking person is able to understand the rationale for the conduct laws desire. For such a person, laws are

not so much a substitution for his judgment as a great convenience
or "salvation" in that they save him the trouble of always choosing
conduct (*Pol* 1310a34–36). In any case, the aim of law should be to
render everyone—the thoughtful and the thoughtless, the rulers
and the ruled, the minority and the majority—supportive of the
regime, for anyone might be the source of its destruction (*Pol*
1294b36–40, 1337a14–17).

Also not appreciated is that Aristotle maintains that laws should
require individuals to exercise their own judgment over many matters of conduct, public and private. Indeed, the aim of the rule of
law is not to command the performance of substantive actions but
to stipulate subscription to the qualitative conditions of civil association.[1] Contrary to Hannah Arendt's interpretation, legislators
are not architects whose aim it is to control or preclude all significant political action but educators whose aim it is to encourage a
way of life.[2] Laws cannot fabricate that way of life because they
cannot make persons choose correctly. They can only try to make
them understand the benefit or virtue of certain choices. As Aristotle says, human beings can only "become good *through* laws [*dia
nomōn*]" (*NE* 1180b25). Accordingly, he believes that the excellence
of the citizens, not simply of the laws, determines the excellence of
a regime (*Pol* 1332a33–35).

---

[1] As Michael Oakeshott explains in "The Rule of Law," in *On History and Other
Essays* (Oxford: Basil Blackwell, 1983), 129.

[2] Arendt, *The Human Condition* (Chicago: University of Chicago Press, 1958), 194–
98, 223–30. See also my critique of Richard Bodéüs's interpretation in the Appendix,
"Premises of Interpretation." Aristotle makes this point also in the last chapter of
Book II of the *Politics*, where he distinguishes between legislators who were "crafts-
men of laws only," such as Draco, Pittacus, and Androdamas of Rhegium, and those
brought about "a regime as well," such as Lycurgus and Solon (1273b32–33). The
difference between the two groups is not, as might be thought, that the first merely
added laws to existing regimes whereas the second founded wholly new regimes;
both groups evidently relied on existing provisions (1273b41–1274a1, b15–24). (This
stands as evidence, of which more follows in this chapter, that Aristotle does not
regard legislators, even such celebrated ones as Solon, as founders of new modes
and orders as did Machiavelli.) The difference is rather, that the laws of Draco,
Pittacus, and Androdamas only prohibited bad actions rather than encouraged
good conduct and government. Aristotle praises Solon's legislation, and although
he is not uncritical of the Spartan way of life, his point is to contrast the two ways of
legislating and to proclaim in favor of bringing about a way of life. In doing so he is
criticizing, as he does elsewhere, the liberal view according to which a regime is
reducible to a covenant. Rule by *lex* or contemporary legislative acts that are merely
legal in intention and scope can achieve only a rights-based alliance; by contrast,
rule by *nomos* aspires to bring about a just and good way of life; see *The Politics of
Aristotle*, trans. Ernest Barker (Oxford: Clarendon, 1948), lxxi–lxxii.

THE RULE OF LAW VERSUS THE RULE OF MEN

If Aristotle deems certain sorts of law or legal provision necessary to the existence of any city, then it seems that he must deem
the rule of at least those laws superior to the rule of men. In fact,
his debate over the question of whether laws or men should rule
supports that conclusion (*Pol* 1286a7–24, 1287a16–b26). The debate
is indeed of less interest for its unsurprising general conclusion—
that both laws and men should rule—than for its finding about the
laws that should rule.

The central points of the debate are as follows. The main advantage of rule by men is that men can deliberate over particular cases;
its main disadvantage is that self-interest, prejudice, or ambition
may influence deliberation. The main advantage of rule by law is
that laws are impartial; its main disadvantage is that laws cannot
judge individual cases. Aristotle raises a couple of red herrings to
make very clear the actual advantage of each sort of rule, which in
turn persuades us of his conclusion.[3] A political order needs both
the discretionary ability of men and the impartiality of laws, because the universal is not just in all cases and men are not always
impartial. What is more, laws and men can rule cooperatively only
if the men are more lawlike and the laws more like men: justice
requires reasonable men and flexible laws (*Pol* 1282b1–6, 1287a25–
27, b5–8, 25–26, 1292a32–34).

This brings us to what is really of interest in the debate. Aristotle
does not conclude simply that laws should rule along with men, but
that only a certain kind of law should be superior to the rule of men.
Laws that a regime cannot persist without should not be replaced by
the rule of men. They should, however, be able to be complemented

---

[3] First, he says in effect that, although one might think that an advantage of rule
by men is their ability to address difficult matters of justice, if laws cannot address
difficult matters, then neither can a human being (*Pol* 1287a23–25). This observation
reminds us that men make laws, but the point is that we should not confuse the
ability to judge particulars with the ability to judge difficult matters. When mea-
sured by the latter, men are no better than laws. Second, one might think that an
advantage of law is that it can oversee many matters at once; but Aristotle suggests
that several persons could do so (*Pol* 1287b8–9). The law-versus-men debate thus
leads to a debate over whether the rule of one or of a plurality is more choiceworthy,
a debate discussed later in this chapter. For now, it suffices to say that, on balance,
Aristotle argues that the rule of some is safer than the rule of one. He thereby puts
to rest the thought that law is advantageous because of the scope of matters it can
address.

by the rule of men—sufficiently flexible so as to be tailored to the particular conditions of a regime. These laws might be thought of as constitutional laws that could be embodied in a document.

In Chapter 6, I investigate the "reasonable men" that should rule along with law and how, apart from habituation by preservative or constitutional laws, Aristotle thinks they can become reasonable.

THE RULE OF LAW

To see that Aristotle means by 'the rule of law' the rule of preservative laws, one must begin with the law-versus-men debate in the *Politics* and then draw on the *Nicomachean Ethics, Metaphysics,* and *Rhetoric.* Aristotle introduces the question of whether law or men should rule with the paradox that passion or prejudice may permeate law; law may be oligarchic or democratic, for example (*Pol* 1281a34–38). In his continuing discussion, he completes the paradox. Law can permeate or influence men in two ways. A man may hold law or a general principle in his mind or may be habituated to the spirit of the laws of his regime (1286a16–17, 1287a25, b25–26). Since law may be impassioned, that habituation may not be wholly desirable. Law may, however, also be dispassionate (1286a17–19, 1287a28–30, 32, b4–5). With this claim, Aristotle clarifies the debate without eliminating the paradox. The rule of law is distinct from the rule of men insofar as it is good law. Aristotle does not need to make his definition of law explicit because both *nomos* and *dikē,* like "law" and "justice," connote rightness.[4] Nonetheless, by the fourth century B.C. the primary sense of *nomos* was "written statute"; like "law" for us, *nomos* had a primarily positivist connotation.[5] Aristotle therefore treats the difference between law and justice,[6] and therewith that between good and bad law, in the *Nicomachean Ethics.*

Aristotle's discussion of natural and legal justice indicates how laws can be impartial even though they are necessarily made by men who are necessarily subject to desire or spiritedness (*Pol*

---

[4] *Politics,* trans. Barker, lxxi.

[5] See H. J. Wolff, "'Normenkontrolle' und Gesetzesbegriff in der attischen Demokratie," *Sitzungsberichte der Heidelberger Akademie der Wissenschaften, philosophisch-historische Klasse,* no. 2 (Heidelberg: Jahrgang, 1970), 68–76.

[6] See also *Politics,* trans. Barker, lxxi.

1286a19–20, 1287a31–32). Being formulated by men, laws may derive from either their passions or their intellect. Insofar as they
derive from intellect or knowledge, they derive from what is universal and unchanging (*NE* V.7, 1180a21–22, b20–22, 25–27,
1141a7–8, 21–25; *Met* 1074b26–28; *Pol* 1332a31–32).[7] Nothing can
guarantee that men will formulate laws objectively, but the activity
of law-making is conducive to their doing so. First, it is a slow
process, allowing time for reflection; unlike commands, laws are
not issued on the spur of the moment. Second, because laws apply
not to present particular cases but to a category of cases in the
future, "love, hate, or personal interest" is less likely, and "the
truth" is more likely, to influence their formulation (*Rh* I.1.7). Third
and most important, legislators formulate laws from "laws resting
on custom" or long-standing precedent. These serve as the political
conduit of natural law (making universals accessible to the non-
noetic) insofar as they are devoid of mere prejudice or opinion.

The debate in Book III of the *Politics* over whether law or men
should rule does not, then, weigh rule by any sort of positive law
against rule by discretion; it weighs rule by a particular kind of
positive law, law based on universal or natural law, against rule by
discretion. Further evidence for this claim is as follows. Aristotle
declares toward the end of the debate that "laws resting on
customs are more authoritative, and deal with more authoritative
matters, than laws resting on writings; so even if it is safer for a
human being to rule than laws resting on writings, this is not the
case for laws resting on custom" (1287b5–8). What are customs (*ta
ethē*) according to Aristotle? In the *Rhetoric*, he observes that there
are two sorts of laws, particular and general. In one place he states,
"By particular, I mean the written law in accordance with which a
city is administered; by general, the unwritten laws which appear
to be universally recognized" (*Rh* I.10.3). Particular appear to corre-
spond with written and general with unwritten laws, or more precisely with unwritten, universally recognized, laws—leaving open
the possibility that there are unwritten, not universally recognized
laws—though it is not clear whether Aristotle would call such laws
particular or general. Later, he clarifies himself: "By particular laws
I mean those established by each people in reference to themselves, which again are divided into written and unwritten; by

---

[7] See also ibid., 366.

general laws I mean those based upon nature" (*Rh* I.10.3). But if general laws are universally recognized unwritten laws, then they must form part of every particular community's unwritten laws. Unwritten laws include both universally recognized laws, laws based on nature, and the unwritten rules of a particular community.[8] Natural law and custom must somehow be fused.

Testimony to the claim that Aristotle believes natural law and custom intertwine is his declaration that a city cannot exist without attending to "the divine" and listing this need, in the same sentence, as both "first" and "fifth" among a city's needs (*Pol* 1328b2–3, 11–12, 1322b31). This declaration makes sense if one invokes two meanings of 'the divine.' A city cannot last unless it heeds the naturally divine precepts, which can be known through reason, and the conventionally divine precepts, which can be known through myths (*NE* 1178b21–23, *Met* 1074b1–14). A city should above all abide by the natural truths. The natural truths, however, reveal paradoxically that human beings need other truths, or piety. Thus, reason or natural law conveys the need for customs.

Although natural law teaches the *need* for customs, customs may or may not particularize natural truths. Customs may be practices people have simply opined to be good (such as a Greek one that men should carry weapons and purchase their wives) or they may be practices people have come to know to be good, expressing natural precepts (for example, that a society cannot exist without rulers and ruled). "Laws resting on customs are more authoritative . . . than those resting on writings" (or contemporary legislation) (*Pol* 1287b5–6) because they are more likely to express natural precepts. Natural precepts are precepts societies cannot last long without heeding; they have therefore already been discovered and become embodied in customs. This implies that legislators should sort out the truly good customary laws from the others. They can go about this by examining "collections of laws and political systems," seeking out those laws that derive from custom or that appear to be ancient and, of those, the laws that are

---

[8] As Martin Ostwald observes, the meaning of *agraphoi nomoi* (unwritten laws) varies according to context in Aristotle's works, referring to both particular and general moral norms. In fact, Ostwald concludes from his study of the phrase in Greek literature that it has no one meaning, referring in various contexts to ordinances sanctioned by the gods or nature, eternal or local moral codes, social pressures, or ritual regulations ("Was There a Concept *agraphos nomos* in Classical Greece?" in *Exegesis and Argument: Studies in Greek Philosophy Presented to Gregory Vlastos*, ed. E. N. Lee, A. P. D. Mourelatos, and R. M. Rorty [Assen: Van Gorcum, 1973], 101–3).

common to all political systems. Thus, they should seek out neither simply ancient laws, nor those that are simply widespread,
but those that are both ancient and widespread—that have stood
the test of time and circumstance (*NE* 1180b20–22, 1181b6–9; *Rh*
I.4.13).

Such a search yields two results. Legislators discover all the laws
or legal provisions that are necessary for a regime to exist; more
precisely, as Aristotle says, they find embodied in ancient, widespread laws what has already been discovered and rediscovered an
infinite number of times (*Pol* 1329b25–34). In addition, they see the
many ways these fundamental laws can be tailored and enacted to
suit various circumstances. In sum, by familiarizing themselves
with traditional constitutional laws, legislators can find the measures that will keep their own regime in existence for the longest
time possible (*Pol* 1288b28–30).

Aristotle therefore clearly opposes the belief, held by the cre-
atively-dressed Hippodamus, that innovation is politically salutary
(*Pol* 1267b22–1268a14). From the progressive's or rationalist's point
of view, new ideas are essential to political progress, and old ideas
impede it; the political solution requires a tabula rasa. To look to or
rely on tradition for answers to the political problem constitutes a
failure of imagination or of creative effort.[9] In contrast, according to
Aristotle, politics calls not for imagination but for prudence, the
ability to detect what works. Indeed, a regime that arises "directly
out of those that exist" (*Pol* 1289a1–4) is more likely than a new one
to be just and to last.[10]

[9] For a critique of political rationalism, see Michael Oakeshott, "Rationalism in
Politics," in *Rationalism in Politics and Other Essays* (London: Methuen, 1962), 1–36.

[10] As Eric Voegelin explains, because law-making cannot alter given material
conditions, "the lawgiver's nomothetic art will be oriented toward perfect actualization but concretely he must be satisfied with the best he can do. . . . Politics as a
nomothetic science, however, did not have the task of transforming the imperfect
forms into the best form. On the contrary, any such attempt was rejected as it would
only lead to disturbances and revolutions. The perverse forms were to be accepted
as they existed historically; and the lawgiver's art should only minimize their evils
in order to preserve and stabilize them. . . . the nomothetic therapy seems to have
no other purpose than to make the perverse form as durable as possible"; *Plato and
Aristotle*, vol. 3, *Order and History* (Baton Rouge: Louisiana State University Press,
1957), 324, 358–59. Clarifying Aristotle's position, P. A. Vander Waerdt explains that
legislators should be guided by a "double teleology"—preservation and the good
life; see "The Political Intention of Aristotle's Moral Philosophy," *Ancient Philosophy*
5, no. 1 (1985), 79, 87–88. Voegelin merely emphasizes that in practice preservation
must be the foremost legislative aim or that "perfection must be understood in
relation to the range of action of a lawgiver" (*Plato and Aristotle*, 323). See also my
discussion of Pierre Pellegrin's views in the Appendix, "The Composition of Aristotle's *Politics*," pp. 224–26.

ARISTOTLE'S ARGUMENT AGAINST CHANGING
PATRIOI NOMOI

Aristotle gives several arguments against overriding traditional
laws (*patrioi nomoi*) (*Pol* 1268b26–1269a27)—laws resting on
custom.[11] As usual, he presents his arguments dialectically, in this

---

[11] Aristotle's arguments may be understood to be commentary on the revision of
the Athenian laws, completed in 403/2 B.C., which involved a debate over resurrect-
ing ancestral laws. The revision incorporated some *patrioi nomoi* but declared others
invalid; see Douglas M. MacDowell, *The Law in Classical Athens* (London: Thames
and Hudson, 1978), 47–48; Martin Ostwald, *From Popular Sovereignty to the Sovereignty of Law: Law, Society, and Politics in Fifth-Century Athens* (Berkeley: University
of California Press, 1986), 165–67, 370–72, 406–16, 514–15. The *patrioi nomoi* were
various sorts of laws—religious, secular, written, and unwritten—but parties to the
debate focused on the ancestral constitutions of Solon and Cleisthenes; see *AC* 29.3;
Ostwald, "Was There a Concept *agraphos nomos?*" 90–91, and *From Popular Sovereignty*, 146, 163–68, 514; MacDowell, *Law in Classical Athens*, 192, 194.
   There was disagreement as to whether those ancient lawgivers had populist
intentions. The populists (*dēmotikoi*) (who prevailed, instituting the regime which
was still in existence at the time of Aristotle's writing) appealed to the ancient
constitutions to justify the continuation of popular sovereignty. Others, led by
Theramenes, appealed to them to remedy what they regarded as the populist
extremism of the late fifth century. Still others, though desiring oligarchy and thus
the demise of populism, blamed Solon for the extreme democracy. Aristotle explains in the *Politics* (II.12) that populists and oligarchs (apparently both those party
to the debate and those among his contemporaries) misinterpret the ancestral constitutions. Addressing the populists, he explains that Solon did not promote populism. Popular suffrage, which should not be confused with allowing the people to
hold office, existed before his time; he only continued it. Furthermore, he extended
only judicial power to the people; that is, he believed that the people ought to have
only the power to elect eligible candidates to office and access to jury seats by way of
a voluntary lottery. As Aristotle says, paraphrasing Solon himself, Solon granted
the people "only the necessary minimum of power." Aristotle goes on to explain
that it was the successors of Solon, the demagogues Ephialtes and Pericles, who
increased the power of the people by perverting the Solonian constitution—for
example, by reducing the powers of the oligarchic Areopagus and paying the
people for jury service, thus encouraging the poor to volunteer for it. By later
approving of Solon's legislation and even ranking him among the best legislators
(*Pol* 1281b21–1282a41, 1318b27–32, 1296a18–19), Aristotle confirms his own views
and his allegiance. He too thinks that Athenian democracy is too populist, but he
criticizes oligarchs for blaming Solon and for not appreciating that Solon's laws
promote the leadership of notables. See *Politics*, trans. Barker, 88 n. 1, 380–81; *The
Politics of Aristotle*, vol. 2, ed. W. L. Newman (New York: Arno Press, 1973), 372–74,
notes on 1273b27, 35, 39; Ostwald, *From Popular Sovereignty*, 370–72, 469; *Aristotle:
The Politics*, trans. Carnes Lord (Chicago: University of Chicago Press, 1984), 253 n.
98.
   The point of this digression is to show that Aristotle's arguments against changing *patrioi nomoi* are consistent with and supportive of his critique of democracy and
his understanding of polity (discussed later in the chapter), and to show that,
although those debating the revision of the laws may have appealed to *patrioi nomoi*
not in order to find historical truth but to promote their own political programs

case presenting first and as persuasively as possible arguments in favor of changing long-standing laws.

The first argument is that, since arts and sciences such as medicine have benefited from moving away from traditional practices, so would politics (*Pol* 1268b34–38). As Jacques Brunschwig points out, Aristotle presents this argument in a "quasi-syllogistic way" (*p* and *q*, therefore *r*) rather than as a simple hypothetical implication (if *p* and *q*, then *r*). Thus, Aristotle's premises are accepted and his argument is contained in the form; hence he announces his conclusion as evident. Aristotle's second argument is that, "in general, all seek not the traditional [*to patrion*] but the good" (1269a3–4). According to Brunschwig, we should not ignore the force of this statement, which results from its underscoring the proposition with which the *Politics* begins—that the city aims at the supreme good—and from the fact that the adjective "patrios" had a "strong laudatory connotation"; that is, Aristotle's contemporaries would have found shocking his denouncing the "blind attachment" of conservationists of the past to the past. Third, Aristotle observes that, because it is impossible to codify everything with precision, "it is not best to leave written [laws] unchanged" (1269a8–9). Brunschwig argues that, since Aristotle does not specify the extent of change written laws may require, we must assume that he would sanction any change—minor or profound—as long as it rendered the law more precise. From these three arguments, "it is evident," Aristotle says, "that some laws must be changed at some times" (1269a12–13).[12]

Next Aristotle presents his arguments against changing laws. First, he explains that a law should not be changed for the sake of effecting only a small improvement, for it would not be worth the consequence of habituating people to the dissolution of laws (*Pol* 1269a15–16). The order law achieves by remaining unchanged

---

(Ostwald, *From Popular Sovereignty*, 372), Aristotle believes that *patrioi nomoi* do contain such truth; their best or indispensable provisions should be preserved, as Cleitophon (who was a member of Theramenes' party) recommended (*AC* 29.3). Aristotle concludes that legislators should err on the side of caution, changing *patrioi nomoi* only incrementally if at all. Thus, it might be said that "Aristotle revives the old conception of *thesmos* [the older Greek word for law deriving from a verb meaning 'to establish permanently'] but rationalises it"; John B. Morrall, *Aristotle* (London: George Allen & Unwin, 1977), 81–82.

12 "Du mouvement et de l'immobilité de la loi," *Revue Internationale de Philosophie* 34, no. 133–34 (1980), 512, 522, 523, 527, 540.

compensates for any small sacrifice of justice, because order is a kind or a part of justice. Thus, he points out that "the argument from the example of the arts is false. Change in an art is not like change in law; for law has no strength with respect to obedience apart from habit, and this is not created except over a period of time. Hence the easy alteration of existing laws in favor of new and different ones weakens the power of law itself" (1269a19–24). Since the premise of the earlier syllogism is false, so is its conclusion. Perhaps not altogether by accident, Aristotle thus avoids risking shock to his contemporaries. Last, Aristotle ends the section by raising and at once setting aside two questions: "If [laws] are indeed to be changeable, are all to be, and in every regime? And by anybody, or by whom?" (1269a24–26). That he does not answer these questions here or elsewhere seems to indicate, as Jacqueline de Romilly observes, that they are rhetorical.[13]

Brunschwig insists, however, that leaving the debate on this note gives a dogmatic interpretation to an aporetic text. For, with respect to even these last remarks, Aristotle is not as conservative as he could be. In saying that laws should remain unchanged if a change would effect only a small improvement, for example, he implies that laws should be changed if the change would effect an improvement that is other than small. Brunschwig also points out that, although Aristotle says in this passage that the only way laws can elicit obedience is through habit, he says in Book V that they may do so also through education. The implication is that, because people can understand reasons for laws, they can obey new laws immediately. Finally, countering Romilly's claim that Aristotle ends the passage by setting aside the problem because the answer to it has become obvious, Brunschwig concludes that he sets aside the problem because it cannot be resolved once and for all. The question of whether it is good to change laws must be addressed continually by legislators in every regime. The real question, then, is not whether laws should change, but where, when, and to what extent. For, Brunschwig argues, according to Aristotle there is no natural law; that is, "in refusing to take invariability as a criterion of naturalness . . . Aristotle does not let the distinction between

---

[13] *La loi dans la pensée grecque: Des origines à Aristote* (Paris: Société d'Édition "Les Belles Lettres," 1971), 220–25.

nature and law become absorbed in the distinction between rest and movement."[14]

A few responses to Brunschwig are in order. First, although in recommending that legislators forgo changing laws just to effect small improvements Aristotle may be implying that they should make changes if great improvements would result, he is not saying that the *changes* should be great. Changes should be made only if a cautious change can bring about a significant improvement (*Pol* 1269a13–14). Second, although Brunschwig is correct to note that laws may elicit obedience by way of education, he does not comment on his own (correct) observation that education through habituation is a necessary condition of living justly. People are not likely to be reasonable without habituation (*Pol* 1253a32–33). Even the best populace should be habituated (*Pol* 1334b8–10): "We need to have been brought up in noble habits if we are to be competent students of what is noble and just, and of political questions generally" (*NE* 1095b4–6). Since regimes should not discount the importance of habit, they should not discount the importance of leaving laws unchanged.

As to Brunschwig's claim that Aristotle does not put forth a doctrine of natural law, it is misleading to conclude that he therefore believes that all law is variable. Aristotle indeed teaches that justice resides in concrete decisions rather than in general rules. Yet, as Leo Strauss points out, "one can hardly deny that in all concrete decisions general principles are implied and presupposed."[15] Aristotle implies that universally valid principles exist when he states that "all is changeable; but still there is such a thing as what is natural and what is not" and observes that "nature" intimates what is "best" (*NE* 1134b29–30, 1135a5). This is not to deny that circumstances may justify suspending these principles but to underscore that political decisions should ensue only from an earnest attempt to uphold them—a difference between Aristotle's and Machiavelli's views. In short, the requirements of natural law do not vary, the requirements of justice do.

Aristotle suggests that earlier "discoveries . . . taught by need"

---

[14] "Du mouvement et de l'immobilité de la loi," 520, 530–35, quotation from 540.
[15] *Natural Right and History* (Chicago: University of Chicago Press, 1953), 159; see also 160–62.

(*Pol* 1329b27–28) intimate the principles of natural right. It has been discovered that all political orders need the following: sustenance, arts, arms, funds, religion, and deliberation (*Pol* 1328b5–16, 1322b29–37). Our ancestors have also discovered that a political order may fulfill these needs by establishing the several kinds of law discussed in the rest of this chapter.

SOFT LAWS: MARITAL, HEALTH, AND POPULATION LAWS

Because as long as human beings are able to, they will supply themselves with food and tools, legislators should aim to bring about a healthy populace; they should in effect superintend the bodies of citizens (*Pol* 1334b25–26). This can be done by way of marital, health, and population laws.

Marital Laws

Marital laws should be conducive to the procreation of healthy offspring and to the health of the couple (*Pol* 1334b32–1335a35, b29–37). If men marry around the age of thirty-seven and women around the age of eighteen, then their bodies are in their primes, their sexual desires are mutual, and their reproductive years coincide.[16] Further, they and their children are more likely to be healthy, since very young mothers often have difficult births, resulting even in their deaths; young men impede their own growth by having intercourse; and very young or old parents tend to give birth to physically and mentally defective children.[17] Finally, par-

---

[16] Although eighteen may seem by late twentieth-century norms too young an age for a woman to marry, Aristotle is in fact arguing against early marriage for women. In Athens at his time it was customary for women to marry around the age of fourteen, the age at which they became legally possessed of their property. He apparently prefers the Spartan custom, according to which women marry a few years later; see W. K. Lacey, *The Family in Classical Greece* (Ithaca: Cornell University Press, 1968), 162.

[17] In the case of children of aged fathers, Aristotle may mean that they are not only physically weak but also subject to emotion (*Politics*, vol. 3, ed. Newman, 476, note on 1335b29).

ents should be sufficiently older than their offspring to benefit them and win their respect but young enough to benefit from their children's assistance in old age.

Laws should not, however, require men and women to marry at certain ages. In fact, couples should "study what is said by doctors and experts in natural [science] in relation to procreation" (*Pol* 1335a39–40); men and women themselves should make an informed judgment as to when to marry and have children. One might infer from Aristotle's discussion that laws should at most make it advantageous for couples to marry at certain ages. Such laws might include a dowry law or a law imposing a fine on all single males over fifty (a modern equivalent being a higher tax rate for single persons).

Marital laws should also encourage monogamy by discouraging adultery (*Pol* 1335b38–1336a2). Adulterers, men as well as women, should be punished if their actions interfere with the conceiving and raising of children. Apparently, punishment should be no more severe than revocation of political privileges, such as eligibility for public office; in any case, the stigmatization should be appropriate to the offense.

Legislators should only loosely legislate or legislate around marital relations, presumably because they are private. To make judgments in such matters for individuals would discourage them from their spousal and parental responsibilities and deprive them of opportunities to use their own judgment, such opportunities being necessary to the cultivation of judgment.

Health Laws

Laws should also encourage fitness through moderate exercise. Moderation is important not only presumably because over- and underexertion impair health but especially because the condition of the body affects one's character or soul and one's ability to pursue liberal activities (*Pol* 1334b25–28). If one is routinized by and sleepy from a schedule of rigorous exercise, like an athlete, then one cannot learn or enjoy liberal pastimes (*Pol* 1335b5–11, 1339a7–10). And if men train all the time, like the Spartans, they are apt to want to prevail over others, a desire that serves war but not the rest of life. Physical prowess and the courageous disposition it engenders are not ignoble, but their nobility derives from their capacity to serve and protect the higher moral and the intellectual virtues.[18] The end of war is peace, and the end of peace, leisure (*scholē*), for which is needed moderation, justice, and the virtues of the mind. Men need moderation and justice especially during peacetime, for good fortune tends to make them arrogant (*Pol* 1333a30–b16, 29–31, 1334a11–b4). Contrary to Arendt's interpretation, Aristotle thus gives no indication that ordinary political life requires citizens to have "a fiercely agonal spirit," that "the virtue of courage is one of the most elemental political attitudes."[19] When legislating health and other laws, legislators should regard temperance as more of an aim than courage, not least because it is required to live privately as well as to live well in public.

Like marital laws, health laws should only encourage rather than mandate certain conduct. Fines should apparently be the severest penalty for noncompliance (equivalent policies exist today, such as higher insurance premiums for smokers). Moreover, positive as well as negative incentives should be used to encourage compliance. The receipt of a blessing, for example, might be made contingent on walking a mile to a temple. Furthermore, it may be appropriate for laws to encourage only select groups to exercise. Oligarchies might fine the wealthy but not the poor for not exercising, for example, since the poor get enough exercise by laboring (*Pol* 1297a32–34); or legislators might deem it appropriate to situate only the goddess of childbirth a mile from the city, thus encouraging only pregnant women to walk the distance every day (*Pol* 1335b14–16).

Legislators should use such devices to bring about not only a healthy populace but the sort of political participation that secures polity or aristocracy (*Pol* 1297a38–b1).[20] An oligarchy should not penalize the free poor for not exercising and should encourage the rich to exercise, for example, in order to give the poor more time to serve on juries or attend political assemblies. Likewise, a democracy should distract the free poor from political participation through similar measures.

---

[18] Plato's Athenian Stranger advises legislators to rank the virtues in the following order: the intellectual virtues, moderation, justice, and courage (the divine goods), and then health, beauty, strength, and wealth (the human goods) (*Laws*, 631c–d).

[19] *Human Condition*, 35, 41.

[20] See also *Politics*, trans. Lord, 258 n. 44.

Population Laws

If marital and health laws succeed, the population increases. Aristotle therefore spends an entire chapter advising legislators to restrict the number of citizens (*Pol* VII.4). He agrees with the common view that a city must be great if it is to be happy,[21] but he believes that the greatness of a city, like that of any other animate or inanimate thing, lies not in its magnitude but in its capacity to perform its function. A huge ship is not great if it cannot sail. The function of any city is to achieve self-sufficiency and order. If it has too few members, it cannot achieve self-sufficiency; if it has too many, it cannot achieve order. Order requires that the rulers fulfill their function, which is to enforce the laws and to make just decisions, and that the ruled fulfill theirs, which is to obey the laws and to elect rulers on the basis of merit. Experience shows, Aristotle says, that overpopulated cities have difficulty securing obedience to the laws. But the point can also be established theoretically: law is a system of order, and orderliness, which is a part of beauty, presupposes limits.[22] Further, rulers cannot rule justly and citizens vote justly unless they are familiar with each other's characters, an unlikely state of affairs in a populous city.[23] Aristotle also theoretically grounds the connection between ruling and population size: ruling and legislating are arts, and like other arts they require suitable materials. A carpenter cannot build a house with three planks, a painter cannot paint a portrait on the side of a barn. He has already made this point with respect to household management: "There is a limit with respect to what exists for the sake of the end" (*Pol* 1257b27–28, 30–31). A last point on behalf of a moderate sized population, very directly connected to a city's preservation, is that it makes it easier to marshal and command forces for war. Many bodies are not sufficient for war; they must be able to be directed.

[21] See also Plato, *Laws*, 742d.
[22] On the connection between beauty, order, and limits, see also *Met* 1078a36 [and b1] and Plato, *Philebus*, 64e, as suggested in *Politics*, vol. 3, ed. Newman, 344–45.
[23] As the Athenian Stranger observes, "there is no greater good for a city than that its inhabitants be well known to one another; for where men's characters are obscured from one another by the dark instead of being visible in the light, no one ever obtains in a correct way the honor he deserves, either in terms of office or justice" (Plato, *Laws*, 738e).

Aristotle recommends two laws as means to limit population: one fixes the number of children allowed to each couple, and one prohibits the raising of deformed children (*Pol* 1335b19–26). If a couple conceives beyond the limit, then the embryo should be aborted (but before "perception and life arises"). If a deformed child is born, then it should be exposed. Aristotle realizes that not all parents would comply with such laws, but he does not say what the consequence for noncompliance should be.

One is thus reminded of his earlier recommendation that legislators leave the upholding of marital and health laws largely to the judgment, or one might say the conscience, of individuals. Good marital, health, and reproductive practices should be more a matter of custom or habit, not only because they are essential to the preservation of a city, but because their being matters for private judgment is essential to the city's goodness.

LAWS TO PREVENT DOMESTIC CONFLICT: ECONOMIC AND PENAL

In addition to a healthy populace, all cities need arms, both to keep domestic peace and to ward off external aggression (*Pol* 1328b7–10). Aristotle indicates his belief that internal discord, in the form of either faction or crime, threatens the existence of a regime more than war does by his greater attention to the causes and prevention of the former. He may have been persuaded of the destructiveness of domestic conflict by Plato, whose Socrates observes that "the name faction is applied to the hatred of one's own, war to the hatred of the alien."[24] In any case, legislators should make sure to establish a police or guard as well as a military.

Causes and Signs of Faction and Crime

If legislators are to institute further measures to preclude civic conflict, then they should recognize its signs, causes, and facilitating circumstances (*Pol* 1302a18–22). The chief cause of conflict is the desire for money and recognition. Men fight with one another even to the point of demanding constitutional change in order to gain or avoid losing either (1302a31–34). Legislators should realize,

---

[24] *Republic*, 470b.

at the same time, that most people probably do not seek both profit and honor, since most tend to prefer one thing above all else, believing that it will bring happiness (*NE* 1095a18–24). In fact, most people prefer money and what it can buy—namely, pleasure—to recognition and what it can bring—namely, power. Consequently, they would usually rather attend to their private business than hold public office (*Pol* 1308b34–37). Appreciating that people prefer to participate in public life to different extents, rather than assuming that everyone wants to, is important to preserving a regime. A practical arrangement would assign offices only to those desiring recognition or power, or, in other words, would accommodate a range of desires for privacy.

In regimes not so arranged, civic conflict is more likely to occur. The chief sign of such trouble, to which legislators should be alert, is the widespread perception of inequality—either when many perceive an inequality of condition, believing themselves to have less wealth or fewer prerogatives than those they consider their equals, or when they perceive an inequality among persons, believing themselves to have the same or less wealth or power than those they consider inferior. Such groups may initiate conflict to gain their perceived due, equality or superiority (*Pol* 1301b26–27, 1302a24–31). The desire for justice does not, however, necessarily coincide with self-interest; men may clash with one another because they think *others* lack their due in wealth or prerogatives (1302a38–b2). Whether seeking justice for themselves or for others, they may be doing so unjustifiably, since their perceptions may be mistaken (*Pol* 1280a9–16, 1282b18–23, 1302a28–29, 40–b1). Most people are poor judges particularly of their own situations; they may not in fact merit what they desire. But they may be mistaken also about the situations of others, who may in fact merit the wealth and prerogatives they have. Aristotle thus implies that legislators should respond to the demands of citizens only if they coincide with those of justice, which is the common advantage (1282b16–18).

Legislators should also recognize the numerous circumstances that facilitate conflict or, one might say, that remind men of their relative material and political status. Rulers may be arrogant, for example, making the ruled want to overthrow them; or they may be fearful from having wronged the people, thus desiring to suppress them further; a person or persons either inside or outside the government may seek preeminence with a view to establishing monarchy or dynasty. These and numerous other situations help give rise to faction (*Pol* 1302b2–5, V.3).[25]

The predominant philosophical point to emerge from this discussion is the distinction between the sense of justice and the feeling of envy. On this point, Aristotle and a contemporary liberal philosopher, John Rawls, agree: they both argue that, though "the appeal to justice is often a mask for envy," a genuine "sense of justice" is not, as Freud claims, "the outgrowth of envy and jealousy."[26] Envy cannot be the basis for, or accompany, the sense of justice, because, like some other feelings such as spite, it does not have a mean; some sentiments, not their excesses or deficiencies, are themselves base (*NE* 1107a9–14). In contrast to Rawls, however, Aristotle does not think that politics should proceed from the assumption of universal rationality.[27] Regimes should educate individuals to recognize that equality of distribution is not the same as justice. Legislators should also realize that education will not eradicate envy and should thus use other means to mitigate it.

The Middle Class

One measure Aristotle recommends to preclude conflict is increasing the middle class (*Pol* 1296a7–9). When the middle class predominates, people perceive existing inequalities to be less great (*Pol* 1295b29–33, 1308b30–31). The poor do not feel as poor because they see that the middle class also has less than the rich, and the rich are less fearful of the poor because they see that the middle class also has property interests. Moreover, those of middling means do not envy the rich because they are not in want and do not perceive themselves as greatly unequal to them. In short, the middle class neither is plotted against nor plots against others. This

---

25 See also *Politics*, vol. 4, ed. Newman, 296, note on 1302a34.

26 *A Theory of Justice* (Cambridge: Belknap, 1971), 539, 540. Rawls summarizes Freud: "As some members of the social group jealously strive to protect their advantages, the less favored are moved by envy to take them away. Eventually everyone recognizes that they cannot maintain their hostile attitudes toward one another without injury to themselves. Thus as a compromise they settle upon the demand of equal treatment. The sense of justice is a reaction-formation: what was originally jealousy and envy is transformed into a social feeling, the sense of justice that insists upon equality for all" (ibid., 539); Rawls cites Freud's *Group Psychology and the Analysis of the Ego*, rev. ed., trans. James Strachey (London: Hogarth, 1959), 51ff.

27 *Theory of Justice*, 530.

makes those of middling means trustworthy, puts them in a position to judge well, and thus makes them worthy of ruling according to both rich and poor (*Pol* 1297a5–6, *DA* 424a6). Both rich and
poor also welcome the rule of the middle class because their alternative, to join forces against it, is not in their interest; depending
on which is in the minority, their collaboration would eventuate in
the submission of one class to the other—the rich would enslave
the poor or the poor would reduce the rich to their level by distributing their property (*Pol* 1296a1–3, b40–1297a5). Furthermore,
there is no guarantee that this new aggregate could predominate
over the middle class.

But how can a regime increase its middle class? We know from
Aristotle's critique of Phaleas's proposal that legislating property
redistribution is not a solution. Aristotle proposes a few ways laws
could help to achieve parity of income (*Pol* 1309a14–25). Although
they should not redistribute the income of the wealthy, for example, they might restrict inheritances to family and allow only one
inheritance per individual. In addition, a regime might allot the
better-paid public offices to the poor. Such laws are desirable in
that they do not alter the fundamental nature of the regime (*Pol*
1296b34–38). But it is doubtful that they alone can effect much of a
redistribution. By raising this doubt, Aristotle reminds us of his
recommendation that all regimes accommodate a market economy.
He helps confirm that he believes the market should effect redistribution when he includes "an abundance of money" on his list
of things a city cannot exist without (*Pol* 1328b10, 1322b32–33). The
constitutional laws of a regime should provide for a market just as
they should provide for a military or any other political necessity.
Maintaining a market is a way of increasing the middle class without weakening the authority of the laws by continually changing
them. Citizens are not likely to resist incremental redistribution
which they largely control and which does not alter the fundamental nature or constitution of the regime.

Aristotle makes clear, then, that the aim of increasing the middle
class is not homogeneity or even increased political participation
but avoidance of civil disobedience and thus preservation of the
regime. Increasing the middle class is a means, not an end; if
measures taken to favor the middle class (such as inheritance and
tax laws) create conflict, then they should not be maintained. The
regime's stability is paramount, and the sign of stability is prevail-

ing support of the regime by its citizens (*Pol* 1309b14–18, 1294b36–40, 1296b14–16).

Criminal Punishment

Another way regimes should safeguard themselves against civil disobedience and other criminal activity is by instituting a penal system. Its presence should deter some of the criminally inclined and its punishments may discourage recidivism.

Aristotle does not seem to recommend severe punishments for crimes, mentioning in the *Politics* primarily fines, exile, and "dishonor" (probably, public stigmatization by revocation of political privileges) as penalties for breaking laws. He does discuss the matter of guarding prisoners but does not give examples of offenses warranting incarceration (perhaps, then, they are few) (*Pol* 1321b40–1322a29, b35). Nor does he mention capital punishment. He apparently thinks that physical punishment other than incarceration is appropriate only for the very young (*Pol* 1336b7–11).

But other arguments compete against these. First, that the many are usually poor (*Pol* 1279b37–38) suggests that fines are a futile way to punish them. Second, the suggestion that beating is appropriate for punishing only the very young occurs in the context of a discussion of the best regime, in which all older persons are virtuous. Third, Aristotle describes "the many" in much the same way that Hobbes describes all human beings—as seekers of pleasure and avoiders of pain. By nature, fear of pain, not shame, motivates them to reasonable conduct. Indeed, in the *Nicomachean Ethics* Aristotle says that "the many" yield (at least initially) not to argument but to force (*bia*) or the threat of force, compulsion (*anangkē*) (1179b11, 28–29, 1180a4–5). Finally, he claims, also in the *Nicomachean Ethics,* that retributive justice entails returning "evil for evil" (1132b34–1133a1), except in the case where one party is an official (1132b28–30), and apparently endorses a proposal put forth by Plato that the pains (*tas lupas*) inflicted to punish a transgressor of the law should be those "that are most opposed to the pleasures he desires" (1180a12–14). Although this implies fines rather than incarceration or other physical punishment for tax evaders, embezzlers, and other 'white-collar' criminals (and presumably an amount proportional to the amount stolen—that is, to the amount of pleasure sought), it implies equally that murder should beget execution, and in the way the murder was carried out,[28] and that the punishment for rape should be castration or some such debilitating measure (today, perhaps pharmaceutical). One is reminded of the injunction in Exodus 21:23–25. But Aristotle advances 'an eye for an eye' not only on behalf of (divine) justice but with a view to deterrence (*Pol* 1332a11–14). He does not present the above extrapolations perhaps because he realizes that a discussion of physical punishments would be unseemly.

In sum, Aristotle's recommendations for preempting domestic conflict—maintaining a police force, increasing the middle class, and instituting a penal system—are designed to maintain obedience to the laws and not otherwise to make better men. One can observe, however, that civil obedience is at least a precondition of virtue, order at least a precondition of justice.[29]

LAWS CONCERNING WAR

A city needs not only to suppress internal conflict but to defend itself against attack from outside (*Pol* 1328b7–10, 1333b40–41). Given that the ability to ward off aggression is basic to the survival of anything, Aristotle's recommendation that a regime institute a standing militia is not surprising. This preservative precaution hardly needs to be pointed out to legislators. What legislators might be less certain about is whether offensive wars are necessary to the survival of a regime. This they must know in order to allocate adequate resources to the military and to have a sense of the extent to which they should prepare a regime for war.

On the one hand, Aristotle denounces the laws of Sparta and Crete for their pronounced concern with domination; they make

[28] The reasoning being that the cessation of the murderer's life by the same means inflicts the amount and kind of pain most opposed to the amount and kind of pleasure the murderer apparently took in the act.

[29] As J. L. Stocks observes about Books IV–VI of the *Politics*, "we are here almost, but never quite, surrendered to that 'cogent expediency' on which in Edmund Burke's view all just government depends." To the extent that Aristotle surrenders in these books to realism and empiricism, Aristotle argues, as Stocks also points out, on behalf "of the relativity of political truth, of the necessity of concessions to democracy, of political institutions as the expression of social and economic fact, the adoption of stability and contentment instead of virtue as the test of success"; "Scholē," *Classical Quarterly* 30 (1936), 186–87.

war a way of life and victory the aim of the regimes. He also gives the impression of disapproving of the Scythians, the Persians, the Thracians, the Celts, and others for admiring and honoring the power to dominate. In the same tone, he reports laws and customs that reward men for killing enemies (*Pol* 1324b5–21). In addition, he points out that it is not lawful to conquer and rule neighboring regimes without regard to their wishes, for it disregards their free status, their ability to rule themselves. It is indeed noble to rule over free persons, but such rule cannot be achieved by sheer might. In sum, a regime preoccupied with war harms both itself and others (*Pol* 1324b22–34, 1333b26–36).

On the other hand, Aristotle says that an offensive war is justified in two cases: when a free people is in need of outside leadership, and when a people has no potential to rule itself (*Pol* 1333b41–1334a2). Assuming the leadership of these peoples is justified because it benefits them. In the first case, Aristotle does not say that the people's consent is required to justify hegemony over them. One might infer, however, that he is suggesting that, once outside leadership has ordered the regime, the people would be grateful to it; that is, their consent would follow rather than precede the intervention. Moreover, by calling such people free, Aristotle implies that such hegemony should be temporary, removed once their ability to rule themselves has been restored. In the second case, since the naturally slavish cannot reason on their own, consent per se cannot be forthcoming. But Aristotle has already made clear that natural slaves do not object to proper mastery. The summary point, however ironic, is that aggression over neighboring peoples is justified only if accompanied, or at least followed, by prudence and moderation. One might observe, however, that although it would be noble for a regime to wage offensive wars in these two instances, it is not clear that it need do so to survive. Nonetheless, one can see that peoples who are not ruling themselves pose at least a threat to a neighboring regime. One can further infer that, if the instability of a neighboring people is great enough, or persists long enough, intervention is not only noble but necessary. In any case, although a regime may or may not be justified in using force against such people for the sake of its own self-preservation, the unpredictability of such people justifies a regime's being *prepared* for an offensive war. Aristotle does not, then, justify so much offensive war as military preparedness for offensive war, as a means to survival.

His teaching to legislators about war might be put as follows. Next to a virtuous populace, the noblest end a regime can achieve is peace. Peace is noble because it facilitates virtue, but it is also necessary for the preservation of a regime. To achieve peace, a regime must be prepared to wage both defensive and offensive wars. But the nature and extent of military preparedness must be compatible with peace and civilian, liberal pursuits. And the nature and extent of any aggression must be such as to allow civilians to continue or at least to return to living in a liberal way. War must always serve peace, and peace, virtue (*Pol* 1325a5–7, 1333a30–b3, 14–16, 29–31, 38–1334a10).[30]

RELIGIOUS LAWS

As noted earlier in the chapter, religion is fifth on Aristotle's list of things that must be present for a city to exist (*Pol* 1328b11–12). Religion should be part of a city, but it should not be part of government (*Pol* 1299a17–19, 1322b18–19). Aristotle is thus among the first political philosophers to advise the separation of church and state. Yet it becomes clear that he does not uphold a strict or modern version of that doctrine. Even his list of a city's indispensable items suggests that religion should be as separate from government as are the military and the economy; laws should establish nonpolitical offices to maintain it.[31] Priests, like generals and market managers, should be accessible and responsive to government

---

[30] Aristotle follows Plato in denying that war is the proper end and most serious business of the polis. See, for example, Plato, *Laws*, 631b and *Republic*, 521a, as recommended by Newman, *Politics*, vol. 3, 332, note on 1325a7; see also 443, note on 1333a35, and Friedrich Solmsen, "Leisure and Play in Aristotle's Ideal State," *Rheinisches Museum für Philologie* 107 (1964), 209.

[31] This is not to say that those holding political office cannot be religious or make the appearance of their being so serve their political objectives. Aristotle indicates that appearing religious can be politically effective when he advises the tyrant: "He must always show himself to be seriously attentive to the things pertaining to the gods. For [men] are less afraid of being treated in some respect contrary to the law . . . if they consider the ruler a god-fearing sort who takes thought for the gods, and they are less ready to conspire against him thinking that he has even the gods as allies" (*Pol* 1314b38–1315a3).

but should function independently. Just as government should be able to command the military to go to battle and to impose higher sales taxes, so it should be able to instruct the religious establishment to induce people to pay revenues, to exercise (*Pol* 1330a8–9, 1335b14–16), or perhaps to have more or fewer children. Such inducements are necessary in ordinary cities because, to recall, most human beings tend to be recalcitrant to reason.[32] The presence of "the gods," or the promulgation of myths that explain their presence, can be as effective in eliciting subscription to the laws as the presence of a police force and a penal system.

But religion is superior to the threat of force (and perhaps therefore listed by Aristotle after arms, second only to political offices) in that it does not seek to suppress passions but to provide a means by which they can be expressed without endangering the regime. Religion can fuse *pathos* and *ethos* without (unlike rhetoric) the use of *logos*. It can therefore move people to comply with the laws without requiring them to follow arguments.

Religion can also render citizens not only obedient to the laws but respectful of authority in general and fearful of shame, attributes belonging to "free persons" (*Pol* 1331a40–b1). It therefore belongs even in the best regime. Since the proximity and counsel of priests tends to edify citizens, Aristotle recommends that most places for worship be conspicuous and near the citizens' recreational area (excepting those places required by religious law to be removed from the city) (1331a24–35). In general, at any rate, legislators should remember that laws should remind citizens of the gods.[33]

In either case, whether serving mere obedience or virtue, preservation or a higher justice, religion should serve the regime, not vice versa; for once religious aims displace political ones, privacy is endangered. Religion that does not recognize the sanctity of the human realm aspires to obliterate the distinction between public

---

[32] See also Leo Strauss, *The City and Man* (Chicago: University of Chicago Press, 1964), 22.

[33] Jean-Pierre Vernant explains that the emergence of the polis in ancient Greece brought about the publicization of religion. Religion was no longer secret wisdom known by priests of a *genē*, but a body of public truths promulgated by official city cults. Temples were open, public, and visibly situated; they and their sacred holdings were to be seen—to be a spectacle providing "a lesson on the gods"; see *The Origins of Greek Thought* (Ithaca: Cornell University Press, 1982), 54–55.

and private. Thus the fundamental laws of a regime should ensure that religion remains civil.[34]

POLITICAL LAWS: OFFICES AND ENTITLEMENT

The last and most important item on Aristotle's list of things a city cannot exist without, "the most necessary thing of all," is a public system of judgment or "offices" (*Pol* 1328b13–14, 1291a22–24, 34–36). The discussion suggests that they are the most important constitutional provision because they compensate for law's inadequacy to judge particulars; the rule of law is perfect or complete (only) in the sense that it provides for its own deficiency (1292a32–34).

Government needs many offices, but only two general sorts—deliberative and judicial. By judicial offices Aristotle means civil and criminal court posts, including juries. By deliberative offices he means the political offices. The deliberative element should have authority over foreign policy (matters of war and peace and alliances), over the laws, over (judicial) cases calling for severe punishment (the death penalty, exile, or confiscation), and over the appointment and auditing of officials (within government as well as appointments to military, religious, bureaucratic, and other such posts) (*Pol* 1298a3–6). Thus, the deliberative offices have legislative and higher judicial functions. What is more, not only "deliberation and judgment concerning certain matters" but "particularly command" characterize political offices (1299a25–28). Aristotle not only assigns an executive function to what he calls the deliberative element but seemingly paradoxically says that its main function is to execute.[35] This makes sense, however, given his teaching that regimes should arise out of those that exist. The fundamental laws of a regime are given to men (in *patrioi nomoi*) to be executed, but their perpetuation and preservative function depend on their being ad-

---

[34] Aristotle's contemporaries also regarded civil authority as more authoritative than religious authority. Civil courts judged violations of religious law, and the religious authorities (for example, the *Eumolpidai* or the *exēgētai*) had no standing in court; the presiding magistrates and juries were secular; see MacDowell, *Law in Classical Athens*, 193; Michael Gagarin, *Early Greek Law* (Berkeley: University of California Press, 1986), 14, 70; Ostwald, "Was There a Concept *agraphos nomos?*" 90, and *From Popular Sovereignty*, 165–71.

[35] See also *Politics*, trans. Barker, 193 n. NN.

justed to circumstances and thus on human discretion. It seems then that nature sanctions the sovereignty of deliberation for the sake of itself—for the sake of perpetuating the actualization of natural law and perpetuating human nature. To perpetuate the actualization of its universals, it is not enough for nature to make them felt or to impose them on human beings; it must give the agents of their actualization some authority over them (*NE* 1134b18–1135a5). Ironically, then, the rule of *patrioi nomoi* is superior to the rule of men in that it accommodates and invites their rule as a means to perpetuate itself; the rule of men is not inimical to but in fact the catalyst of the rule of law. In sum, Aristotle wants to demonstrate that there cannot be purely executive, legislative, and judicial functions. Executors must judge, and legislators and judges must execute.[36]

The Preservative Tasks of Rulers

Aristotle's references to both "legislators" and "political rulers" (or "experts in politics") in his political works proposes a division of labor within the deliberative offices, evidently between those who have authority over the laws—the preservative laws—and those who rule otherwise. Like legislators, other rulers should seek to preserve the regime.[37] In chapter 8 of Book V of the *Politics*, Aristotle discusses the preservative tasks of rulers.

First of all, for a regime to exist, its inhabitants must perform specific actions necessary to the regime's functioning. The objective of political rule, which issues commands, is to ensure the

---

[36] For related and similar points, see Harvey C. Mansfield, Jr., *Taming the Prince: The Ambivalence of Modern Executive Power* (New York: Free Press, 1989), 46–71; 53–65 is an in-depth analysis of deliberating and judging as presented in Book IV of Aristotle's *Politics*; for a longer version, see Mansfield's "The Absent Executive in Aristotle's *Politics*," in *Natural Right and Political Right*, ed. T. B. Silver and P. W. Schramm (Durham: Carolina Academic Press, 1984), 169–96. Mansfield points out that the need for the sovereignty of deliberation is why the deliberative offices must be plural (*Taming the Prince*, 58, 71). Mansfield explains reason's sovereignty as follows: "Deliberation in [Aristotle's] account, unlike modern scientific reason, does not make its way solely on the basis of its own premises to create its own sovereignty. For Aristotle, deliberation must deal with things beyond human power and somehow bring them within human power. While facing the difficult, perhaps indeterminate, question of what is beyond and within human power, Aristotle does at least avoid the necessity embraced by the modern schema of claiming that we are sovereign even when we give no thought to the matter at hand" (ibid., 54).

[37] Not even political activity is wholly divorced from necessity; political rule, like mastery, cannot then be the noblest of activities (*Pol* 1325a26–27).

performance of such substantive actions. But it can achieve this only if rulers and subjects recognize the authority of the laws by subscribing to them. In that the activity of ruling postulates association in terms of laws (*Pol* 1270b29–31), it must seek to preserve them. The commands of rulers should not transgress the laws even in a minor way, for minor transgressions eventually transform the regime (*Pol* 1289a19–20, 1307a40–b6, 30–34).[38] It should be observed that rulers are thus responsible for seeing that the activities law mandates as private remain private.

That ruling presupposes law indicates that the validity or authenticity of commands derives from law. An authentic command reflects the spirit of the laws; oligarchies issue oligarchic commands, democracies democratic ones, and so forth.[39] Simply, an authoritative, or just, command respects or expresses law (*Pol* 1289a18–19).[40] As Aristotle explains, there are two sorts of good political order or, literally, good rule according to law (*eunomia*): when the laws of a regime are obeyed, and when they are both obeyed and the best (*Pol* 1294a4–6).

The next most important preservative task of rulers is to maintain good relations with one another and with the ruled. The first they may achieve by treating one another "in a democratic spirit of equality." As Aristotle says throughout his political works, democratic principles should obtain among the equally capable; the best place for democracy is *within* government or the governing class. Office holders might restrict their tenure, for example, to give their peers turn in office or a particular office. (This tenure should, however, be the longest possible to take advantage of experience; *Pol* 1261a38–39.) In aristocracies and oligarchies, such a rotational policy prevents the concentration of power in a particular family; in democracies, it prevents the rise of demagogues (*Pol* 1308a3–7, 10–24).

In Book IV of the *Politics*, Aristotle hints that the best way for rulers to maintain good relations with the ruled is to maintain the latter's privacy. He explains that proper political rule should direct all or a part of the citizenry only in certain matters, such as war or

[38] In this sense, political rule differs from household rule, which is not confined to interpreting rules but carries the prerogative of making and changing them.
[39] Or, as Oakeshott explains, "competence to command belongs to an office, a *persona* identified in terms of rules" ("The Rule of Law," 130).
[40] See also *Politics*, trans. Lord, 256 n. 3.

the supervision of children (1299a20–22). But in chapter 8 of Book V, he explains more ways rulers should keep the ruled content. They should appoint to political posts those among the ruled who demonstrate leadership ability or ambition (1308a7–9), for example. Such appointees as well as those already in government should, however, be advanced by degrees, not only to test their ability to uphold certain responsibilities but to prevent old boy networks, nepotism, and the like (1308b10–18). In addition, rulers may assign the least authoritative, nonpolitical offices to the ruled. The well-off in a democracy and the poor in an oligarchy could, for example, be assigned to religious, military, bureaucratic, judicial,[41] and penal posts (1322b31–36). Nonetheless, these posts differ with respect to the amount of "experience and trust" they require and should be distributed accordingly. Aristotle implies that a regime may safeguard itself against civil disobedience not only by instituting a police, a penal system, and a free market economy but also by distributing civil service appointments or pseudo-political power among the ruled. This should satisfy desires among them for recognition. It should be noticed, however, that rulers, not laws, should distribute authority to the ruled (on an ad hoc basis); such distribution should not be a constitutional provision or, as we would say, a right. At any rate, Aristotle advises rulers not to appease the ruled generally by granting them political power (1309a31–32, 1321a31–32), for this would not preserve the regime. Finally, rulers should also (indirectly) treat the ruled fairly by keeping their own salaries moderate (1308b31–33).

In the remainder of the chapter, Aristotle lists other general preservative measures. Rulers should keep alive or not try to dispel fears about the security of the regime that grip a populace, for such fears make the latter more protective of and willing to defend the regime. Rulers should intervene in disputes among the distinguished members of a regime, for these can escalate into faction.[42] Rulers should adjust property qualifications for office to take into account fluctuations in the value of currency.[43] And they

[41] The Athenians selected juries by lot from a permanent group of six thousand volunteers; see M. I. Finley, *Democracy Ancient and Modern*, rev. ed. (New Brunswick: Rutgers University Press, 1985), 117.

[42] For instances of such disputes and possible modes of intervention, see *Politics*, vol. 4, ed. Newman, 388, note on 1308a31.

[43] See *Politics*, trans. Lord, 262 n. 75.

should rely less on devices than on the laws to control who participates in the regime. This apparently miscellaneous list of tasks
might be condensed into the general maxim that rulers should err
on the side of caution, or always rule conservatively.

The Expert in Politics

Rulers can best achieve their conservative objectives if they employ a conservative mode of discourse. By employing this mode,
which is rhetoric properly understood, they will persuade the
ruled to obey their commands or policies. Since proper rhetoric
combines *logos* with *ethos* and *pathos,* a rhetorician not only demonstrates his point logically but reveals his character and appeals to
the characters and emotional state of his audience (*Rh* I.2.3). An
effective appeal requires accepting uncritically, not examining in
Socratic fashion, the common opinions of an audience or the public
morality.[44] A ruler who refuses to accept this morality but proceeds
to try to persuade is a mere sophist or dogmatist. One who insists
on examining prevailing beliefs is not an expert in politics but a
philosopher or skeptic.

Rhetoric, then, depends on the character of a populace, which in
turn depends on the nature of the laws.[45] In contrast to the Soph-
ists, Aristotle implies that law must regulate the arts because the
reason inherent in law, unlike the reason inherent in the arts, is of
the highest sort.[46] For the art of ruling to subordinate itself to the
rule of law, it must—like the other arts—recognize its limits (*Pol*
1257b25–28). Experts in politics should not try to remake the world
with causes or ideologies. Their virtue and justice relative to the
regime and affection for it compel them to carry out the laws (*Pol*
1309a34–37, 1270b29–31), issuing commands only over particulars

---

[44] Larry Arnhart, *Aristotle on Political Reasoning: A Commentary on the "Rhetoric"*
(DeKalb: Northern Illinois University Press, 1981), 38, 41, 153–54. Put technically,
the rhetorician constructs a proof; however, although the body of this proof, the
enthymeme, is like the logical syllogism employed in dialectic (*Rh* I.1.11), it incorpo-
rates *ethos* and *pathos* in order to create trust or belief (*pistis*) in the audience. The
rational can embody the emotional without becoming irrational (ibid., 21, 22, 34,
114–15). On Aristotle's claim that the rhetorician should employ *logos, pathos,* and
ethos together, see also William M. A. Grimaldi, *Studies in the Philosophy of Aristotle's
Rhetoric* (Weisbaden: Franz Steiner, 1972), especially 58; Mary P. Nichols, "Aristotle's
Defense of Rhetoric," *Journal of Politics* 49, no. 3 (1987), 664–68.

[45] Arnhart, *Aristotle on Political Reasoning,* 24, 75.

[46] Strauss, *City and Man,* 23–24. Strauss cites *NE* 1094a27–b6, 1180a18–22; cf.
1134a34 with *Pol* 1287a28–30.

to achieve equity (*NE* 1137b27–32). In addition to love for the regime, love for their work—not an agonistic desire for power—motivates them (*Pol* 1309a35), though industry may look like the quest for power to others.[47]

Aristotle's conception of political rule thus contrasts with the prevalent unreflective liberal view, derived primarily from Hobbes and Locke, according to which "power is the capacity . . . to subordinate the wills of others to one's own will" and is a "cause of antagonism in society." On this view, "the more one man's desire for power is satisfied, the more will his fellows' wish for it remain frustrated."[48] Aristotle instead teaches that rulers can in fact satisfy the ruled by exercising their power prudently, can even make them glad to be ruled and to be able to attend to their own affairs (*Pol* 1321a31–39, 1297b6–8, 1308b34–37).

Monarchy versus Aristocracy

If, as Aristotle seems to imply, only the prudent should be entitled to hold the political offices, then should not a human being whose prudence surpasses that of everyone else be entitled to hold all the offices—that is, to be king? Indeed, according to P. A. Vander Waerdt, Aristotle argues that if there exists a man so virtuous as to be able to govern alone, he should do so, for this would allow all citizens to devote themselves to the liberal arts.[49] It is indisputable that the rule of one supremely virtuous man appeals to Aristotle (*Pol* 1284b32–34) and likely that it appeals to him for the reason Vander Waerdt suggests, but Aristotle indicates several problems with such an arrangement, the main one being that, unlike a plurality of offices, a single office cannot be counted on to ensure the sovereignty of deliberation.

First, who should be king is not likely to be evident, for "it is not as easy to see the beauty of the soul as it is that of the body" (*Pol* 1254b39). Second, because of this difficulty, even good men may not agree on who is preeminent among them. Third, even if an outstanding man were detected and unanimously nominated to rule, he would be reluctant to claim the honor of ruling over all, preferring to give the honor to a friend (*NE* 1169a29–30). One

---

[47] For a similar point, see Mansfield, *Taming the Prince*, 49.

[48] As this view is explained by Roberto Mangabeira Unger, *Knowledge and Politics* (New York: Free Press, 1984), 64–65.

[49] "Kingship and Philosophy in Aristotle's Best Regime," *Phronesis* 30, no. 3 (1985), 249–73.

might point out that, just prior to explaining this man's willingness to give up riches, honors, and offices to friends, Aristotle says that he "would choose . . . to live nobly for a year, rather than for many years in a chancy way" (*NE* 1169a23–24). Thus, Aristotle does not logically (or psychologically) exclude the possibility of a sequence of short-term monarchs. Men might also agree more readily to be ruled by one man for just a year. On the other hand, the rule of even the best man might improve over time (*Pol* 1261a38–39). And the assumption of the existence of several exceptional men is suspicious since, according to Aristotle, it is not evident that we should assume the possibility of the existence of even one who is "like a god among human beings" (*Pol* 1284a11, b30–31). Even if we suppose with Vander Waerdt, as it seems we should, that Aristotle is recommending for king one whose virtue is heroic rather than philosophical,[50] such virtue seems to be unattainable by Aristotle's own account. Vander Waerdt seems to argue that, although "heroic virtue . . . transforms men into gods and places them beyond the sphere of human virtue and vice," such virtue is nonetheless humanly possible because it "is an excess of [human] virtue (*aretēs huperbolē*)."[51] But Aristotle indicates that this superhuman virtue must remain an aspiration, for every human soul necessarily has the passionate element (*Pol* 1286a18–20), which is able to pervert or twist even the best men (*aristous andras*) (1287a28–32); not even their passions always accord with virtue.

Aristotle therefore favors aristocracy over monarchy: "The judgment of a single person is necessarily corrupted when he is dominated by anger or some other passion of this sort, whereas it is hard for all to become angry and err at the same time" (*Pol* 1286a33–35). If, then, there are several persons who are "excellent in soul, just like the single person," they should rule, since they would be "more incorruptible" than the individual (1286b2–3, 1286a31–33); in other words, "if it is just for the excellent man to rule because he is better, two good persons are better than one" (1287b12–13).[52] Accordingly, Aristotle describes the regime in

---

[50] Ibid., 266–68. Aristotle cannot mean to propose that the philosophically virtuous person rule, because philosophy and politics are two different ways of life (*Pol* 1324a25–32).

[51] "Kingship and Philosophy," 267.

[52] Thus it is not the case that Aristotle thinks the outstanding man should rule "regardless of the natural character or excellence of his subjects" (ibid., 249).

which virtue is honored above all as an aristocracy, not a monarchy (1273a41–b1, 1278a18–20), and states: "If, then, the rule of a number of persons who are all good men is to be regarded as aristocracy, and the rule of a single person as kingship, aristocracy would be more choiceworthy for cities than kingship . . . provided it is possible to find a number of persons who are similar" (1286b3–7).[53]

The Status of Democracy

Legislators cannot assume that several persons equally preeminent in virtue exist in most regimes; it would be "a work of chance" if they existed in any regime (*Pol* 1332b16–23, 1331b21–22; *Rh* I.1.7). What qualification, then, should preservative laws establish for holding office? Only virtue legitimately entitles human beings to rule others, but a city needs wealth and manpower (*Pol* 1296b17–19); since virtue is scarce, regimes should allow also the wealthy and the people (those who are neither wealthy nor virtuous) to hold offices. It should be noticed, first, that this argument for allowing those who are less than virtuous authority does not appeal to justice or fairness (only persons who are similar deserve equal treatment; *Pol* 1332b27). Second, as I explain in the next section, Aristotle does not think that all those allowed authority should be allowed the same kind and amount of authority. Third, he cautions us not to confuse a system that grants all free persons entitlement to participate in the regime with democracy. Democracy does not, in theory or in practice, allow all to rule.[54]

Aristotle arrives at the formal definition of democracy by reasoning (1) that democracy is the opposite of oligarchy, (2) that oligarchy is rule by the propertied, and therefore (3) that democracy is rule by those who lack a significant amount of property or are poor (*Pol* 1279b7–9, 17–19, 39–40). Even in actual democracies not everyone, but rather the majority, rules (*Pol* 1291b37–38, 1317b3–7). Moreover, the majority is—not by definition but by accident—

[53] Vander Waerdt cites this passage in support of his claim that both kingship and aristocracy are acceptable to Aristotle, and that their "relative rank . . . accordingly depends upon which of them is better suited to promote the way of life of the best regime" (ibid., 255). It appears rather that their relative rank depends on whether one of them is unrealistic. For arguments that Aristotle does not intend his notion of supreme monarchy to be a practical proposal, see W. R. Newell, "Superlative Virtue: The Problem of Monarchy in Aristotle's 'Politics,'" *Western Political Quarterly* 40, no. 1 (1987), 159–78, especially 161, 170, 175; Mansfield, *Taming the Prince*, 23–45, 62, 70.

[54] See also Mansfield, *Taming the Prince*, 56.

poor (*Pol* 1280a3–4).[55] There is therefore confusion about what democracy is; it is rule by the poor, but since the poor are also many, it is thought to be rule by the many (*Pol* III.8). The many in particular reject the definition of democracy as rule by the poor, believing that number constitutes a just claim to rule. They maintain that whatever the majority resolves is just, since each of the citizens has a say. In their view, majority rule is a mark and defining principle of a free regime (*Pol* 1317b3–11, 1291b34–38).

In addition to empowering the poor majority, democracy in principle allows one to live as one wants. Like most human beings, democrats regard freedom as the greatest good. But they reason that, since not living as one wants is characteristic of a person who is enslaved, living as one wants is characteristic of a person who is free. Thus, they prize freedom of expression above all else—above wealth, family, and virtue. From their presuppositions that living freely is the greatest good and living as one wants is living freely, they claim the right to political freedom; that is, they claim that living freely requires freedom from any government interference and, failing that, the freedom to rule and be ruled in turn. They accept rotational rule because, in distributing authority to every citizen without regard to personal merit, it upholds the democratic notion of justice as equality (without regard to equality in what things) (*Pol* 1317a40–b4, 11–17; *NE* 1131a12–29).

Notable characteristics of democracy include "election to all offices from among all"; "having all offices chosen by lot, or those not requiring experience and skill"; "having offices not based on any property qualification, or based on the smallest possible"; "the same person not holding any office more than once, or doing so rarely"; "having all offices of short duration . . . where . . . possible"; and "having all or [persons selected] from all exercise judicial functions" over "the greatest and most authoritative matters" (*Pol* 1317b17–1318a3). Thus, many offices do not require any knowledge, experience, or wealth, and most offices, because of their short tenure, do not enable one to acquire any knowledge, experience, or wealth. In other words, in a democracy an ignorant, inexperienced, and poor majority rules.[56]

Yet this characterization does not take into account Aristotle's

---

[55] See also Strauss, *City and Man*, 36.
[56] Or, as Strauss reasons, "if democracy is rule of the poor, of those who lack leisure, it is the rule of the uneducated and therefore undesirable" (*City and Man*, 36).

discussion of the merits of collective judgment, which points out that, although the individuals constituting most multitudes lack virtue, they may by acting in concert surpass in virtue and thus judgment individuals superior in virtue (*Pol* 1281a42–b5). This cannot, however, be said about all multitudes, since some are beastly (1281b15–20). That a multitude only *might* have good judgment means that it is not safe to have it fill the highest offices, for it might commit injustices or simply make mistakes (1281b26–28).

In sum, it becomes clear that Aristotle indicts democracy, and even more particularly the democratic character: "Low birth, poverty, and vulgarity" characterize the many (*Pol* 1317b40–41).[57] Lacking self-restraint and prudence and insisting that living by no standard is the best standard, they live deviantly. Democracy is thus itself, in a word, a deviation (*Pol* 1279b4–6).

Polity

The form of regime second best to aristocracy is polity, in which the minority—the wealthy and the virtuous—as well as the majority are entitled to hold office. But Aristotle's critique of democracy compels one to wonder why the majority should be given entitlement to any authority. Aristotle answers that, if a regime denies the multitude prerogatives, then it would be "necessarily filled with enemies," risking rebellion (*Pol* 1281b28–30). Moreover, a multitude, regardless of its other positive or negative attributes, is a multitude of bodies, which a city needs for defense. Defense may not be forthcoming if the multitude is dissatisfied with the regime. Here the thought arises that, if the multitude were shrewd, they would stake their claim to rule not on majority opinion or freedom but on "military virtue" (*Pol* 1279b1–2).[58] But the many believe that the only way to serve themselves is to rule themselves, not to contribute to the needs of the regime.[59]

---

[57] This remark is bracketed by Alois Dreizehnter in *Aristoteles' Politik* (Munich: Wilhelm Fink Verlag, 1970) and others (see *Politics*, vol. 4, ed. Newman, 503, note on 1317b38; *Politics*, trans. Lord, 265 n. 8), indicating an interpolation.

[58] Especially since military virtue involves more than brute strength; by Aristotle's account, it involves at least *thumos* (see Chapter 6, "Political Virtue: Virtue Redefined") and perhaps also *sōphrosunē*. Vernant argues that these are two opposite military virtues; the warrior of the Homeric epic needed *thumos*, the hoplite, *sōphrosunē* (*Origins of Greek Thought*, 63).

[59] In claiming to rule themselves regardless of benefit, they reveal their tyrannical stubbornness. To the extent that a regime permits such assertion of will or "freedom," it shares in tyranny (Mansfield, *Taming the Prince*, 48–49).

Although Aristotle's conclusion—that a regime, in order to survive, should allow money and free birth as well as virtue to entitle human beings to office—is a concession to the scarcity of virtue, a practical argument, he believes that a regime should seek justice or proportionate equality as much as possible within the limitations imposed by nature or chance. It may do so by making its deliberative offices open only to the virtuous or educated and the other, predominantly judicial offices open to others.[60] Such a policy may contribute to the duration of the regime as well. But polity is a durable form of regime also because it can be tailored to the attributes of a particular populace: in some polities, more offices must be open to free birth than to wealth or virtue; in others, more to wealth than to virtue. Still, legislators should aim for a good mixture: "It should be possible for the same polity to be spoken of as either a democracy or an oligarchy"; but where possible a polity should "be spoken of most particularly as aristocracy" (*Pol* 1294b15–16, 1294a23–24).

Polity lies between democracy and aristocracy, then, in recognizing but differentiating all claims to office.[61] Democracy overlooks that a city cannot be self-sufficient without expertise (*Pol* 1277a5–11, 1273b5, 1261b14–15). How can individuals be "partners and helpers" to one another[62] if none is very good at anything because all are at once free to live as they want but required to be available for political office? Falling short of self-sufficiency, not to say justice, democracy is not a durable sort of regime (*Pol* 1332b28–29, 1253a1, 1326a12–13). By contrast, polity is more viable (*Pol* 1294b34–40).

How can a regime distribute the most important offices to those worthy of them without instilling resentment and provoking unrest among those not worthy of them? Aristotle indicates that this task may be less difficult than it might seem. Contrary to Hobbes's later claim, not all people have an unceasing desire for power after

---

[60] Thus, we see that Aristotle agrees with Solon (see note 11, pp. 102–3).

[61] Insofar as modern democracy recognizes merit—for example, requires lawyers, judges, and other civil servants to pass exams, or requires officials to be elected rather than chosen by lot—it "would have to be described with a view to its intention from Aristotle's point of view as a mixture of democracy and aristocracy"—in other words, as polity (Strauss, *City and Man*, 35). Because Aristotle realizes that the intention of elections (or exams) may not be fulfilled, he would consider them only a theoretically aristocratic mechanism (see *Politics*, vol. 2, ed. Newman, 374, note on 1273b39).

[62] Plato, *Republic*, 369b–c.

power. In fact, "no one would ask for office unless he were honor-loving" (*Pol* 1271a15–16).[63] Desire for political recognition is not universal; some desire gain or pleasure instead or more. Legislators should not assume, then, that those not honored with office or an important office will be envious of or hostile toward those so honored.

Three sorts of people in particular prefer not to participate in political life. First, the poor would in fact rather work than either hold office or go to war.[64] They "are even glad if someone leaves them the leisure for their private affairs [*tois idiois*]" (*Pol* 1308b35–36, 1318b12–17, 1297b6–12). Second, the well-off are not always inclined to public service; having to or preferring to manage their business affairs, they sometimes swear that serving would cost them financially or impose other burdens.[65] Since the interests of the wealthy should be spoken for, a regime should not allow them to decline office, even if they pay a fine for not serving (1297a19–20). But it can be inferred that, if a regime is more in need of their money than of their service (or the services of all of them), then it should make the wealthy's preference and ability to pay work to its advantage. Third, those who shun public service the most are the philosophical, those who find the greatest happiness in the activity of the intellect; for such activity thrives in solitude (*NE* 1177a12–b2, *Pol* 1267a10–11).

It should be observed that, although these different sorts of people desire particular ends—subsistence, wealth, thought—they all desire the opportunity to pursue a good. Privacy is, strictly speaking, a means to fulfill their desires; but insofar as means are bound to their ends, these people desire privacy itself as much as their particular ends. Further, insofar as the pursuit of their ends requires some form of virtue—industry, prudence, or the highest human capacity—they all desire privacy as Aristotle wishes us to

---

[63] Fortunately for regimes, there are people who are both virtuous and want to perform public service (*Pol* 1291a34–b2, 1324a29–32; *NE* 1177a30–31); "actions directed to honors and to what makes one well off are very noble in an unqualified sense. . . . they are providers and generators of good things" (*Pol* 1332a15–16, 18). Aristotle is not disparaging "honor-loving" per se.

[64] Assuming that, as was the case in Athens, the per diem compensation for public service was less than what could be gained or earned in a working day (*Pol* 1297b11–12, 1318b13–16). There would, however, be those among the poor who would prefer the compensation to work—the elderly, the very poor, and, one might add, the lazy (see Finley, *Democracy*, 118).

[65] See *Politics*, trans. Lord, 258 n. 45.

understand it. The paradox that the human desire for privacy makes political life possible thus emerges.

If there are, and surely there are, some among the less virtuous who demand to participate in political decision making, then legislators might do the following: either allow some number from the multitude to be elected to the deliberative body, or allow the people to consider issues that have already been considered by the members of a preliminary council, a council of law guardians or some such office. "In this way the people will share in deliberating but will not be able to overturn anything connected to the regime" (*Pol* 1298b27–32).[66]

One might point out that, although the limited participation of the less virtuous serves the regime, the nonparticipation of the philosophical is not desirable; legislators should not welcome philosophers' reluctance to perform public service and should contrive a way to make them serve. But such demands are counterproductive, since public service interferes with the activity of philosophy. Rather, then, legislators should figure out a way for a regime to benefit from the wisdom of philosophers without invading their privacy. And perhaps Aristotle has suggested the way—by encouraging legislators to learn from ancient law or custom. For if we assume that the presence, writings, and teachings of philosophers influence ways of life,[67] then those ways of life as embodied in laws and customs may transmit the political teachings of philosophers. Philosophers perform their public service posthumously by leaving a legacy of political ideas. Thus, a regime may leave philosophers undisturbed while benefiting from philosophical wisdom. By leaving philosophers alone, then, a regime ensures its future or longevity.

---

[66] As Mansfield observes, "in advising that the power of rejecting be conceded to the demos, Aristotle recognizes the naysaying *thumos* of human beings; and also, without making a point of it, he admits the necessity of decrees despite the sovereignty of deliberation." In other words, Aristotle concedes the power of human nature and nature "to decree limits to human choice." Thus, choice "must rest content with having the first word" (*Taming the Prince*, 57–58).

[67] See Chapter 6, "Leisure: Private and Public Good," pp. 163–64.

6

POLITICAL EDUCATION:
A PREFACE TO JUSTICE

Although the virtues of the rule of law are considerable, Aristotle has revealed or suggested in discussing them at least five reasons why the rule of law needs to be complemented by the rule of men. Those reasons, to the extent that they are separable, can be summarized as follows. First, the rule of law needs human discretion to render it practical or serviceable and thereby ongoing; men will not continue the rule of law unless it can be tailored to promote the survival of particular regimes. Second, law is not fully able to determine to what it applies; human discretion needs to define the boundaries of practical affairs, or interpret the law. Law may, for example, declare its authority over military and religious matters, but human beings must decide what these matters are.[1] Third, laws need human discretion to address the recalcitrance or refusal of a populace to obey them. Fourth, both the preservation and the justice of regimes call for human judgment to improve the rule of law by purging it of overly simple, barbaric, and foolish laws created by simpleminded populaces; "at Cyme, for example, there is a law concerning cases of homicide, to the effect that the accused shall be guilty of murder if the plaintiff can provide a certain number of witnesses from among his own relatives" (*Pol* 1268b39–1269a8, *Met* 995a3–6). Finally, equity or fairness (*epieikeia*), the best sort of justice, calls for human discretion since law can issue judg-

---

[1] The Athenians undertook this task when they reinscribed their legal code in 403/2 B.C.; see Douglas M. MacDowell, *The Law in Classical Athens* (London: Thames and Hudson, 1978), 47–48, 160–61, 194.

ments only about categories or classes of cases. Strictly speaking, Aristotle explains in the *Nicomachean Ethics, law* is not defective; it is correct to uphold the universal by automatically appealing to the usual case or precedent because this is its function. But the irregularity of practical matters is such that universal judgments cannot correctly apply to all of them. Thus, human discretion must sometimes either rectify a law itself by qualifying it or suspend its operation by issuing a decree in its place. From the perspective of equity, then, the universality of law is its defect (*NE* 1137b13–29).[2]

If human beings are to compensate for the rule of law's inadequacies without overruling its proper authority—that is, if they are to help law preserve the regime—then they must be educated in the spirit of the laws—"If the laws are popular, in a popular spirit, if oligarchic, in an oligarchic spirit" (*Pol* 1310a12–18). The education that is important from the political point of view is apparently not an education in complete virtue but in political virtue: "All those who take thought for good order [*eunomia*] give careful attention to political virtue and vice" (*Pol* 1280b5–6).

My first aim in this chapter is to explain the attributes that together constitute political virtue according to Aristotle. I discuss the qualities that citizens in their capacity as citizens should have as well as the qualities needed by rulers in particular. In the best regime, civic virtue and the ruling virtues coincide in all citizens; ordinarily, however, those with ruling virtues are relatively few. My second aim is to explain the means Aristotle proposes for cultivating political virtue in human beings, to make them good citizens and good rulers. Finally, I consider the discovery of those means, or the political role of philosophical virtue, and thus show that complete virtue is in fact more politically important than political virtue insofar as it is in a sense the source of the latter.

POLITICAL VIRTUE: VIRTUE REDEFINED

As if in response to the question, what is political virtue? Aristotle writes: "If it was correctly said in the *Ethics* that the happy life is

---

2 Like Kant, Aristotle is saying that not law but practical affairs disappoint; unlike Kant, he is nonetheless persuaded of the ability of human discretion to discover an approximately reasonable, or a kind of reasonable, course of action in the irregular circumstances of life.

one in accordance with virtue and unimpeded, and that virtue is a mean, then the middling sort of life is best—the mean that is capable of being attained by each sort of individual. These same defining principles must also define virtue and vice in the case of a city and a regime" (*Pol* 1295a35–40). If a city ought to follow that way of life that stands as a mean to it, then it follows that a citizen ought to follow that way of life that stands as a mean to the regime. Good citizens are, then, more virtuous than the regime in which they live. For example, whereas the best form of democracy is the most moderate form with respect to the extreme form, the best democrat is moderate with respect to the standards set—not by the extreme form of democracy—but by the most moderate form of democracy. The best democrats, then, even more than the best democratic laws, recognize claims in addition to freedom and equality. What enables citizens to be more moderate than the laws under which they live is civic virtue. The elements of civic virtue enable them to temper their foremost political desire (for freedom, equality, economic equality or preeminence, power or dominance).

The civic virtue exercised by the citizens in the best regime, like ordinary civic virtue, partakes of the mean. But this mean is the true mean. Civic virtue that upholds the true mean is moral virtue simply. The character and conduct of the citizens in the best regime are then 'extreme' in that they always, in public and in private, are morally virtuous.

Not all citizens in ordinary regimes partake of the civic mean and thereby surpass the laws in goodness. Indeed, some are not even as good as the laws, for private upbringing and character often influence them more than the laws: "It has happened in many places that, although the regime insofar as it is based on the laws is not a popular one, it is governed in popular fashion as a result of the [citizens'] character and upbringing [*tēn agōgēn*]. Similarly, it has happened elsewhere that the regime insofar as it is based on the laws tends toward the popular, but through the [citizens'] upbringing and habits tends to be oligarchically run" (*Pol* 1292b12–17). Likewise, we can infer that some citizens surpass the standard of civic virtue for their regime. In short, because of nature and nurture, the virtue of citizens in the same regime varies; a zealot may live next door to a *spoudaios*.[3]

---

[3] Although Aristotle makes no reference to nature here, it is possible because of his use of *agōgē* in addition to *ethos* that he means by the latter the natural temperament or inclinations of individuals.

Aristotle has suggested three reasons for regimes to cultivate in their citizens political virtue that goes beyond mere obedience to the laws. First, the laws themselves may not be good; to follow the way of life they set forth may be to live licentiously or acquisitively, for example. Second, even if the regime is the moderate form of its type, citizens can effect the better sort of *eunomia*, which goes beyond the observance of laws as such. Third, an education in civic virtue has more potential than the laws to remedy a bad character and upbringing and to enhance a good character and upbringing.

According to Aristotle, civic virtue comprises five main qualities: (1) self-restraint or temperance, (2) trustworthiness and a capacity to trust, (3) thoughtfulness, judgment, or prudence, (4) spiritedness, and (5) goodwill, or the capacity for concord. In educating citizens not simply in the spirit of the regime but in the spirit of the mean relative to it, a regime twice redefines virtue—moving away from the true mean, and back again toward it.

Self-Restraint or Temperance

Citizens in any regime should resist the impulse to steal, whether need or want generates that impulse (*Pol* 1267a2–5). Most need the help of education to check their desires (*Pol* 1266b29–31). Ideally, education should dissuade persons from even coveting excessive possessions or from "money-loving." As noted in Chapter 4, one should desire wealth only in order to meet needs and to be generous to others.[4]

In the modern liberal view, as derived especially from Hobbes, the concept of good or goodness collapses into that of want or interest such that "the sole measure of good that remains is the wants of an individual or some combination of the wants of individuals revealed by the choices they make. The good has no existence outside the will."[5] According to Aristotle, the will is only one part and the least noble part of the soul. It becomes more noble not as it recedes but as it accords with the rational, more noble, part of the soul (*Pol* 1333a16–29; *NE* 1098a7–8, 1102b28–31). Thus, educa-

---

[4] Aristotle makes the following distinctions. Those without self-restraint, or the self-indulgent (*akolastoi*), do not resist their desires that are inconsistent with virtue (for example, they want to loaf instead of write their term paper and so loaf); the self-restrained or continent (*engkratoi*) resist such desires (they want to loaf but write their term paper); the temperate (*sōphronēs*) have only desires consistent with virtue (they want to write their term paper instead of loaf) (*NE* 1102b26–28, 1119a1–18).

[5] Roberto Mangabeira Unger, *Knowledge and Politics* (New York: Free Press, 1984), 67–68.

tion should not suppress but ennoble the passions of citizens. This benefits not only the regime but the individual, in saving him from the futility of trying to satisfy his untempered passions and from the resulting lost opportunities for a complete life.

Trust and Trustworthiness

Citizens should be trustworthy so that trust may be forthcoming among them. Trust should predominate for many reasons, but mainly because a regime cannot last unless its citizens trust each other enough to let others rule. Since it is just to distribute offices according to merit, citizens need to trust each other's judgment about what constitutes merit or virtue (which is why the rich and the poor do not let each other rule) (*Pol* 1326b14–18, 1297a4–6). If such trust does not prevail, then offices will change hands only by usurpation. Similarly, unless trust prevails, the ruled may not abide the decisions of the rulers; offices will lose their power to command.

The prevalence of trust also safeguards a regime against the rise of a tyrant or demagogue; when citizens are divided, one who wants to rule only for personal advantage can easily rise to power. Citizens heed such a person because, though not serving their interests, he does not serve the opposition's interests either. In contrast, when citizens are united or trust one another, they together distrust one who appears unworthy of ruling. In other words, the trusting and trustworthy—that is, the respectable—do not submit to the rule of a tyrant out of distrust of the alternative, rule by their fellow citizens. Consequently, "[tyrants] make war on the respectable as being harmful to their rule"; a shrewd tyrant knows that "a tyranny will not be overthrown before some persons are able to trust each other" (*Pol* 1314a17–23).

Finally, citizens should be trustworthy enough to keep agreements and trust others enough to keep them, for a city cannot exist without agreements of all kinds. To live together citizens must agree at least not to violate each other's persons or property and to exchange goods (*Pol* 1280b29–32). "For the most part [the wealthy] are more trustworthy regarding agreements" (*Pol* 1283a32–33)—perhaps because the wealthy, being less needy than others, do not attempt to cheat or swindle to procure what is not theirs legally or by agreement. At any rate, the opportunity for gain, being an opportunity to satisfy needs, especially invites persons to be untrustworthy.

For trust to prevail, "the citizens must necessarily be familiar with [*gnōrizein*] one another's qualities" (*Pol* 1326b16–17). Human beings trust one another only if they deem the other's character sound, and they cannot render such a judgment without being familiar with the other. Perhaps Aristotle is saying that citizens need, not to know each other personally,[6] but to recognize in each other desirable, trust-eliciting qualities. In any case, he observes that a tyrant, in trying to undermine or preempt trust among his subjects, will do everything possible to render or to keep them unfamiliar with each other—such as prohibit academies, intellectual gatherings, and athletic, social, and religious functions (*Pol* 1313b3–6).[7]

Thoughtfulness, Judgment, or Prudence

A third salient element of political virtue is thoughtfulness, judgment, or prudence. According to Aristotle, the Greeks, being as a race more endowed with thought (*dianoētikon*) than peoples of cold countries, govern themselves in a manner much superior to the way northerners govern themselves and show, also in contrast to northerners, the ability to rule others (*Pol* 1327b24–33). Thought (*dianoia*) appears then to be a necessary condition of prudence (*phronēsis*), the capacity to rule and to be ruled (*Pol* 1277a14–16, 25–27, 1333a11–13). If thought is presupposed by, but is not the same thing as, prudence, then perhaps what Aristotle means by it is thoughtfulness—that quality that compels one to think, or one might say calculate, before doing or acting. It would thus complement both technical skill (*technē*) and prudence (*phronēsis*), the two lower-order intellectual faculties (*NE* 1139a6–12, 1140b35–1141a1). It is better, for example, to think to shut off the water before fixing the plumbing and to think before issuing a decree. Having done so does not mean, however, that one knows how to fix the pipes (has *technē*), or knows what action is good for the country (has *phronēsis*). Without thoughtfulness, then, people are less inclined to heed others or to be guided to virtue (*Pol* 1327b36–38)—preferring to act rather than to listen or think—and less inclined to make sound judgments or rule well—preferring quick to deliberate decisions.

---

[6] Ernest Barker claims that Aristotle means the opposite; see *The Politics of Aristotle* (Oxford: Clarendon, 1948), 292 n. 3.

[7] Carnes Lord's explanation of *scholai* ("leisured discussions") and *syllogoi scholastikoi* ("meetings connected with leisure"); see *Aristotle: The Politics* (Chicago: University of Chicago Press, 1984), 263–64 n. 104.

Aristotle seems to be saying that good political order requires citizens who have some degree of caution and are thus willing to consider or, as the case may be, reconsider decisions before executing them. That the Carthaginian oligarchs allow the people to challenge some of their proposals is not commendable insofar as it is a deviation toward democracy (*Pol* 1273a4–13) (though advisable as a safeguard against discord); nonetheless, it evinces the oligarchs' willingness to reconsider their decisions before making them law. Without such reconsideration, there cannot be decisions that deserve to be called judgments. And, as we have learned from Aristotle, without judgments human beings cannot live together; even if an association is constituted of all those persons needed to furnish the necessities of life—such as weavers, farmers, shoemakers, and builders—"there must necessarily be someone who assigns and judges what is just [*krinounta to dikaion*]." Indeed, in the sense that we should consider the soul of an animal to be more important than its body, we should, to recall, consider the part of the city that judges or deliberates (whether over judicial or political matters) to be more important than even those parts that provide food, clothing, and shelter (*Pol* 1291a22–28).

It seems, on the one hand, that regimes cannot make their populaces thoughtful, because thoughtfulness appears to be a natural virtue that "must [already] be present [*ta men huparchein*]" in a city (*Pol* 1327b19–20, 1332a28–29). On the other hand, Aristotle indicates that thoughtfulness makes people yield easily to virtue (*Pol* 1327b36–38). Perhaps he is saying that, insofar as legislators cannot create thoughtfulness, it is a natural endowment; but insofar as they can transform it into good judgment or deliberation and, in some persons, even prudence (the ability to carry out deliberative decisions; *NE* 1140b20–21, 28), it is a (supremely important) political virtue.

Spiritedness

In addition to being self-controlled, trustworthy, and thoughtful, citizens should also be spirited (*enthumon*). If they are not, their fate may be that of the Asians—perpetual subjection and enslavement (*Pol* 1327b27–29). Spiritedness protects a people against enslavement because, one might surmise, it is fierceness, or a readiness to fight. The spirited man is not by nature aggressive, but rather he is willing to be so. Perhaps Aristotle is agreeing with the Athenian

Stranger that "every real man should be of the spirited type, but yet also as gentle as possible. For there is no way to avoid those injustices done by others that are both dangerous and difficult, or even impossible, to cure, except to fight and defend oneself victoriously, in no way easing up on punishment. This, every soul is unable to do, if it lacks a high-born spiritedness."[8] But Aristotle criticizes Plato for depicting the guardians of his city—who, like dogs, attack outsiders—as too harsh. One should not be harsh even to strangers, Aristotle says. It appears, moreover, that spiritedness in his view is nothing like fierceness, for "spirit . . . is the capacity of the soul by which we feel love." Hence it is "a thing expert at ruling [archikon]" us (Pol 1327b38–1328a1, 7–8).

If, however, spiritedness is the capacity that feels or is aroused by affection (ho thumos estin ho poiōn to philētikon), how does it allow the Greeks to remain free and self-governing (Pol 1327b40–41, 31–33)? Perhaps it makes them "keenly alive to the obligations of friendship"[9] or, more broadly, protective of what is their own. Human beings feel affection for what is their own and dear (Pol 1262b22–23), and when the objects of their affection are threatened spirited human beings become aroused, ready to protect what they hold to be good.[10]

The spirited person is, then, harsh only in reaction to those behaving unjustly (adikountas) (Pol 1328a10). Otherwise, it appears, he is gentle. Aristotle therefore agrees with Plato but emphasizes that it is not unfamiliarity per se but injustice that arouses the spirited man—who is not like the dog who attacks all strangers but the tame dog, the dog who attacks when he senses a danger or threat to his masters, those he "owns."[11] Like the tame dog, he is noble, not beastlike (Pol 1338b29).

In being a disposition to protect what is one's own and dear—what is private—spiritedness is not a mere willingness to fight, an ability to be piously cruel, or even spite. It is rather a moral sensibility or posture, a loyalty to what is not simply one's own but one's own and dear or thought to be good. It is the disposition or

---

[8] Plato, Laws, 731b.
[9] Politics, trans. Barker, 296 n. 3.
[10] Hence children, being, as Aristotle and Socrates observe, "full of spirit straight from birth" (Plato, Republic, 441a; Pol 1334b22–24), often cling fiercely to things that are theirs or that they believe to be theirs.
[11] Plato, Republic, 375e.

feeling that, in Aristotle's view, human beings properly have toward those things that are truly private. Being a loyalty or commitment to what is good and one's own, it is the disposition that someone may have about not only intimates and friends (*Pol* 1328a1–2, 10–11) but also the activity of philosophy.[12]

Thus, spiritedness is not in Aristotle's view blind or simple patriotism. Esteem—for friendships, family, a way of life—moves human beings to protect themselves. Spiritedness thus springs from or is attached to judgment.[13]

That spiritedness is aroused by threats to what people esteem means that it manifests itself variously. Friends and intimates "choke with rage" (with good reason) when what they have with one another is slighted (*Pol* 1328a5, 13–14); citizens who esteem their way of life go to war if attacked; and one who esteems the contemplative life, like Socrates, protests if it is threatened. Although such individuals may not themselves be victorious, their spiritedness shows itself until their end, for spirit is an "indomitable thing [*aettēton*]" (1328a7).

Goodwill

If spiritedness is a commitment to what is held dear, then it is inseparable from affection (*Pol* 1327b40–41); and since spiritedness motivates people to defend their regime, it is not surprising that affection or friendship (*philia*) is "the greatest of good things for cities" (*Pol* 1262b7–8). But friendship is also a great good for cities in that it seems to hold them together (*NE* 1155a22–23) by safeguarding them against civic conflict (*Pol* 1262b8–9), encouraging voluntary sharing of possessions (*Pol* 1263a38–39), and rendering them more than alliances (*Pol* 1261a24–25, 1280a31–35, b29–31). For these reasons, Aristotle appears to be against diluting friendship between citizens (*Pol* 1262b15–16).

Still, as people become closer and their claims of friendship increase, their spiritedness becomes more easily aroused (*Pol* 1328a1–2)—suggesting that where friendship exists between citizens the potential for civic conflict is great. Moreover, much of Book II is devoted to the point that too much unity destroys a city (e.g., *Pol*

---

[12] Ibid., 376c.

[13] It is perhaps because spiritedness is a kind of moral virtue that farmers should not be of a spirited stock (*Pol* 1330a27); that is, those who are spirited should be not farmers but citizens.

1261a16–21, II.2–6). So Aristotle's statement against dilution of friendship in cities is in fact a statement against an excess of affection, a condition certain to bring about such dilution (*Pol* 1262b10–16).

The friendship Aristotle deems the greatest good for cities is then a particular species of friendship—namely, concord (*homonoia*) (*NE* 1155a24–25). Concord lies between enmity on the one hand and (other types of) friendship on the other (1155a25–26, VIII.3). It is unlike enmity because goodwill (*eunoia*) characterizes it; but it is unlike the other types of friendship (for utility, pleasure, and virtue) because the goodwill is not reciprocal (1155b33–34). Goodwill between citizens is not reciprocal because it is not the (mutual) appreciation of specific qualities (such as beauty, wealth, or goodness) by specific persons but is rather appreciation of a general attribute of all (or most) persons. As Aristotle explains, "many a person has goodwill to those whom he has not seen but assumes to be decent or useful, and one of these might have the same goodwill toward him. These people, then, apparently bear goodwill to each other, but how could we call them friends when they are not aware of each other's regard?" (1155b34–1156a3, 1157b18–19).

Concord appears, then, to be conducive to or expressed in law-abidingness, in that abiding the law—not killing, robbing, or otherwise harming others—is an expression of goodwill, a recognition of the decency or at least usefulness of others (insofar as living with others in peace rather than enmity facilitates living). That concord may stem from a recognition of simply the usefulness of other citizens indicates that it is close on the spectrum of friendship to utilitarian friendship. But to call it utilitarian friendship would be in Aristotle's view to overstate what it is, since it does not satisfy specific needs or wants. Not rooted in particularity and thus proximity (*NE* 1157b10–13, 19), concord is a diffuse, watery kind of association.

Although Aristotle does not think that citizens can reciprocate goodwill, he does think that they should reciprocate equality (*Pol* 1261a30–31), that is, equality of treatment: "Men seek to return either evil for evil—if they cannot, they feel they are in the position of slaves—or good for good—if they cannot, no exchange takes place." In short, "proportionate reciprocity holds together a city" (*NE* 1132b31–1133a2). Aristotle thereby suggests the conclusion

that concord, insofar as it is manifested as law-abidingness or respect for the law, makes possible the dispensation of rewards and
punishment, or justice. Understandably then, legislators are more
concerned about (political) friendship than about justice (*NE*
1155a23–24).

The Ruler's Virtues: Prudence, Temperance, and Justice

Rulers should have all the virtues of a good citizen, but they
should have especially prudence (not simply thoughtfulness or
judgment), temperance (not simply self-restraint), and justice (not
simply goodwill).

Rule is not, properly speaking, rule in Aristotle's view unless
those ruling possess prudence. As explained in Chapter 5, a regime may have to establish other qualifications for office, but it
should make prudence a qualification for as many offices as possible and especially for the most important ones.

Prudence is the defining virtue of a ruler according to Aristotle
(*Pol* 1277a14–16, 23, b25–26) for two reasons. First, it is the faculty
that translates, by good deliberation, judgments into actions (*NE*
1143a7–10, 1140b3–7, 15–16, 1141b12–14, 21), thus enabling the
ruler to issue (good) commands (*epitaktikē*) (*NE* 1143a8).[14] In presupposing judgment, prudence distinguishes the ruler from the
clever incontinent or evil man, who can also obtain his desired end
(*NE* 1142b18–20).[15] In presupposing judgment and effecting it,
prudence distinguishes the ruler from the man of understanding
(*sunesis*), who can neither judge by himself[16] nor actualize a judgment (*NE* 1143a13–15). Finally, in actualizing judgment, prudence
distinguishes the ruler from the man of judgment (*gnōmē*), who is
capable of rendering judgments alone and thereby of holding true
opinion (*doxa alēthēs*) but cannot apparently effect judgments (*NE*
1143a8, *Pol* 1277b28–29). In distinguishing between the man of un-

[14] See also Eric Voegelin, "What Is Right by Nature?" in *Anamnesis*, trans. and ed.
Gerhart Niemeyer (Notre Dame: University of Notre Dame Press, 1978), 67, 69–70
and, acknowledging Voegelin, Ronald Beiner, *Political Judgment* (Chicago: University
of Chicago Press, 1983), 74–75.

[15] Both the prudent and the clever man can, by deliberating or calculating correctly (*orthōs*), figure out the means to achieve a certain end; but only the prudent
man deliberates well (*eu*)—that is, nobly (*kalōs*) (*NE* 1143a14–15)—because the
means he arrives at effect a good end (embodied in judgment) (*NE* 1142b18–22, 27–
33, 1143a26, 28–35).

[16] At *NE* 1143a9–10, Aristotle states that "understanding judges," but then he
explains two lines later that it judges "what someone else says" (1143a13–15).

derstanding and the man of judgment, Aristotle seems to be drawing a distinction between those members of a regime who are only able to be unquestioningly law-abiding and those who are able to hold and voice their own, perhaps critical, judgments of the regime.[17] Aristotle suggests that yet another sort of citizen might exist—those who have the capacity to be prudent but prefer to engage in theoretical speculation, speaking out against the regime only if and when it threatens their preferred activity.[18]

Prudence is also the defining virtue of a ruler, according to Aristotle, because it effects what is good for the whole. It is the ability "to deliberate nobly about . . . what conduces to the good life in general" (NE 1140a25–28, 1141b12–14). Rulers do not deliberate about what the good life *is*, for it is impossible to deliberate about what does not vary (1140a31–32, 1141b10–11); rather, they deliberate about the means to obtain it, which do vary. But, in order to deliberate about these, they must have in view the end (1141b11–12). Not being able to arrive at what is universally good on their own (1141a29, b14–15, 1142a25–26), they seek to learn it, as has been explained, from law (1141b24–26) which embodies to varying degrees the insights of the wise. In deciding what to command or decree, rulers consider the law and the particulars at hand.[19] If the

[17] The likelihood that persons of judgment would criticize their regime is presumably a function of the number and authority of prudent office-holders. That any regime can have both critical and uncritical members is possible and likely because understanding and judgment are natural endowments (NE 1143b6–7). Voegelin seems to collapse judgment (*gnōmē*), which Aristotle discusses in NE VI.11, and understanding (*sunesis*), which Aristotle discusses in NE VI.10, when he states that "*synesis* is the virtue of right judgment and understanding (*kritike*)" and explains that the *sunetos* (not also the man of *gnōmē*) is different from the *phronimos* because he cannot act effectively. Or, he subsumes *gnōmē* under *phronēsis*. In any case, he does not address *gnōmē* in his discussion of *phronēsis* ("What Is Right by Nature?" 69–70). Although Aristotle does use *krisis* (judgment or discrimination) to describe the activity issuing in understanding (*sunesis*) (NE 1143a10, 14, 15, 30) and in judgment (*gnōmē*) (1143a20, 23, 30) and says that both *sunesis* and *gnōmē* concern particulars (1143a28–29), the fact that he uses two different words cannot be ignored; the strongest case for accounting for it seems to be the difference between following another's reasoning and reasoning on one's own (the latter easily subsumes the former). This interpretation is supported further by what seem to be distinctions between understanding, judgment, and prudence: "There being two parts of the soul that can follow a course of reasoning, [prudence] must be the virtue of one of the two, namely, of that part which forms opinions. . . . But yet [prudence] is not only a reasoned state" (1140b25–26, 28).

[18] In the best regime, citizens have actual prudence when ruling and latent prudence when being ruled (Pol 1277a13–14, 20–23).

[19] My point is contrary to Ronald Beiner's suggestion that the prudent man does not consider codified principles (Political Judgment, 73).

law does not stipulate what would be fair, they rectify this deficiency by prescribing what they deem fair rather than what is legally just (1137b19–27, 1140b4–6, 1143a31–33). Accordingly, prudence shapes legislative wisdom and politics (1141b24–28).

In effecting what is good for the whole, the ruler displays justice, for justice is by definition the exercise of virtue in relation to others (*NE* 1129b25–27, 32–1130a1; *Pol* 1277b16–18). Good citizens too are just, but not fully, since they lack the capacity, not to ascertain what is good for the whole, but to effect it.[20] Having the justice characteristic of being ruled (*Pol* 1277b18–21), good citizens apparently attend largely to their own affairs.

Prudence also presupposes temperance. The word *sōphrosunē* (temperance) derives from *sōzein* (to preserve, maintain) and *phronēsis* (prudence); we imply by the word *sōphrosunē*, Aristotle says, that "it preserves one's prudence [*sōzousan tēn phronēsin*]" (*NE* 1140b11–12). Again, good citizens too are moderate, but in a way befitting being ruled (*Pol* 1277b18–21), which may mean that self-restraint suffices for the ruled, at least in most regimes.

THE GUIDING PRINCIPLES OF POLITICAL EDUCATION: "THE POSSIBLE AND THE PROPER"

Having reviewed the nature of political virtue, we can now turn to the ways of cultivating it. On the one hand, Aristotle declares, "education relative to the regimes" is "the greatest of all the things" that makes regimes last (*Pol* 1310a12–14). On the other hand, in advising all cities to try to realize as much as possible the happy, that is, the virtuous or noble life, he indicates that the aim of education should be to make citizens as virtuous as possible (*Pol* 1323b30–36, 40–1324a2, 12–13).[21] Taken together, these two prescriptions repeat the claim that the virtue that citizens should have should constitute a mean relative to their regime. Education should form characters supportive of the regime yet should also prepare and encourage individuals to actualize their human potential. In calling for the actualization of potential, Aristotle is, one should remember, calling not only for excellence but for diversity,

---

[20] Strictly speaking, then, politics is properly the domain of rulers not citizens.
[21] See the Appendix, "The Composition of the *Politics*," pp. 221–26.

since a city's existence depends on the preservation of differences not inimical to virtue (*Pol* 1261a24, 29–30). In short, education must make persons at once excellent citizens, excellent human beings, and excellent individuals.

It should be noticed that, in advising an educational solution to the problem of realizing the end of the city, Aristotle implicitly rejects the characteristically modern judgment that institutional remedies to political problems are more realistic than educational ones. In Aristotle's view, institutional regulation is not to be preferred because it at least jeopardizes the actualization by human beings of both excellence and talent or individuality. It is neither realistic nor desirable to try to achieve political unification through uniformity.[22]

If an educational system is to preserve difference or choice and foster excellence or the making of good choices, then it should not expect the same level of performance from all. Uniformity of achievement results only if the standard of achievement is set by the capabilities of the least capable, which may be no standard because, as Socrates and Aristotle note, "there may be persons who are incapable of being educated and becoming good men" (*Pol* 1316a10–11). At the same time, education cannot without cost to its effectiveness ignore the limitations nature insists on imposing on individual human beings. In short, it must accommodate the inequality that is and will continue to be a feature of all regimes at all times (*Pol* 1316a11–14).

Since the extent to which individuals can actualize virtue (*aretēs energeia*) ranges from not at all to completely (*Pol* 1328a37–40), education should adopt as guiding principles the two aims that individuals should undertake for themselves—namely, "the possible and the proper [or fitting; *to te dunaton kai to prepon*]" (*Pol* 1342b17–20). Yet fourteen lines later (1342b33–34), concluding the last paragraph of the *Politics*, three principles—"the mean, the possible, and the proper [*to te meson kai to dunaton kai to prepon*]"—are recommended to guide education. Why Aristotle adds this third term to his initial list of principles, and what he means by these three terms, deserves consideration.

---

[22] See Leo Strauss, *Natural Right and History* (Chicago: University of Chicago Press, 1953), 193–94, which contrasts the ancient view of institutions with the views of Hobbes and Kant; and Eric Voegelin, *Plato and Aristotle*, vol. 3, *Order and History* (Baton Rouge: Louisiana State University Press, 1957), 323.

What Aristotle means by "the possible" as a guiding principle for education seems evident: it would be absurd to ask of human beings what nature prevents them from achieving or makes unreasonably difficult for them to achieve. Five-year-olds should not be expected to learn geometry, for example. What is "proper" for human beings to undertake also seems clear enough: that which is beyond the merely possible in the direction of excellence, but not beyond attainment by the individual. Five-year-olds have the potential to learn table manners and the alphabet and should therefore be encouraged to actualize their moral and intellectual virtues in these ways. Furthermore, although Aristotle states here that age indicates the potential of human beings (*Pol* 1342b20), his earlier observation that human beings are unequal at birth (*tōn gignomenōn pantōn*) (*Pol* 1316a13–14) testifies that the human capacity for virtue is not a function of age alone. It may well be proper for some five-year-olds to learn geometry.

Requiring individuals to undertake activities that they are able to undertake but that are not easy for them to undertake would seem to be a sufficient, twofold principle for designing educational media. Why then does Aristotle conclude that "the mean" should also be a guiding principle? He in effect accounts for this third term by providing, between his first and second lists of guiding principles, two examples of what education should require which illustrate aiming for the mean in education; taken together they serve to illuminate the meaning of "the possible" and "the proper." The first example proposes that the elderly not be required to sing high-pitched harmonies because of the difficulty of their doing so. And since the young will become older, they too should practice the moderate activities that become those who are older (*Pol* 1342b20–29). We are thus cautioned against overreaching in matters of education; there is a difference between virtue and ambition (*NE* 1125b18–25) (a teaching that did not guide J. S. Mill's education). The second example submits that children's music both entertain and discipline them (*Pol* 1342b29–33),[23] perhaps inspiring controlled and repetitious movement. Here Aristotle tacks in the opposite direction: education should make demands on, not simply

[23] Reading *paidia* ("play") rather than *paideia* ("education") and taking *kosmon* to mean "order"; see *Politics*, trans. Lord, 271 n. 32 and *The Politics of Aristotle*, vol. 3, ed. W. L. Newman (New York: Arno Press, 1973), 573, note on 1342b31.

amuse or occupy, human beings (*NE* 1177a2–3). Taken together, the examples thus illustrate the double entendre of "the mean": the mean is both not-the-extreme and excellence itself (*NE* 1107a6–8). What is reasonable includes what is difficult. The last paragraph of the *Politics* therefore exhibits symmetry and communicates the tension implicit in the activity of reaching for excellence which legislators, other educators, and individuals should keep in view.[24]

The Means of Political Education: Habit and Reason

The two guiding principles of education constitute only part of the knowledge required for establishing a good form of education. Legislators must know also the means the principles should direct. Knowing how to induce people to undertake what is both possible and proper for them presupposes, according to Aristotle, knowing what affects or moves the human soul. A legislator must be, then, not just anyone (*tou tuchontos*) but a knower (*tou eidotos*) of the soul (*NE* 1180b25–27).[25] Legislators must know that the human soul has a nonrational part that responds to habituation and a rational part that responds to reasoned argument, to "listening" (*Pol* 1332b1–3, 7–8, 10–11). To what should the nonrational part be habituated and to what should the rational part listen? Aristotle maintains that, since the appetites and desires are inferior to reason, they should be induced to harmonize with it (*Pol* 1333a16–24). Habit should engender the moral virtues, since "none of [them] arises in us by nature" (*NE* 1103a17–26). As for reason, it should be persuaded to be as active as possible (*Pol* 1333a24–30).

Equipped with the two guiding principles and the knowledge that habituation and argument can improve human beings, legislators developing a system of education should set out to discover (1)

---

[24] The symmetry may be summarized as follows: (1) the possible and the proper stipulated as aims for individuals (lines 17–20); (2) first example: illustration of the possible as the mean qua middle (20–29); (3) second example: illustration of the proper as the mean qua excellence (29–33); (4) the mean, the possible, and the proper stipulated as guiding principles for education (33–34). If the paragraph is an interpolation, as some scholars contend (see *Politics*, trans. Lord, 271 n. 33), it is nonetheless consistent with Aristotle's reasoning.

[25] This claim is merely a logical analogue of the claim that, for example, those who care for and train horses should have knowledge of horses (*NE* 1180b27–28).

what kinds of habituation effectively improve which age groups
(for a good upbringing is not sufficient to render human beings
virtuous—even adults need to be induced to practice good habits;
NE 1180a1–4); (2) what mixture of habituation and argument is
appropriate for the adult population in question; and (3) what the
most attractive ways are to induce good habits and to get people to
think and study; people are more apt to comply if their doing so
yields some sort of pleasure (*NE* 1172a25–26). If legislators discover
these things, then they will have figured out how to encourage
moderation (not stoicism), teach trustworthiness (not mere ad-
herence to principles), cultivate judgment (without undermining
political friendship), and foster goodwill (without impairing judgment or diluting spiritedness).

EDUCATION BY HABITUATION

In the *Politics,* Aristotle chooses to discuss the division of the soul
in Book VII, which concerns the regime governed by virtuous men.
He may thereby be suggesting that even men with the best
natures, falling short as they do of being gods, can benefit from
habituation; insofar as even they have appetites and desires that
occasionally work against the actualization of reason, they can benefit from a disposition that ensures the actualization of reason especially in such circumstances (*NE* 1180a22–24, *Pol* 1287a32).

Although one might accept that habitual conduct does not necessarily signify the relinquishment of reason,[26] one might nonetheless wonder why, apart from the sake of political order or from the
point of view of intellectual virtue, reason requires actualization,
whether habitual or otherwise. Aristotle's abbreviated answer is
that there is a sense in which action completes reason: one cannot
be said to *know,* say, the truth of a precept unless one abides it in
practice (*NE* 1179b2–4).[27] Aristotle would, then, agree with the
Athenian Stranger that "what really makes a difference in education—not only of the young but of ourselves—is not so much the
precepts one gives to others, as the way one exemplifies the pre-

---

[26] Of course, it may sometimes signify this, since following a habit or disposition
is not always the best thing to do.
[27] For Aristotle's unabbreviated answer, see Chapter 8, "The Relation between
Moral and Intellectual Virtue," pp. 198–202.

cepts one would give to another, in one's conduct throughout life."[28] In fact, Aristotle says that what distinguishes a good from a bad political system is whether it forms good habits in its citizens (*NE* 1103b3–6).

A good disposition may save the virtuous from infrequent lapses of reasonableness, but most human beings must normally rely on their dispositions (*NE* 1179b4–16). Arguments about human goodness seem to affect those who are young and good-natured and even to inspire those among them who have an inborn yearning for what is noble, but they do not affect most people. Reason or speech alone—lectures, discussion, or writings—cannot impel most people toward nobility and goodness, because they have never experienced the true pleasure that accompanies virtuous activities. Having no conception (*ennoian*) of virtue or thinking wrongly that they do know what others mean by virtue (and having a wrong conception, understandably finding it repellent), they have no sense of honor and therefore no sense of shame. Consequently, they live by pursuing pleasures and avoiding pain without consideration of whether the pleasures in which they indulge are true ones.[29] If base activities give them pleasure, then they refrain from them only if they are afraid of suffering the (legal) penalties attached to them. In short, the many, especially but not only when young, find it difficult because they find it unpleasant to live with even moderation and perseverance (*NE* 1179b31–1180a5). Inclined neither to ascertain what limits they ought to impose on themselves nor to impose voluntarily any such limits on themselves, they need lawmakers and laws to do both of these things for them. The many need laws and an education enforced by law not so much to become noble or excellent but to become self-restrained and thus orderly.

Aristotle seems nonetheless to agree with Plato that some among any multitude would become, as a result of proper habituation, receptive to argument and excellent: "Legislators should exhort people to virtue and urge them forward for the sake of what is

---

[28] Plato, *Laws*, 729c.

[29] Thus, the function of the sense of shame is to promote goodness or excellence in an individual. Similarly, according to Freud, the sense of guilt enables a person to live with others insofar as it checks aggressive impulses. Aristotle and Freud thus agree that shame or conscience is civilization's handmaiden; see Freud, *Civilization and Its Discontents* (New York: W. W. Norton, 1961), 78–94.

noble, on the assumption that those who have been promoted in goodness by the formation of habits will respond" (*NE* 1180a5–8). Because there may be a variety of natures even among the many, all regimes should contain a form of education that prepares them for and invites the pursuit of excellence.

Habituating Children: Physical and Moral Supervision

The formation of habits preparing individuals for further education should begin before they are required to obey the laws directly, when they are children. Since children's reasoning powers are latent (*Pol* 1260a12–14), their upbringing should focus on developing their bodies through gymnastic and sports (*Pol* 1334b25–26, 1338b4–8). The body should be developed, not for the sake of the body itself (health), for the sake of competition (honor), or for the sake of the defense of the city (courage), but for the sake of the whole soul (1334b27–28, 1338b9–16). Light (noncompulsory) exercise serves the soul by making the body more resistant to fatigue and illness that could later distract the soul from its proper work (1338a19–20, b40–42, 1335b8–11).

Since the appetites and desires can, as much as fatigue and illness, interfere with thinking, they too should be disciplined. Teaching children what they should find repellent and what they should love (*Pol* 1340a15) is in fact a way to promote the later development of their minds, since they will come to love all things noble.[30] Before puberty, this habituation should take the form of monitoring what children hear and see, so that they do not acquire an element of rudeness or meanness (1336b2–3). Parents or others overseeing children at home should assume this responsibility until children are seven years old; once the regime begins to supervise children, this responsibility becomes also that of legislators and public supervisors of children. Adults should prohibit children from, for example, using or hearing foul words, looking at unseemly pictures, hearing lampoons (*iamboi*), seeing comedies, or spending time with the household slaves (1336a39–b23).[31] The young should not be exposed to base things in general, and they

[30] See also Plato, *Laws*, 653b.
[31] Lampoons are indecent and abusive verses recited at festivals of Dionysus; see *Politics*, trans. Lord, 269 n. 81, which refers the reader to Aristotle's *Poetics* 1448b24–49a15.

should be kept away especially from anyone or anything that is depraved or hostile (1336b33–35).

According to Plato and Aristotle, it is futile to try to regulate children's conduct by reasoning with them. When a child becomes capable of reasoning he will understand that he was forbidden certain things because children are especially impressionable (*Pol* 1336b33).[32] Moreover, his "passions can in consonance with reason affirm that they have been correctly habituated in the appropriate habits" and, as the Athenian Stranger explains, "this consonance in its entirety is virtue."[33]

Habituating the Young and Adults: Music Education

When children near puberty, after they have learned the useful skills of writing and drawing (*Pol* 1337b23–26), their moral education should assume the form of music (*mousikē*), "the assumption being that, just as gymnastic makes the body of a certain quality, so also is music capable of making the character of a certain quality by habituating it to be capable of taking pleasure in the right sort of way" (1339a21–25, 29–31, 4–5). Having the young actually participate in music—play instruments and sing—is the most effective way to habituate their souls to the moral virtues music represents.[34] Yet also adults should listen to music for the sake of their characters (1340b20–39). Indeed, Aristotle implies that music can promote the five elements of civic virtue—moderation, trustworthiness, thoughtfulness or judgment, spiritedness, and goodwill. This can be seen in both his confirmation that music is morally educative and his definition of "music."

In addition to the possibility that "music contributes something to virtue," Aristotle raises the alternatives that music, like sleep, drinking, and dancing, is "for the sake of play and rest," and that it "contributes in some way to pastime and prudence" (*Pol* 1339a14–21, 25–26, b13–14). In that "music is one of the greatest of pleasures," it qualifies as a form of play, relaxation, and pastime (1339b14–20). Yet, that "in some way it contributes to the character and the soul" is also evident, for "we become of a certain quality," "we are altered in soul," when we hear music. This is so because

---

[32] Plato, *Republic*, 378d.
[33] Plato, *Laws*, 653b.
[34] Carnes Lord, *Education and Culture in the Political Thought of Aristotle* (Ithaca: Cornell University Press, 1982), 97–98.

rhythms and tunes imitate or are like qualities pertaining to character. They may evoke anger, serenity, valor, frenzy, passion, or composure, for example. Music has the power to make us feel similar to what we hear. In fact, although we hear only "imitations of characters," these can produce in us a condition close to the true character—sad songs tend to make us sad. Therefore, to ennoble our characters, we should play, sing, or listen to music that inspires nobility (1340a6–12, 18–25, 38–39, 1342b1–3, 12–17).

Music is an ideal medium for producing good character because it can also arouse pleasant feelings;[35] having a good character means in part liking, desiring, or having pleasant feelings toward good things (*Pol* 1340a14–18). Thus, enjoying good, beautiful, or noble music over time habituates a person to experience pleasure in good, beautiful, or noble things in general. When not partaking in music, such a person seeks out good things (or judges correctly), for these have become enjoyable.[36]

From Aristotle's claim that certain sorts of music can create or inspire in a performer or listener corresponding sorts of character, one might infer that music can therefore inspire the civic virtues. Indeed, to repeat, he says that music can inspire moderation or steadfastness and courage or spiritedness (*Pol* 1342b12–17). That it can elicit sociality or goodwill is obvious and a main reason why human beings accompany their social gatherings and pastimes with singing or performed music, especially cheerful music (1339b21–24).

But can music inspire trustworthiness and thoughtfulness or judgment? In fact, Aristotle indicates that judging or critically evaluating music improves moral judgment (*Pol* 1340a14–18). But this seems most implausible; developing technical or aesthetic judg-

---

[35] Things we taste and touch can produce pleasure but do not seem to affect character; what we see, like what we hear, affects the soul and can produce pleasure, but Aristotle claims that pictures and statues cannot affect character as much as music because they are "not likenesses" but "indications of characters" (*Pol* 1340a28–35; *Politics*, vol. 1, ed. Newman, 363). Aristotle might have judged differently had he lived in the age of photography.

[36] See also Plato, *Republic*, 401d–e. On Aristotle's point, see also *Politics*, trans. Barker, 343 n. 3; *Politics*, vol. 1, ed. Newman, 363, 368, 372; Lord, *Education and Culture*, 93. Newman explains that, "in order fully to understand the importance of the part assigned by Aristotle to music in the development of the *spoudaios*, we must bear in mind that to him, unlike some modern moralists, a man is not really virtuous unless he finds pleasure in the exercise of virtue. It is precisely this identification of the good and the pleasurable that music is the earliest means of producing" (368).

ment, such as the Spartans claim to have done (1339a42–b4), does not seem to improve one's moral character necessarily. Aristotle even says that citizens should not partake of music with a view to becoming experts or professionals.[37] They should not perform in contests or attempt to execute difficult music, for such training impairs bodies for military service and diverts attention later from civic duties and the pursuit of knowledge. What is more, undertaking a musical education for the sake of becoming a professional, of playing for an audience, corrupts its educative purpose, since one plays not for one's own virtue but in the spirit of a laborer trying to please others (1341a5–13, b8–18). At the same time, Aristotle says that citizens should not simply enjoy music, like children, slaves, and even some animals (1341a13–17), thus returning us to the notion that music affects the soul by engaging thought.

How music may affect moral judgment beyond habituating the soul to what is noble—how it may be said to teach or educate—becomes evident once one appreciates that by music Aristotle does not mean merely audible harmony but also poetry. He says, for example, that music is pleasant "both by itself and with melody" (*Pol* 1339b20–21) and speaks of "tunes by themselves" or "harmonies" and "rhythms" (1340a38–40, 13–14, b17–18, VIII.7). The flute, he argues, should not be taught because it "prevents speech" and educating "the mind [*tēn dianoian*]" (1341a24–25, b2–8). Most telling, he declares in his discussion of music education that "one should learn and become habituated to nothing so much as to judging in correct fashion of, and enjoying, respectable characters and noble actions" (1340a16–18)—not only tunes but a story may imitate or portray characters. Aristotle must mean that by evaluating the characters and deeds depicted in a poem (or literature), one may learn moral lessons. Thus, he agrees with Odysseus that music is the best pastime (*diagōgē*) (1338a21–22, 28)—literally, the best way "to lead across life."[38]

Aristotle may deem music—with or without tunes—the best pastime because it compels reflection about ethics, but he characterizes the experience of listening to it less as an intellectual than as

---

[37] For the claim that Aristotle does not think music should promote technical or aesthetic judgment, see Lord, *Education and Culture,* 74–75, 99–103.

[38] In other words, "*diagōgē* rightly understood . . . is fundamentally 'ethical' or 'educative' activity" (ibid., 103). Credit for observing that Aristotle's concept of *mousikē* includes poetry and that he believes that it can affect the soul is due to Lord (ibid., 65–66, 86–89, 103, 109, 139–41).

a moral experience.[39] For example, he says that "all who listen to imitations apart from rhythms and tunes themselves come to experience similar passions" (*Pol* 1340a12–14). In fact, music can morally improve human beings not only by way of teaching or education (*paideia*) but also by way of purification or catharsis (*katharsis*) (1341b36–38). Just as certain sorts of tunes calm the soul by way of making it frenzied (1342a7–11), so certain forms of poetry—especially tragedy and comedy—may temper human beings by making them suffer the painful consequences of excessive passion.[40] Human beings become more thoughtful less by analyzing than by vicariously experiencing moral dilemmas.

In conjunction with characterizing music education as a fundamentally moral education, Aristotle indicates that music education should also assume the form of theater (*Pol* 1342a16–18). These two points suggest that music education is suitable for any free adult populace. This is not to say that all citizens everywhere would profit morally from attending tragedic or comedic public spectacles; their individual natures, private upbringings, and even the nature of the laws would bear on the educative effect of theater. Nonetheless, public musical spectacles achieve a politically salutary effect even when "vulgar persons and laborers" listen to them, insofar as they keep them occupied and entertained when they are not working (1342a15–22).[41]

In sum, Aristotle brings us to the conclusion that "music" is the best way to promote civic virtue in citizens. The right kind of music can render souls, particularly but not only youthful ones, temperate, spirited, goodwilling, and noble (of good judgment and trustworthy) (*Pol* 1339b24–25, 1340b10–13, 30–31). Citizens habituated by music throughout life and also by the laws when adults (*NE* 1180a1–3) develop virtue that stands as a mean relative to the regime.

---

[39] Ibid., 65–66.

[40] Ibid., 173–77 (Lord makes several references to Aristotle's *Poetics*); see also 34–35. Lord's explanation makes clear that the *katharsis* poetry effects is not simply the release of emotions in a harmless manner, which would only moderate rather than purify or eliminate the passions (see especially 176 n. 54). Thus, one can see why Aristotle thinks that poetry is superior to religion as a means to bring about civic virtue.

[41] On the theater, see ibid., 202 n. 27. For the claim that Aristotle thinks that music is the best pastime for mature citizens, see 34, 73, 83–84, 93–96, 102, 112, 147, 152.

Leisure: Education in Reason?

The previous chapter discussed the ways that laws should superintend the bodies and conduct of adults. But habituation alone, even if effected from the beginning until the end of a life, cannot make a human being good. A complete education, one that enables a human being not only to be a good citizen but to rule both self and others—one that completes a human being—must include leisure (*scholē*).

That Aristotle does not define *scholē* may be due, as J. L. Stocks suggests, to the term's having been in popular use at the time of his writing. Aristotle did not need to explain to his audience that by *scholē* he meant spare time, without pressing duties, spent in voluntarily undertaken schooling or study.[42] Nor did he need to point out the three main elements of leisure: freedom from labor, autonomy, and education. According to Friedrich Solmsen, Aristotle did not even need to persuade his audience of the value or necessity of leisure, for the Peloponnesian War had some twenty-five years before the founding of Plato's Academy generated in a portion of Athenians "a longing for the quiet of leisure." Plato and Aristotle discovered not the value of leisure but the best content for it.[43] They took it on themselves, perhaps in response to what they perceived as a need, to articulate the essence and communicate the spirit of leisure, to rank and explain its nature and constitutive elements—which they took to be (1) economic security (freedom from the necessity to labor), (2) psychological freedom (freedom from worries and cares), (3) a condition of quietude or peace[44] and thus freedom from even political activity, (4) self-direction, or "time for oneself,"[45] and (5) education. Declaring that education should be the essence of leisure, Plato and Aristotle sought to explain what sort of education leisure should entail and why.

In the following discussion, I show or suggest the emphasis Aristotle places on each element of leisure. I note where he may

[42] J. L. Stocks, "Scholē," *Classical Quarterly* 30 (1936), 181.

[43] "Leisure and Play in Aristotle's Ideal State," *Rheinisches Museum für Philologie* 107 (1964), especially 201, 204, 206. On who the Athenian quietists were and how they manifested quietism (*apragmosunē*), see L. B. Carter, *The Quiet Athenian* (Oxford: Clarendon Press, 1986).

[44] As its etymological root ("to halt or cease") implies; see Sebastian de Grazia, *Of Time, Work, and Leisure* (New York: Twentieth Century Fund, 1962), 12.

[45] Stocks, "Scholē," 181; Grazia, *Of Time, Work, and Leisure*, 12.

have derived his thoughts from Plato's account, but I do not seek to distinguish their contributions systematically.[46]

What Leisure Is Not

To understand Aristotle's conception of leisure, one should first note that he contrasts leisure to occupation (*ascholia*): *scholē* and *ascholia* are as different as peace and war (*Pol* 1333a30–32, *NE* 1177b4–6). *Ascholia* means approximately "busyness," not "labor," for which there is the more specific *ponos*. Because labor keeps one busy, *ascholia* technically includes labor, but it generally means any necessary activity one would rather not do.[47] In the *Nicomachean Ethics* Aristotle allows that political actions can be noble and great but calls them unleisurely (*ascholoi*) (1177b6–18). Politics in his view appears to be a combination of the necessary and the noble and no part of leisure.

Because leisure is not for the sake of the necessary (*Pol* 1333a30–36), one cannot be busy meeting one's needs and be at leisure. One must have wealth enough to have not only free time, but the amount of time that holding political office demands; "a moderate amount of property" is insufficient (*Pol* 1273a24–25, 1291b25–26, 1292b25–29).[48] But Aristotle indicates that one does not need great wealth to have the time to rule when he proposes that government support the respectable who are poor when they are ruling (1273a32–b7). Indeed, if leisure is not busyness, then it must require not having wealth in an amount that demands constant upkeep, guarding, or managing. Being at leisure requires having that amount of wealth that fosters indifference toward it.[49]

In opposing leisure to occupation, Aristotle at once excludes play (*paidia*) and relaxation or rest (*anapausis*) from his conception of leisure. Human beings play or amuse themselves in order to relax

[46] Solmsen proposes that Aristotle's contribution is to advocate incorporating *scholē* into the city as an education for all citizens, against Plato's intention to confine *scholē* to the philosopher's school ("Leisure and Play," especially 206–7).

[47] See Grazia, *Of Time, Work, and Leisure*, 14–15.

[48] For discussion on the point that it is hardly fair to attribute to class prejudice Aristotle's contention that wealth is a requirement of leisure, see Solmsen, "Leisure and Play," 218.

[49] Thus, Grazia captures not the letter but the spirit of the philosophers' ideal of leisure when he explains that "commodities are irrelevant. A walk outdoors will do. As the *Republic* opens, Socrates goes to the house of a rich old man named Cephalus. It took no show of commodities to get him to make the visit. To lure Socrates all you needed was the promise of conversation. How Cephalus's house looked or was furnished had little importance" (*Of Time, Work, and Leisure*, 348).

or rest, but they need to relax or rest only after they have been busy or exerted themselves (*Pol* 1337b38–39). Play or recreation is not, in other words, for its own sake, but for the sake of relieving one from occupation. It is necessary because one cannot work constantly (*NE* 1176b34–35). Play should thus be regarded as simply a remedy to occupation (*Pol* 1337b41–42)—its complement (not its opposite) and never an end in itself. "Indeed, it would be absurd if the end [of life] were amusement, and one were to exert oneself and suffer throughout life in order to amuse oneself" (*NE* 1176b28–30).

Similarly, leisure is not spare time to do as one pleases or to be idle or licentious. Aristotle makes this point at least four times in the *Politics*. In Book I he remarks that nomadic shepherds "derive sustenance from domesticated animals without toil [*ponos*]" "and so have leisure [*scholazousin*]," yet he calls their way of life "the idlest [*argotatoi*]" (1256a31–32). He is not praising them for having found a way to live that frees them from labor but criticizing them for failing to live in a truly leisurely fashion. In Book II he remarks that, although the serfs in Thessaly and the Spartan helots apparently had time to prepare an attack on their masters, they cannot be said to have had leisure for they lived constantly awaiting the opportunity for ambush (1269a38–39). Thus, time spent merely waiting is not leisure. In the same chapter, Aristotle relates the unfortunate situation that arose in Sparta. The Spartan men, having become self-controlled and accustomed to observing rules as a consequence of their military training and actual combat, were evidently well-prepared to receive further instruction in virtue during peacetime (1270a1–6, 1334a24–25, 1269b19–21).[50] In contrast, the Spartan women, having no experience of military life, lived "licentiously in every respect and in luxury," refusing to abide by the laws, both when the men were away at war and after they returned, during peace (1269b22–23, 1270a1–2, 6–9). Aristotle makes clear that he is not raising this example to denounce women in general or even the Spartan women. The issue is not the propensity of one sex or the other for licentiousness. Nor is his aim to blame any particular party for the situation that arose (1270a9–11), though by explaining what led to the women's way of life he is in effect excusing *them*. Rather, he is saying, first, that human beings

---

[50] Yet Aristotle later denounces the Spartan men for "not knowing how to be at leisure" (*Pol* 1271b2–6). He thereby indicates here, in Book II, that military experience is not the right sort of preparation for leisure and thus makes us anticipate his discussion of laws and music as proper modes of habituation.

must learn how to use free time. The Spartan regime should have educated its women about spending time in the way that becomes human beings. Second, this example indicates that people should know how to be at leisure during both war and peace. Aristotle implies that, had the women known how to be at leisure when Sparta was at war, they would have been able to rule themselves; had they known how to be at leisure during peace, they would have known how to be ruled. Leisure, it appears, teaches how to rule and be ruled; it appears to promote political virtue. Finally, Aristotle distinguishes leisure from spare time to do as one pleases in Book VIII, where he observes that "being at leisure . . . seems to bring in itself pleasure, happiness, and living blessedly" (1338a1–3), for "the happy life seems to be a life expressing virtue, which is a life involving serious actions, and not consisting in amusement" (*NE* 1177a1–3). If being at leisure brings happiness, then it cannot also mean simply living as one likes. In summary, as Sebastian de Grazia notes, "[although] in some cases it seems that leisure is another word for spare or free time, . . . one senses a different element, an ethical note, a hint that spare time when misused is not leisure."[51]

But what exactly is this ethical element? By opposing leisure to occupation, Aristotle may be suggesting that leisure's ethical component is the opposite of occupation's ethical component. Leisure's ethical component, whatever else it may or may not be, is not necessary tasks accomplished or products produced. In light of Aristotle's claims that "life is action not production" and "man is by nature a political animal" (*Pol* 1254a7, 1253a2–3), one might speculate that leisure is ethical because it is purely social or exemplary of species life. Perhaps Aristotle is implying what Marx stated explicitly—that the life "*opposed* to [man's] material life" is "the *species life* [*Gattungsleben*]," which is man's perfected political condition. According to Marx, to be human and free requires being conscious that one is a member of a species and living in accordance with that consciousness. Perhaps Aristotle is suggesting that leisure instills this consciousness and way of life.[52]

51 *Of Time, Work, and Leisure*, 13.
52 Karl Marx, "On the Jewish Question," in *The Marx-Engels Reader*, ed. Robert C. Tucker (New York: W. W. Norton, 1972), 31–32. In his brief discussion of Marx's concept of leisure, Grazia notes that "Marx seems to have been groping for a fresh expression of the classical concept" (*Of Time, Work, and Leisure*, 350–51).

On this account, leisure's value lies in its capacity to render individuals fit for community life. Not necessary to individual survival, it appears nonetheless necessary to collective survival. But Aristotle places leisure among the noble, not the necessary or useful (*Pol* 1333a30–b3); leisure is not for the sake of something else, even the body politic. What is more, the happiness human beings find in leisure varies according to their individual natures and characters (*Pol* 1338a1–8). By contrast, leisure understood as the fulfillment of oneself through species life presupposes that happiness is the same for all.

What Leisure Is

According to Aristotle, one cannot live pleasurably, happily, and blessedly or be at leisure without complete virtue (*Pol* 1338a1–3, *NE* 1100a4–5), which requires habituation and education—since habituation engenders the virtues of character (*ethikēs*), and teaching, the virtues of thought (*dianoētikēs*) (*NE* 1103a14–17, 31) (though nature contributes the potentiality to both sorts of virtue; *NE* 1103a23–25, 1179b21–23; *Pol* 1331b24, 29–41).

By saying that music is the best pastime in leisure, Aristotle implies that there are other such pastimes (*diagōgai*). "Subjects of education," "sorts of learning . . . for their own sake," should be studied in leisure (*Pol* 1338a9–12). Carnes Lord points out a forward reference (*Pol* 1338a30–37) and Book VII's introduction to education as evidence that the missing chapters of Book VIII discussed the liberal arts other than music.[53] Aristotle also associates leisure with the development of sciences unrelated to utility, of which he gives the mathematical sciences as an example (*Met* 981b21–26). Taken together, this evidence all but confirms that Aristotle means by "leisure" the liberal arts, or "culture."[54]

That he intends philosophy or contemplation to be counted among the liberal arts is clear, since he says that leisure provides the full range of happiness (*Pol* 1338a1–9).[55] But perhaps it would

[53] *Education and Culture*, 150.

[54] See also Leo Strauss, *The City and Man* (Chicago: University of Chicago Press, 1964), 31; Lord, *Education and Culture*, especially 19, 23–24, 29, 180, 198–202.

[55] Lord maintains that Aristotle uses "philosophy" both in the precise sense, meaning "theoretical speculation," and "in a looser sense of what would today be called 'culture'"; this implies that Aristotle sometimes uses "philosophy" to mean leisure and thus sometimes subsumes theoretical speculation under philosophy (*Education and Culture*, 199–200, 202). This interpretation solves more difficulties

be more precise to say that the liberal arts should prepare those who are capable for contemplation, in particular by instilling in them a love for learning or thoughtful activity for its own sake; for Aristotle does not expect that even all the best persons have the capacity for contemplation (*Pol* 1331b39–41, 1333a25–30).[56]

What good men can develop is good judgment and eventually prudence (*Pol* 1277b25–29; *NE* 1142a14–16, 1143a29–31). Since each man judges well what he knows, Aristotle reasons, the best way for him to become "a good judge in general" is for him to receive "an all-round education" (*NE* 1094b28–1095a2). Such an education is both possible and proper for those human beings with an adequate nature and habituation (*Pol* 1332a38–40, 1291b25–30). Each would benefit from leisure in accordance with his own disposition (*Pol* 1338a7–9).[57] If citizens follow a course of liberal education enforced by law when young, and as a result of that education voluntarily avail themselves of culture when adults, then a city becomes unified in the way and to the extent that Aristotle thinks a city should (*Pol* 1337a21–27, 1263b31–37).

LEISURE: PRIVATE AND PUBLIC GOOD

Benefiting the individual through education, leisure appears to be a private good. Indeed, as Solmsen maintains, Aristotle leaves the impression that leisure should promote primarily not civic-mindedness or the virtues of citizenship but private happiness.[58] By encouraging citizens to become good judges in general, leisure encourages them to reflect not only on the best way of life relative to their regime but on the best way of life simply. A complete liberal education asks students to become not good citizens but good human beings.

---

than it creates, but one should not lose sight of the fact that Aristotle sometimes means by "philosophy" contemplation or theoretical speculation of the highest sort; for example, reading "philosophy" as "culture" does not, as Lord argues, make sense of Aristotle's claim that "philosophy [is required] with a view to leisure [*philosophias de pros tēn scholēn*]" (*Pol* 1334a23) if leisure is itself defined as culture. I explain the respect in which contemplation is required with a view to leisure at the end of this chapter.

56 See also Solmsen, "Leisure and Play," 218; Lord, *Education and Culture*, 64, 199.

57 See also Grazia, *Of Time, Work, and Leisure*, 348–49.

58 According to Solmsen, Aristotle thus reveals sympathy for Hellenistic over classical tendencies ("Leisure and Play," 219–20).

But by becoming through leisure good human beings, individuals in fact become exemplary citizens in that they develop, insofar as they have deliberated about what is good for human beings, prudence (*NE* 1141a23–28, b8–9), the virtue enabling one to rule (*Pol* 1277a14–16, 29–31).[59] By providing leisure, then, a regime furnishes itself with potential rulers, increasing its chances for just rule. Evidently, "there is a need for leisure both with a view to the creation of virtue and with a view to political activities" (*Pol* 1329a1–2).[60] Aristotle seems to agree with the Athenian Stranger that a true education is one "that makes one desire and love to become a perfect citizen who knows how to rule and be ruled with justice," and that all other sorts—such as education "that aims at money, or some sort of strength, or some other sort of wisdom without intelligence and justice"—are "vulgar, illiberal, and wholly unworthy to be called education."[61] In sum, because leisure serves the public through the private, Aristotle suggests that all regimes incorporate it (*Pol* 1273a32–35, 1333a30–b3).[62]

Since leisure aims to cultivate both political and complete virtue, it aims to develop in particular the capacities that most characterize those forms of virtue. It has become evident that prudence (*phronēsis*) is the leading capacity of political virtue, since it most enables one to rule; and Aristotle says in Book VI of the *Nicomachean Ethics* that wisdom (*sophia*) leads among the intellectual virtues (1141a16–17) and thus completes virtue. A brief discussion of prudence and wisdom should, then, illuminate the objectives of leisure.

Prudence and wisdom differ radically in that "the content of wisdom is always the same, but the content of prudence is not"

[59] See also Lord, *Education and Culture*, 177–79.

[60] This statement works against P. A. Vander Waerdt's thesis that citizens in the best regime would not rule (see Chapter 5, "Political Laws: Offices and Entitlement," pp. 124–26).

[61] Plato, *Laws*, 643e, 644a.

[62] Grazia points out that the classical ideal of leisure "has been deformed almost everywhere" because leisure and democracy are not compatible: "The point at which the deformation is most obvious is in the idea that leisure is owed everyone and everyone can benefit from it in equal measure. The educators try to say that leisure and democracy were destined for each other. To the Greeks, who were more liberal than we in the matter of bedfellows, these two would still be strange partners" (*Of Time, Work, and Leisure*, 348–50). Aristotle advocates introducing leisure into inferior regimes, not because he thinks that everyone has a right to it and can benefit from it equally, but because he thinks that everyone has a duty to better themselves and that it is in the interest of government to provide the means for them to do so, since a liberally educated citizenry is perhaps the best means by which inferior regimes can be incrementally transformed into better ones—polities or aristocracies.

(*NE* 1141a24–25, *Met* 1074b26–27). The content of wisdom never changes, because it comprehends what is highest by nature (*NE* 1141a22–23, 34–b3). The content of prudence changes because it addresses human concerns. Prudence is the faculty with which human beings deliberate about what is good for themselves (*NE* 1141a23–28, b8–9). It is also the faculty that effects what is good for human beings (1141b12–14, 1140b1–4) and therefore lends itself to both political science and politics (1141b24–1142a10). Prudence is closer to the virtues of character than it is to wisdom, is more like a moral than an intellectual virtue, for three reasons. First, the prudent, in order to put into practice what is good for human beings, must engage the moral virtues (*NE* 1178a16–19). Second, the work of prudence requires human beings as objects or recipients of action and human things such as money, power, and freedom (1177a30–32, 1178a24–b3). To perform its work it needs, so to speak, to be complemented both internally and externally. Third, prudence is like a moral virtue in that it serves wisdom (*NE* 1145a6–11); it does not have command over the intellect.

In contrast, because the faculty of wisdom (*nous*) aims to grasp the truth about the first principles, to understand what accounts for scientific knowledge (*NE* 1141a3–8, 17–20, b2–3), its activity is self-sufficient; the wise person is the most self-sufficient of human beings, being able to contemplate (*theōrein*) alone (*NE* 1177a32–b1). For such a person external goods "are even hindrances" (1178b3–5, 1179a1–5).[63] Nonetheless, the experience of constancy is a happy one: "We think happiness has pleasure mixed into it; and the activity in accordance with wisdom is admittedly the pleasantest of the activities in accordance with virtue; at any rate, philosophy seems to have pleasures marvellous for their purity and enduringness, and it is to be expected that those who know will pass their time more pleasantly than those who search" (1177a22–27).

The best human life, then, paradoxically requires turning away from merely mortal thoughts and striving as much as possible to live in accordance with the most excellent, powerful, and valuable thing in a human being; one should try to become, in a word, immortal (*athanatizein*) (*NE* 1177b31–1178a2). Exercising one's di-

---

[63] Aristotle acknowledges that the person who contemplates of course needs the sorts of external goods necessary for living as a human being, interacting virtuously with others (*NE* 1178a24–25, b5–7). For further discussion of contemplation, see Chapter 8, especially "Intellectual Virtue and Contemplation," pp. 193–98.

vine element to approach immortality requires not acting or speaking much at all. Speeches and deeds cannot confer immortality because they must, like all particulars, pass away.

Why, then, from the city's point of view, should leisure encourage contemplation? It has been argued that according to Aristotle becoming a good or prudent human being requires simply considering through leisure the virtues of the supreme way of life, not necessarily leading that way of life. By evaluating the contemplative life (perhaps Socrates'), citizens would come to realize that those who engage in "those speculations [theōrias] and thoughts [dianoēseis] that are for their own sake" are also acting well and moreover in the most self-sufficient way available to human beings (Pol 1325b12–21, 29–30, 1325a32). On this reading, a liberal education should work to preempt the forming of or eradicate the common prejudice that philosophers are inactive parasites. Citizens examining the contemplative life would also conclude that a regime must allow citizens to choose that way of life if the regime's intent is, as Aristotle says it should be, to allow and facilitate the happiness of which each is capable. In sum, by appreciating the complete coincidence between virtue and freedom and thus that philosophers set the standard for choice, citizens would become gentlemen.

Aristotle hints nonetheless that philosophy can make a direct, substantive contribution to the city when he states that "philosophy [is required] with a view to leisure" (Pol 1334a23). Apparently, philosophical insights are required to establish the best form of education, one that produces good rulers and good human beings. Perhaps the single most important insight needed for the task is that human beings are part divine, part not-divine (NE 1177b26–28, 1178a6–7; Pol 1333a16–18).[64] Only philosophers can know the full meaning of this universal truth because they are able to experience the divine (NE 1177b26–31, 1178a22); only this perspective illuminates the limitations and the potentialities of a bifurcated existence. By understanding the divine, a philosopher under-

[64] Nature repeats in humanity the "irreducible duality" that characterizes "the whole of nature" for the sake of the principle of the whole: if human beings did not make "due allowance" to "the grossly necessary" and "surrender to the incorruptible nature"—if they did not try to resist gross nature to the extent permitted by the incorruptible—political life would be incompatible with the whole of nature; Joseph Cropsey, "Political Life and a Natural Order," in Political Philosophy and the Issues of Politics (Chicago: University of Chicago Press, 1977), 227.

stands the whole of nature (*Met* 1074b3) and therewith the relation between human beings and the natural order. He sees the truths that characterize this relation, such as that "all partnerships aim at some good" (*Pol* 1252a4); "nature makes nothing in an economizing spirit" (1252b1–3); "everything is defined by its work and its capacity" (1253a23); things diverge toward either ruling or being ruled (1254a21–36); nature intends but does not achieve a correspondence between the quality of bodies and that of souls (1254b27–33); and nature makes mere life sweet (*Pol* 1278b25–30). A philosopher understands the reasons for these truths insofar as he sees the unity of the whole of nature.

In understanding the natural truths, a philosopher sees how human beings should be educated so that they may harmonize with the natural order. And, although he is not inclined to establish the requirements of education through legislation—that is, to partake in the legislative process—he may transmit his knowledge of the natural truths through private teaching and writing, as did Socrates, Plato, and Aristotle himself, thus influencing the ways of life of those who listen and comprehend, and thus influencing future legislation.

7

Private Friends
and Public Citizens

Like education, friendship improves the quality of life by requiring virtue (*NE* 1155a3–4). Also like education, friendship is a public and a private good; neither cities nor individuals can live well without it. Thus, contrary to the modern view, Aristotle believes that friendship is properly the concern of political science. He says not only that friendship should be a concern of legislators but, in further contrast to the modern perspective, that it is a necessity (1155a4–5). Not only can regimes and individual human beings not live well, they cannot survive, without friendship. That political orders require offices or a system of ruling in order to last implies, in fact, that they require friendship of a sort. In this chapter I explain the types of public and private friendship Aristotle deems essential to a regime and to an individual human life.

Friendship Defined

After observing that friendship is both a necessity and a good, Aristotle continues his introduction to the subject in the *Nicomachean Ethics* with several other observations, with a view to defining friendship (1155b13–18, 28–1156a5). First, friendships differ with respect to not simply the amount but also the kind of affection or love involved. We can tell what kind of affection a friendship involves, or what kind of friendship it is, by the object or end toward which it is directed. Also relevant to defining friendship is whether the affection is reciprocated. If it is not, then the relationship is not friendship (for we do not say there can be friendship with wine, with someone whom one does not know, or with someone who is not aware of one's affection).

Reciprocity as a criterion of friendship is, however, problematic in that among examples of kinds of friendship are the relationship between parents and offspring and that among citizens, or "concord" (NE 1155a16–26). It is not evident that infants or all children reciprocate affection or that all citizens know one another. Indeed, Aristotle says much later that we should set apart relationships between relatives and those between citizens from the other sorts of friendship (1161b12–15). Yet, that he uses these examples to introduce the subject of friendship and takes them up later seems to indicate that we should not set them apart from other sorts of friendship. Apparently, that they may be characterized by an absence of reciprocity does not sever them entirely from the category of friendship. Moreover, as human beings know from experience, and as Aristotle will say, reciprocity is sometimes a feature of both of these kinds of relationships (in good families and among good men who are citizens). The question arising then is, what more clearly both qualifies and disqualifies kinship and concord as friendship? Perhaps Aristotle believes that they each qualify as friendship because they are the relationships that perpetuate cities but do not qualify insofar as neither kind of relationship is chosen.[1]

According to Aristotle, only three kinds of friendship are reciprocal—friendships of utility, of pleasure, and of virtue (NE 1156a7–10). The first form when persons discover that they can supply each other with useful things; the second, when parties find pleasure in one another; and the third, when people love one another for the other's self or character. Yet human beings regard as useful what seems good or pleasant to them (1155b19–26). Thus, generally speaking, there are only two species of friendship. One yields pleasure and the other is good in itself.

On one hand, then, Aristotle's introduction to friendship appears to serve the purpose of simplifying a complex topic. It introduces five species of friendship—kinship, concord, utilitarian

---

[1] Among relationships of kin, only the marital relationship results from choice; but even it arises out of natural desires (see Chapter 1, "Affection," pp.25–27).

friendship, pleasure-based friendship, and true friendship—but gives the impression that there are only two categories of friendship. On the other hand, relative to what follows, the introduction seems misleading and incomplete. Aristotle teaches later that kinship and concord are not negligible forms of relationship and that there is a sixth sort of friendship—namely, friendship with oneself. Perhaps one should regard Aristotle's introduction as neither a simplification nor an oversimplification of what is to come but as a statement to the effect that, of all the sorts of friendship, the two that are most properly speaking friendships are those that are both chosen and private.

KINSHIP

Although friendships founded on pleasure and virtue appear to rank at the top of Aristotle's hierarchy, friendship with relatives or kinship is first, in time, for human beings. Our first friends are our parents and siblings. Aristotle observes this, in effect, at the beginning of the *Politics,* by describing the household as being prior to the city in time.

Our first friendships, then, are characterized by inequality. Each household member has a different virtue (*aretē*) and a different function (*ergon*) and, consequently, "each does not get the same thing from the other" (*NE* 1158b17–20). Indeed, it is clear that the benefits a child receives from its parents far exceed those the parents receive from the child. Most notably, the child receives its very being from the parents—or, more specifically, from the father. But the child also receives nurture and education (*NE* 1161a16–17). In contrast, the child can reciprocate at first merely by being the likeness that its parents sought to bring into being (in order to leave behind) (*Pol* 1252a28–30). Somewhat later, children can reciprocate by honoring, obeying, or loving their parents (*NE* 1161b24–26). But it seems that offspring cannot reciprocate in any other way until they are adults, for only then can they provide their parents with means of support and present what they have made of themselves to them (that one's offspring is prospering seems to be for some mothers a sufficient return) (*NE* 1165a21–23, 1159a28–33). By showing affection in these ways to their parents, offspring in a sense equalize the vast inequality between themselves and their parents (1159b1–2) and thereby render their friendship with them lasting and decent (*epieikēs*) (1158b21–28).

Even apart from the latent effort to reciprocate on the part of the offspring, there is a sense in which household relationships are theoretically just, for the claims of justice are proportionate to desert (*NE* 1161a21–22). Aristotle implies that the balance of claims rather than the balance of actual benefits constitutes the essence of the household's justice (for offspring could never do enough to repay the debt of their existence; 1163b15–21).

In describing family relationships in terms of the worth, merit, or virtue of the parties, Aristotle indicates that they have, not rights against each other, but duties or responsibilities toward one another (*NE* 1159b35–1160a3, 1161a16–17). Parents have a duty to nourish and educate their children; children, to honor parents; brothers, to speak freely and share possessions with one another (1165a24–30). These duties are fulfilled naturally: "Parents love their children as part of themselves"; "children love their parents as the source of their beings"; and brothers love one another because they are born of the same parents, have the same upbringing, are similar in age and are (thus) equals (1161b18, 1161a3–5, 1161b30–1162a1, 9–14). Moreover, the natural feelings of the parents match, or enable them to fulfill, their greater duties (1161b19–26, 1168a24–27, 1167b34–1168a9). Parents love their children more and more quickly than children do their parents, since they know with more certainty that their children are theirs than do the children know their parentage (hence also the reason mothers love their children more than fathers). Further, since children are a natural bond between parents, it is in the interest of their union to care for them (1162a19–25). In sum, perhaps Aristotle is saying that "there are, strictly speaking, no natural rights—only rights we confer upon each other out of natural inclination and commitment."[2]

Aristotle acknowledges nonetheless that differences among family may arise when expectations are not met (*NE* 1163a24–26). Fathers may disown sons and brothers may hate each other (*NE* 1163b18–19, *Pol* 1328a15). Indeed, since the claims among intimates

---

[2] Nel Noddings, *Caring: A Feminine Approach to Ethics and Moral Education* (Berkeley: University of California Press, 1984), 120.

are great, there is a chance that some will feel slighted (*Pol* 1328a1–4). It appears, however, that family members should strive to do what they can to acknowledge or return benefits received (*NE* 1163b15–18). That one's duties may be imposed by nature, rather than freely chosen, does not then seem in Aristotle's eyes to warrant failing to fulfill them. In other words, the household demands upholding virtue.

Friendships of Utility

In comparison to his generally sanguine and inspiring portrait of kinship, Aristotle's description of ordinary friendship is cynical, or at least true to life. At the same time, he indicates that even common friendship has standards that the parties should try to meet.

Most people befriend others because they perceive a benefit to be obtained by doing so (*NE* 1156a10–12). Such friendship derives, then, from a felt or perceived need or lack (1159b12–14). Since people's needs and wants change, and their ability to fulfill the needs and wants of others changes, these friendships are characteristically always coming in and out of being (1156a20–24, 1158b4, 1159b10–11). But there is nothing absurd (*ouden atopon*) about this; it is in fact reasonable (*eulogon*) that affection should cease when the attributes that we loved exist no longer (1165b1–4). Yet, that Aristotle takes pains to point out that it is not strange for such friendships to die suggests that parties to these friendships are often disappointed or shocked when they do. Aristotle's remark reveals, in other words, that the many do not want their friends to change, for even the betterment of a friend may threaten his or her usefulness to another.

The durability of utilitarian friendships is apparently a function, not only of the presence of desired attributes in the friends, but also of whether the respective ends sought are the same and whether the ends derive from the same source (*NE* 1157a3–6). A friendship in which the ends sought are not the same is especially fragile; if only one of the two different needs from which the friendship arose ceases to exist, then so does the friendship. For example, a person without a car seeks transportation to work, a fellow employee with a car seeks someone to talk to on the way; if the first gets his own car, then for him the utility of the friendship disappears. If, however, they both seek conversation for the drive, then they continue to ride together even if they both have cars. But if one wants to talk only about sports and the other only about politics, then their ride sharing does not last long. By contrast, if two people both seek entertainment on Saturday evenings (the same end), and both want to play cards (they find entertainment in the same source), then the friendship has prospects for continuing. In this respect friendships of utility do not differ from other sorts of friendship: the more the parties are alike, the longer the friendship lasts (1158b1–3).

Those who are friends for the sake of utility tend not only to terminate eventually (in spite of their wishes) their association (*NE* 1157a14–15) but also to distrust one another (1157a20–24); to prefer not to live together (1156a27–28); and to accuse and reproach each other (1162b5–6). But this, again, is reasonable or to be expected (*eulogos*), "for these friends deal with each other in the expectation of gaining benefits. Hence they always require more, thinking they have got less than is fitting" (1162b16–18). Furthermore, base or inferior people (*phauloi*) tend to form friendships of utility or pleasure, since they are not able to like one another for their characters (1157b1–3). On the one hand, these observations characterize friendships of utility in a negative way and seem even to contradict Aristotle's opening assertion that "friendship is a virtue or involves virtue" (1155a3–4). Aristotle admits in fact that those who associate for the sake of utility are friends only by analogy or similarity, "for it is in virtue of something good and something akin to what is found in true friendship that they are friends"—that is, since pleasure, utility, and equality also characterize true friendship (1157a30–32, b4–5, 34–1158a1, 33–34). On the other hand, Aristotle says that those who tend to form friendships of utility are the old, the young, those in their prime, the rich, the poor, those in positions of authority, the clever, those who desire honor, the ignorant, the learned, the beautiful, the ugly, young lovers, those in mourning, those who do business, gift givers, and cities (1155a6–16, 1158a27–33, 1159a18–21, b11–16, 1162b25–34, 1171a29–30). Thus, friendships of utility are necessary to living. Aristotle tempers his more negative comments about friendships of utility also by suggesting that, even in these associations, standards of conduct should obtain: "If we can we should return the equivalent of what we have received . . . or even more" (1163a1–2, 16–20, b15–

18). This would be just; for then people would be compensated for what they lack (1163b1–5).

FRIENDSHIPS OF PLEASURE

Friendships of utility may yield pleasure and have other things in common with friendships of pleasure, but they are not the same species of friendship as the latter (*NE* 1157a33–35). Friendships of pleasure are similar to those of utility in that they too tend to dissolve if what yields pleasure ("the bloom of youth," for example) passes away. Pleasure-based friendships are, however, much closer to true friendship because "both parties get the same things from each other and delight in each other or in the same things" (1158a18–20). Such friends give each other willingly and generously the pleasure they both find satisfying, and they rarely accuse or complain, "for both of them get what they want at the same time if they enjoy spending their time together; and someone who accused his friend of not pleasing him would appear ridiculous, when he is free to spend his days without the friend's company" (1162b13–16). Moreover, everyone, even people who have everything, needs pleasant friends or pleasure; people "wish to live with someone" (1158a23, 1155a5, 1171b27–28). Evidently, this category of friendship includes romantic love and erotic passion (1156b1–3, 1157a12–14, 1158a11–12).

Friendships of pleasure not only are very close to true friendship, they also may become true friendships. Romantic or erotic liaisons are apparently more likely to become so, for "many [lovers] remain friends if they have similar characters and come to be fond of each other's characters from being accustomed to them" (*NE* 1157a10–12). Similarly, the natural inclination of men and women to form couples—which generally yields useful and pleasurable partnerships (since each sex has its proper virtue)—may also eventuate in friendships based on virtue (*aretē*) if the parties are decent (*epieikeis*) (1162a16–17, 24–27).[3] Aristotle seems to discourage any dis-

---

[3] It is therefore misleading to say, as does Jean-Claude Fraisse, that "Aristotle dispels all assimilation between friendship and a passion, in the modern sense of the word. If *philia* is not a *pathos*, to the extent to which it is not passive, it is still less a fit of passion, or, like Platonic *eros*, a form of *mania*, of delirium"; see *Philia: La Notion d'amitié dans la philosophie antique* (Paris: Librairie Philosophique J. Vrin, 1974),

tinction between a person's qualities and character, both of which may give one pleasure, when he points out in Book I of the *Politics* the apparent mixing by nature of the various kinds of souls with various kinds of bodies (1257b27–39). It is futile to try to establish what falls under the category of qualities and what under that of character because it is "not easy to see the beauty of the soul" (1254b38–39). Only when nature fulfills its intention of uniting beautiful bodies and beautiful souls (1254b27–28) is beauty of body an indicator of beauty of soul; but in that case, as Harvey C. Mansfield, Jr., implies, it remains difficult, or is especially difficult, to separate bodily from soulful qualities because the former distract one from the latter.[4] In any case, loving or taking pleasure in the qualities along with the character of a person does not diminish that love precisely because a person's qualities are a part of him or her. Accordingly, in seeking partners people should "seek friends who are good as well [as pleasant], and good for them too; for then they will have everything that friends must have" (*NE* 1158a26–27).

Aristotle's portrait of friendships founded in pleasure stands in some contrast to his description of utilitarian friendship. Still, neither of these sorts of friendship is in itself good or bad: "It is possible for bad people as well [as good] to be friends to each other for pleasure or utility, for decent people to be friends to base people, and for someone with neither character to be a friend to someone with any character" (*NE* 1157a16–18). Aristotle is not denouncing either friendships of utility or those of pleasure but saying perhaps that one should enter into these friendships at the right time, with the right people, and in the right way (*NE* 1106b19–24, 1104b25–26). If so engaged in, private relations afford opportunities for gain, pleasure, and virtue.

---

198. Indeed, as Klaus Oehler explains, "pleasure plays such an important role in Aristotle's analysis of life, because in his eyes pleasure indicates the very existence of life and makes contact with an ultimate reality and hence, in describing the highest form of existence as a living thing, he comes to the conclusion that its activity is pure, uninterrupted pleasure." Moreover, "all beings strive for pleasure following a divine element in their nature. In doing so they are striving for a higher degree of self-awareness and self-knowledge, because pleasure is experience of life itself"; see "Aristotle on Self-Knowledge," *Proceedings of the American Philosophical Society* 118, no. 6 (1974), 505.

4 *Taming the Prince: The Ambivalence of Modern Executive Power* (New York: Free Press, 1989), 308–9 n. 31. And Mansfield, pointing out that the Greek work *kalos* can mean "noble" or "beautiful," suggests that in Aristotle's view "beauty of soul is not separable from beauty of body" (66, 308 n. 31).

SELF-LOVE: PUBLIC AND PRIVATE FRIENDSHIP

It is perhaps the most private relationship of all that affords the greatest opportunity for virtue, and therewith pleasure. The person who truly loves himself "gratifies the most authoritative part of himself [*heautou tǭ kuriōtatǭ*], obeying it in everything" (*NE* 1168b30). A human being is, Aristotle explains, like a city or any composite whole insofar as that person seems to be, above all, the part that is able to direct or guide (1168b30–35); hence he who follows this part becomes or realizes himself. In short, the finest thing one can do for oneself is to live according to reason (*kata logon* or *meta logou*) (1169a5, 1).

Most people, however, harbor two misconceptions about self-love. On the one hand, they think that true self-love means being satisfied with or approving of oneself. To love oneself is, in this view, to believe that one is decent (*NE* 1166b3–4). It means not being hard on oneself or believing that 'I'm okay.'[5] But, Aristotle objects, if this were true self-love, then almost everyone could be said to have achieved it, for the many, "base though they are," also appear to approve of themselves (1166b2–3). On the other hand, people distinguish self-approval from self-love and equate the latter with selfishness. They reproach those who award themselves "the biggest share in money, honors, and bodily pleasures" (1168b15–17) and think that those people are displaying self-love. At the same time, the many think that being good to oneself means pursuing all opportunities for external goods; self-love is, in their view, self-gratification (thus, the many both reproach and indulge in selfishness). In Aristotle's view, the equation of self-love with selfishness has in particular corrupted the notion of self-love.

Aristotle agrees that greediness or common selfishness is reproachable but objects that it is not self-love properly understood (*Pol* 1263a41–b4). The selfish person aims to gratify only his desires and feelings, following the nonrational rather than the rational part

---

[5] Martha Craven Nussbaum captures this disposition, which is popular to cultivate today: "I am dissatisfied with my life. I feel that I am not reliably exercising excellences that are valuable to me. . . . I join a religious group or go in for some fashionable kind of therapy, with the result that I emerge feeling quite at peace and contented with my state, although my objective situation has not improved"; "Shame, Separateness, and Political Unity: Aristotle's Criticism of Plato," in *Essays on Aristotle's Ethics*, ed. Amélie Oksenberg Rorty (Berkeley: University of California Press, 1980), 398.

of his soul (*NE* 1168b19–23). A base man should not, therefore, be encouraged to love himself, "for he will harm both himself and his neighbors by following his base feelings" (*NE* 1169a14–15, 1130a5–7). He will harm others by taking from them or taking advantage of them; he will harm himself by being led now by this desire, now by that one.

The person who truly loves himself is not so conflicted. His composure results from knowing that a human being may secure the highest satisfactions or greatest rewards by doing what is reasonable and noble. Being one with himself (*homognōmonei heautǭ*), he in fact desires what is noble (*oregesthai tou kalou*) (*NE* 1166a13–14, 1102b26–29, 1169a5–6). This means, generally, acting in accordance with the interests of one's friends and country (1169a18–20). It may mean giving up wealth or power, dying for the sake of others, or, most paradoxically, letting others instead have the opportunity to act nobly (1169a25–36). Perhaps most striking, such a human being (*spoudaios*) "will choose intense pleasure for a short time over mild pleasure for a long time; a year of living nobly over many years of undistinguished life; and a single noble and great action over many small actions" (1169a22–25). For such a human being, the private is anchorage for a noble life, the resource that makes self-sacrifice and public service possible.

One might say, then, that self-love is the most ambitious and greatest form of moral friendship in that it serves the public and the private. In mediating between the two, it bestows the greatest moral goods on both the city and the self-lover (*NE* 1169a8–11).

TRUE FRIENDSHIP

In choosing the *Nicomachean Ethics* to address the subject of friendship, Aristotle indicates that friendship is, in Jean-Claude Fraisse's terms, "not cosmological, not metaphysical, not even directly political, but specifically ethical, and this springs . . . from the sense itself of the word *philia*"; *philia* is possible only between one human being and another.[6] Or, one might say, Aristotle reveals in his choice of the *Ethics* that friendship is a private activity:

6 *Philia*, 193, 195–96.

it is untouched by rulers and legislators insofar as it can arise only from individual initiative and discrimination. For this reason, Aristotle is especially concerned to persuade human beings to pursue the best forms of friendship. Those who are virtuous should aspire to achieve true friendship—the third form of chosen friendship he discusses in Books VIII and IX.

What is true friendship? If a good man loves himself by obeying the rational part of his soul, and if, as Aristotle says, a good man's friend is "another self" (*NE* 1166a31–32, 1170b6–7), then maybe a good man accrues friends by inducing others to listen to his reason. This follows, however, only if the others are nonrational, for only then does the relationship mirror that found within the soul of a good man, which is a sort of friendship. And then it is necessarily a lesser friendship, like that between master and slave (*Pol* 1255b13).

If a good man's friend is like the good man, then the friend too must be self-loving in the correct way, and being a friend to him must mean facilitating or not impeding the friend's being self-loving. Insofar as loving someone for being morally virtuous means loving that person for a stable, perhaps even permanent, quality (*hē d'aretē monimon*) characterized by right desire (*NE* 1156b12–13, 1139a22–23), it seems that a friend loves another for who the other *is* and does not want the other to change. Yet "life is action not production," from which one might infer that an active, changing friend would enhance life; moreover, it has been shown that *lesser* friendships depend on what friends produce for each other. Should human beings wish their friends to change or not, according to Aristotle? He answers, in effect, that one should wish a friend not to grow or develop in any way but to become more adept at taking into account moral considerations. Moral virtue is, after all, not only a state of character (*NE* 1106a11–12, 1157b6–7) but right action involving good deliberation. Acting well (*eu prattein*) depends on good deliberation (*euboulia*), which "is correctness of deliberation as regards what is advantageous, arriving at the right conclusion, in the right way, and at the right time" (*NE* 1142b27–28). The good man "judges everything correctly" and "sees what is true in each case" (*NE* 1113a29–30, 34). The good man loves another for the other's disposition to act well *and* ability to do so. Unconditional friendship is, then, an oxymoron. One may love a friend for who that friend is, but this includes the friend's capacity to enact his or her virtues and thus realize his or her potential.

Does true friendship prohibit failures in conduct? Must a friend, to remain a friend, always approve of one's conduct? According to Aristotle, true friendship may survive failures in conduct if they result from the agent's ignorance or if they are in fact only perceived failures. Virtuous agents usually do what virtue requires, but they may involuntarily act contrariwise, out of ignorance—doing neither the action they supposed, nor to the person, nor with the means, nor for the result they supposed (*NE* 1135a31–b2, 12–13). In contrast, "a voluntary act would seem to be an act of which the origin lies in the agent himself when he knows the particulars that the action consists in" (*NE* 1111a22–24). Only voluntary actions, then, are blameworthy (1135a20–21, b25). Thus, one may disapprove of a friend's inappropriate or unjust actions without ending the friendship because one sees that ignorance accounted for them—that the friend did not wish them at all (1113a17–18)—and that the conduct was thus an aberration.[7]

Friendship also entails appreciating that one may not know the reasons for or choices leading to a friend's conduct. Although one can judge another's character by the choices that person makes (*NE* 1112a1–2), to know what someone's choices are means knowing what deliberations went into them, for choice by definition involves deliberation (1112a15–16). If one does not know the reasoning and thought (*logou kai dianoias*) that went into someone's choices, then one can only hold opinions about those choices; "we opine what we do not quite know" (1112a8). Friendship requires openness to the possibility that one may not know the reasons, or all the reasons, for a friend's choices. Although among the virtuous a friend is like another self (*NE* 1170b6–7), moral virtue does not enable one to live a friend's life. Indeed, moral virtue entails recognizing that one cannot understand another's conduct just as the other does; thus, true friends give their friends the benefit of the doubt. Julia Annas's contention that Aristotle does not recognize

---

[7] Confidence in another's character, which allows for such aberration, also renders friendship immune to slander; "for it is not easy to trust anyone speaking against someone who has been tested by oneself for a long time; and among good people there is trust, the incapacity ever to do each other wrong, and all the other things expected in a true friendship" (*NE* 1157a21–24).

"the irrational element in friendship, which can lead us to like and love people of whom we strongly disapprove,"[8] thus seems misleading, for Aristotle's conception of friendship accommodates the two vulnerabilities to which conduct, to the extent that it issues from choice making, is (perhaps inevitably) subject. Certainly we should infer that friendship thrives when friends approve of both the conduct and character of one another, but at the same time Aristotle gives us hope that it can survive at least the ignorance of the choice maker and the ignorance of the friend judging the choice maker. Indeed, friendship can withstand these because it is, in part, conviction that another has the capacity to make good choices. Just as one wishes oneself good and fitting things, such as health, wealth, and prosperity, because one believes one will use them well, so one wishes (though not quite as much) a friend good and fitting things because one believes that the friend will use them well (*NE* 1157b31–32, 1159a5–12, 1166a19–22). Friendship then includes, but is more than, feeling: "Love [*philēsis*] seems to be a feeling, friendship [*philia*] a fixed disposition; for love can be felt even toward soul-less things, but mutual love involves choice [*proaireseōs*], and choice springs from a fixed disposition" (1157b28–31).[9] The choice to enter into and sustain a relationship represents conviction about another's character.

[8] "Plato and Aristotle on Friendship and Altruism," *Mind* 86, no. 344 (1977), 550.

[9] There is debate over Aristotle's concept of *proairesis* (choice). The prevailing interpretation maintains that he uses the term both in exclusive reference to means and in reference to means that always aim at an end. The debate concerns the apparently contradictory claims that virtuous men choose actions for their own sakes (*NE* 1105a28–33, 1144a18–20) and that choice results from deliberation *(bouleusis)*, which is always about how to achieve an end (*NE* III.2–3, VI.2); see Alfred R. Mele, "Choice and Virtue in the *Nicomachean Ethics*," *Journal of the History of Philosophy* 19, no. 4 (1981), 405–6. Arguing that choice is always toward *(pros)* ends, Mele notes Aristotle's claim that one can judge a man's character better by his choices than by his actions (*NE* 1111b5, 1110b31, 1117a5, 1163a22, 1164b1) and provides the following example: "Suppose that a just agent wants to do what is just in a situation in which he has, say, damaged a tool that he has borrowed. He deliberates, and judges that the just thing to do is to give the owner five dollars to cover the cost of repairing the tool (perhaps as opposed to buying the owner a new tool, or repairing it himself). Now, our just agent obviously does not give the owner five dollars simply for the sake of giving it to him: nor does he intend by giving him the money merely to bring about that the tool is repaired. Rather, his primary intention in giving him the money is plainly to *do what is just*. . . . Though our agent's giving the owner of the tool five dollars may not be a *means* (in the ordinary sense of the word) to his doing what is just, it is done with the *intention* of doing what is just, and, in this sense, is *pros* his doing what is just—that is, *pros* his *end*" (409). Although Mele's analysis is correct as far as it goes, it implies too narrow an

Despite the vulnerabilities of conduct, it is, as noted, a good indicator of character in Aristotle's estimation. In fact, it seems that *only* the phenomena of aberrations and apparent aberrations in conduct allow one to see the difference between conduct and character. Aristotle would say, accordingly, that pressing the distinction between conduct and character any further is analytically over-zealous.

It is difficult, if not impossible, not only to divide a person into constituent parts, but to distinguish loving another from loving oneself; "for the good man in becoming a friend becomes a good to his friend," so if one loves him, one is loving what is good for oneself (*NE* 1157b33–35, 1156b12–14). As W. D. Ross explains, Aristotle suggests "that the self is not a static thing but capable of indefinite extension. . . . a man may so extend his interests that the welfare of another may become as direct an object of interest to

understanding of what Aristotle means by an end. According to Aristotle, a human being's end is a life lived well. Attaining this end may require doing more than what is just (for example, doing what is noble). What is more, one may not be able to judge, given a particular set of circumstances and apparent responses to those circumstances, whether an agent acted virtuously. Such a judgment may not even be possible before the agent has finished living, for a virtuous response may mean waiting for the right set of circumstances in which to respond.

Let us take two examples. Suppose one scholar borrows a copy of the *Federalist Papers* from another and, just before he returns it, spills coffee on it. Since the copy was full of the owner's marginal notations and underscoring, buying the owner a new copy or giving him money will not compensate for the damage done. The borrower thus chooses to do nothing but apologize. But he does so in hope of compensating later, in some way, for the mishap. It is in continuing relationships that a human being can be judged virtuous or not.

Another example illustrating that a virtuous person's end must be understood broadly as a life lived well is that of a student who judges himself indebted to his mentor. The student knows that gifts or invitations are only tokens of appreciation, not repayment for his mentor's years of advice, criticism, and recommendation letters. Indeed, he sees that he may come closest to repaying his mentor by living a life that reflects serious consideration of what his mentor has imparted to him.

Although a life lived well undeniably includes the realization of other ends (doing what is just in particular instances), it may take the course of a person's lifetime to reveal the goodness of that life and thereby of all the particular choices (*NE* 1098a18–20). In sum, according to Aristotle one aims at what is unconditionally complete, for an end worthy in itself of pursuit is more choiceworthy than "ends that are choiceworthy both in themselves and for the sake of this end" (*NE* 1097a28–34). And the "absolutely final" end, which is always pursued only for itself and never as a means, is happiness, activity of the soul in accordance with virtue (1097b20–21, 1098a12–14). Hence "choice springs from a fixed disposition" (*NE* 1157b31).

him as his own welfare."[10] Yet, in loving him, one is helpful to him, gives him pleasure, and wishes him good things (1156b13–15, 1157b35–36). Indeed, friendship "seems to consist more in loving than in being loved" (1159a27–28, 33–35). Self-love that takes the form of loving another thereby compresses egoism and altruism. In Aristotle's view, only maternal love, and then apparently only in some cases, approaches selfless love (1159a28–33). One thus wonders if inequality permits selflessness. In any case, because the good are equal in virtue (1159b2–4), they are capable of fostering each other's virtue (and thereby, in effect, of returning virtue) (1159b2–7), and because they are virtuous they try to return more than they receive.

The moral standards inherent in true friendship are, however, tacitly self-imposed, for "if one idolizes or imposes excessive moral demands on one's friends, one may well be betrayed unintentionally by the overburdened person."[11] In fact, true friends do not demand even predictable behavior, but rather constancy of judgment (which may naturally generate an expectation of—but still not a demand for—predictability). In other words, to repeat, friendship depends on confidence in another's character. Having this confidence, one expects that the other will honor the friendship, and in this way only does a friend expect certain conduct (not to be lied to, humiliated, betrayed) from a friend. However,

> these kinds of friendships are likely to be rare, since such people are few. Moreover, they need time and familiarity; as the proverb says, men cannot know each other till they have 'eaten [a peck of] salt together'; nor can they accept each other or be friends until

[10] *Aristotle: A Complete Exposition of his Works and Thought* (New York: Meridian, 1959), 224–25. Similarly, though deeming Aristotle's view of friendship deficient in this regard, Gregory Vlastos states: "[Aristotle's] intuition takes him as far as seeing that (a) *disinterested affection for the person* we love—the active desire to promote that person's good 'for that person's sake, not for ours'—must be built into love at its best, but not as far as sorting this out from (b) *appreciation of the excellences instantiated by that person;* (b), of course, need not be disinterested and *could* be egoistic"; "The Individual as Object of Love in Plato," in *Platonic Studies* (Princeton: Princeton University Press, 1981), 33 n. 100. Thus, Vlastos and Julia Annas (acknowledging him), criticize Aristotle for not distinguishing between "loving a person for himself," "truly as an individual," and loving him "as a bearer of desired qualities"; see Annas, "Plato and Aristotle," 550.

[11] Judith N. Shklar, *Ordinary Vices* (Cambridge: Belknap, 1984), 142.

each appears worthy of friendship and has won the other's trust. Those who are quick to treat each other in friendly ways wish to be friends but are not friends, unless they are also worthy of friendship and know each other to be so; for though a wish for friendship may arise quickly, friendship does not. (*NE* 1156b24–32)

Alternative Conceptions of Political Friendship

Whereas true friendship is difficult to achieve, civic friendship is not. Aristotle believes that the standards for public interpersonal conduct should be lower than those for private interpersonal conduct. At the same time, unlike some modern political philosophers, he does not think that civic relationships must be founded only on the lowest human common denominator. Presenting a concept of civic friendship that reflects the dual nature of man, Aristotle surpasses the attempts of political thinkers who followed him to provide a useful concept on which to model public relationships. A brief consideration of a sample of those attempts underscores the merits of Aristotle's conception.

The most notable attempt to define civic friendship after Aristotle's is St. Augustine's. The latter's formulation of Christian fraternity falls short of adequacy, however, because it does not characterize the relationships among most citizens. According to Augustine, only those who love God can love their fellows, love of God is a consequence of God's grace, and the blessed are few. Neither their reason nor their moral dispositions motivate the chosen to love others; rather, grace compels them to love others because they are children of God.[12] To love one's neighbor is simply one way to show one's love of God. The motivation for fraternity must be one's love of God, not of men, for "if we love the world, it will separate us from the love of God which is charity. . . . Two loves there are, of the world and of God: if the love of the world dwells in us, the love of God can find no entrance. The love

---

[12] Saint Augustine, *The City of God*, trans. Marcus Dods (New York: Random House, 1950), XIV.7, 448; see also Herbert A. Deane, *The Political and Social Ideas of St. Augustine* (New York: Columbia University Press, 1963), 80.

of the world must depart, the love of God come in to dwell: make room for the better love."[13]

Since "love of the world" dwells in most men, they do not reciprocate the love the blessed show to them. The best that can come from lovers of this world is a love of earthly glory. According to Augustine, this sort of love should not be wholly denounced, for it manifests a capacity to defer gratification, a quality needed also by Christians. It parallels the Christian temperament also in being mindful of the judgment of others. But this merit of the love of glory is at the same time its significant weakness, for it makes it "the slave of *human* praise"; that is, consciousness of the judgment of other human beings easily becomes pride, "the beginning of sin." The earthly city should therefore not promote the love of glory as civic virtue.[14]

In fact, Augustine dashes all hope of any semblance of virtue becoming the norm. In his estimation, the lovers of this world want "to draw the others into punishment with them." Being "by the contrariety of their aims . . . enemies to those who turn unto God," they try to deceive and seduce them into loving the things of this world.[15] The wicked not only try to diminish the fraternity existing among the good but create conflict among each other in their quests for power and possessions. Men are not even simply social or political, for original sin made them grasping. Therefore, according to Augustine, the norm can never be either true virtue or civic virtue; rather, misery will prevail.[16]

St. Thomas Aquinas provides a more sanguine portrait of Christian civic virtue, but since he draws heavily from Aristotle his conception of civic friendship does not represent well an alternative to Aristotle's. Turning to Machiavelli, however, one finds a unique conception of political friendship. Yet, on inspection, one discovers that it suffers from one of the same defects as Augustine's—namely, that it cannot be a widespread phenomenon. Whereas in Augustine's view political friendship can exist only

[13] Augustine, "*In Epistolam Ioannis ad Parthos Tractatus Decem,*" II.8, as cited in Deane, *Ideas of St. Augustine,* 260–61, n. 85; see also *City of God,* XIV.28, 477.

[14] *City of God,* V.15–19, 165–73; XII.6, 385; XIV.13, 460–62; quotations from V.19, 173 (emphasis added) and XII.6, 385.

[15] From several works by Augustine; see Deane, *Ideas of St. Augustine,* 261 nn. 87, 91; text reprinted on page 32.

[16] Augustine, *City of God,* XV.4, 481–82; see also Deane, *Ideas of St. Augustine,* 33, 260 n. 79.

among the elect, in Machiavelli's view it can exist only between ruler and ruled. According to Machiavelli, a truly great leader knows how "to give men a feeling of security and win them over with the benefits he offers." He should elicit the support (*favore*), indeed, the friendship (*amico*) of the common people by comforting his subjects (for example, "with the hope that these bad times will not last long"), by defending them in bad times (a prince should always maintain his own arms and well-trained troops), and by being reservedly compassionate (a prince's conduct "should be of a sort tempered by prudence and kindness"). Indeed, criticizing Agathocles, who rose to political leadership by guile and bloodshed, Machiavelli says, "It cannot be called ingenuity to kill one's fellow citizens, betray friends, be without faith, without pity, without religion; all of these may bring one to power, but not to glory. . . . his vicious cruelty and inhumanity, together with his infinite iniquitous deeds, do not allow him to be counted among the most outstanding famous men."[17]

Yet Machiavelli admits that he is really recommending that a prince merely *seem* good; it is harmful to *be* "compassionate, faithful, humane, upright, religious" but useful to *appear* to be so. Appearing to have these qualities rather than actually having them allows a prince to change "according as the winds of fortune and the fluctuation of things command him." To appear to be "all compassion, all faithfulness, all integrity, all kindness, all religion," one "must not separate himself from the good."[18] Yet this counsel is simply instructional, not intended to encourage a prince to pursue knowledge of the good for its own sake.

Moreover, Machiavelli indicates that a prince should win friends not only by insincere means but for insincere ends. He should seek the friendship of subjects and allies (that is, potential subjects) for assistance in adverse times and "as a ladder up" to more power in fortunate times.[19]

Political friendship requires, then, in Machiavelli's view, excep-

---

[17] *Machiavelli's "The Prince": A Bilingual Edition*, trans. and ed. Mark Musa (New York: St. Martin's Press, 1964) VIII.74–75; IX.80–81; X.88–89; XIII.116–17; XVII.136–37; VIII.68–69.

[18] Ibid., XVIII.146–49.

[19] Ibid., IX.80–81; Niccolò Machiavelli, *The Discourses*, ed. Bernard Crick, trans. Leslie J. Walker, S. J., rev. Brian Richardson (New York: Pelican Books, 1970), II.1, 273; see also Harvey C. Mansfield, Jr., *Machiavelli's New Modes and Orders: A Study of the Discourses of Livy* (Ithaca: Cornell University Press, 1979), 214–15.

tional ability and exceptional power, excluding the ordinary from sharing in it among themselves. But even if citizens could achieve this kind of friendship, one would then have to consider the desirability of all citizens regarding one another as ladders to power—a thought that brings Hobbes's views to mind.

In Hobbes's *Leviathan* one finds the claim that men are disposed to fight one another for gain and glory. Whether they actually fight or not, "men have no pleasure . . . in keeping company, where there is no power able to over-awe them all." But even with a sovereign erected by the people to keep peace, men experience only sensations toward one another, not 'goodwill' or 'friendship.' Such are merely names designating whether we feel a desire or an aversion toward someone or something, and whether such objects are present or absent. To the extent that friendship exists among citizens, then, it is desire for society fulfilled, that is, "*love . . . for society*"—which we name "kindness." Sounding somewhat like Machiavelli, Hobbes declares further that one of the main uses of speech is "to make known to others our wills and purposes, that we may have the mutual help of one another." Thus, kindness among Hobbesian citizens appears to arise when the need for transaction arises.[20]

This brief review should give an idea of the kinds of difficulty conceptions of civic friendship in the history of political philosophy present. Other philosophers present similar problems. One finds in Locke's "law of nature" and Rousseau's "general will" the basis of a kind of civic friendship, but one that arises, like Hobbesian kindness, by way of the affirmation of individual will.[21] "Ethical life" for Hegel and "species life" for Marx include kinds of civic friendship, but like Augustinian fraternity they presuppose the transformation of human beings—not by grace, but by history or material circumstances. "Reason" must reconcile subjective interests with the common good, or the state must whither away. In summary, the weaknesses of these various conceptions of civic friendship are multiple and cross-cutting: some are limiting, mak-

---

[20] Thomas Hobbes, *Leviathan or the Matter, Forme and Power of a Commonwealth Ecclesiasticall and Civil*, ed. Michael Oakeshott (Oxford: Basil Blackwell, 1946), XIII.81–82; VI.31–32, 35; IV.19.

[21] On the essential affinity between Hobbes, Locke, and Rousseau, see Joseph Cropsey, "'Alienation' or Justice," in *Political Philosophy and the Issues of Politics* (Chicago: University of Chicago Press, 1977), 48.

ing friendship the prerogative of the few (Augustine, Machiavelli); some volatile, making friendship essentially self-serving (Machiavelli, Hobbes, Locke); and others require the metamorphosis of human nature, making friendship unlikely (Augustine, Rousseau, Hegel, Marx). The ways Aristotle's conception surpasses these I leave largely for the reader to discern.

CONCORD: FRIENDSHIP AMONG CITIZENS

Political friendship includes a relationship among citizens and a relationship between rulers and ruled. That Aristotle discusses the first kind of political friendship, which he calls concord (*homonoia*), in the *Nicomachean Ethics*, and the second in the *Politics*, gives rise to the thought that friendship between rulers and ruled presupposes concord. In this section and the next I substantiate that speculation.

Concord Defined

In the middle of Book IX of the *Nicomachean Ethics*, Aristotle provides a concise operational definition of concord: a city is in concord if people are like-minded as to what is in their interest, choose the same means to effect their interest, and act on their common resolutions (1167a26–28). One should notice that concord is an attribute of a city (*tas poleis homonoein*). For concord to exist, "all together" or the whole, not every citizen, needs to be like-minded (1167a30–31).

General agreement need not be forthcoming about all matters, but only about important (*megethei*), practical matters (*ta prakta*), the interests and concerns of life (*ta sumpheronta kai ta ton bion anēkonta*) which can in fact be resolved or realized (*NE* 1167a24–26, 28–30, b3–4). Thus, for concord to exist, citizens do not need to be in general agreement as to whether, for example, the earth is flat or spherical. This can be resolved, but neither its resolution nor whether people generally find its resolution persuasive bears on political life. Similarly, concord does not imply general agreement about whether an act of creation or evolution accounts for the existence of man, both because political order does not require it and because there appears to be no way to resolve it. Conversely, concord does imply general agreement as to the large practical matter of what the ends of political association should be: economic equality, empire, freedom or opportunity, order, safety, or justice, for example. Likewise, concord is general agreement not only about ends but also about means (1167a27): how many will rule, who is eligible to rule, how they will be selected, what prerogatives they will have, criteria for citizenship, what rights citizens will have, how disputes will be resolved, and whether and how these procedural matters can themselves be changed. But concord also implies *acting* on common resolutions (1167a28–31); that is, concord accommodates disagreement about ends and means which does not impede or prevent government from functioning. According to Aristotle's definition, disagreement among citizens about important constitutional matters constitutes discord only if it interferes with political operations such as the making and upholding of policy and elections. Hence "a city is in concord when the judgment of all decrees that offices should be elective, or they should form an alliance with Sparta, or that Pittacus should rule when he himself is willing" (1167a30–32). Pittacus must be willing to rule because otherwise the decree cannot be effected.[22] As long as faction does not obstruct government, a regime can be said to be in concord.

This condition does not mean, however, that where suppression succeeds there is concord; China was not in concord in 1988 nor was Romania in 1990 nor the Lithuanian Republic in 1991. Indeed, the act of suppressing signifies that dissent has and is interfering with actions of government. Moreover, in Aristotle's view, there cannot be political friendship where there is no justice (*NE* 1161a10–11, 32–34). But this condition does not imply either that governments should never suppress popular uprisings or should always enact the policies citizens want; rather, for there to be concord there must be justice (1161a10–11). Insofar as justice presupposes order, government should try to appease citizens, but to the extent that their demands contravene justice it should ignore them.

The Nature of the Human Propensity for Concord

One who disagreed with everyone about everything would be "like the man rebuked by Homer, 'clanless, lawless, hearthless' " (*Pol* 1253a4–5). Such a person would also be like Hobbes's man, for,

---

[22] H. Rackham contends that Pittacus must be willing because concord means unanimity and Pittacus would otherwise be a dissenting voice; see *Aristotle: Nicomachean Ethics*, rev. ed., trans. H. Rackham (Loeb Classical Library, 1934), 542, n. a; conceivably, however, Pittacus could vote against himself but agree to rule if elected.

as Aristotle observes, "the one who is such by nature has by this fact a desire for war, as if he were an isolated piece in a game of chess" (1253a6–7). But such a person would be exceptional in Aristotle's view, for he maintains that human beings generally have a natural inclination to form cities, since alone they are not self-sufficient. They are, moreover, equipped by nature to form them, for the basis of cities is shared moral perceptions, and nature gives human beings both the capacity to perceive what is good and evil, just and unjust, and the capacity, in speech, to exchange those perceptions (1253a14–30). Aristotle is not saying that exchanging moral perceptions results necessarily in sharing them. Nor is he, as Alasdair MacIntyre contends, blind to "a Sophoclean insight—that it is through conflict and sometimes only through conflict that we learn what our ends and purposes are."[23] Aristotle defines judgment, what prudence effects, as "the right discrimination of the equitable" (*NE* 1143a20); in its attempt to discover what is equitable, good judgment addresses conflicting goods. Aristotle is not saying, however, as Bernard Yack contends, that because man has the capacity for argument he "is therefore an argumentative animal." Yack goes too far in criticizing MacIntyre's interpretation, contending that Aristotle maintains that political communities are based not on common moral perceptions but on argument about them. In Yack's view, Aristotle's citizens argue about "general standards of justice and goodness," about the very thing that, Aristotle implies, makes their disputation and decision making possible.[24]

Although human beings have the capacity for argument and do argue, Aristotle would say, they realize that it is in their self-interest to agree on at least general standards of goodness and justice. Concord does not require a human being to transform or rationalize his subjective will insofar as it allows for the expression of significant moral differences, which presupposes the retention of individual judgment. Concord cannot, however, accommodate "particularly violent distrust and conflict," for it would obstruct the autarky of citizens, that which the community should serve according to Aristotle.[25]

23 *After Virtue: A Study in Moral Theory* (Notre Dame: University of Notre Dame Press, 1981), 153.
24 "Community and Conflict in Aristotle's Political Philosophy," *Review of Politics* 47, no. 1 (1985), 97–98, 102, 105–6.
25 Yack, "Community and Conflict," 106; see also 102, 107, 109; see also Cropsey, "Justice and Friendship in the *Nicomachean Ethics*," in *Political Philosophy*, 262.

The self-interested desire for concord is thus connected with a desire for privacy; one cannot achieve autarky without pursuing private activities, and the absence of concord makes private pursuits more difficult. Accordingly, by preserving and fostering privacy and private activities a regime promotes concord. Persons who enjoy personal friendships, family, household matters, business, the liberal arts, and contemplation do not invest their well-being in the political community; having less at stake in public matters, they are not inclined to violent confrontation. Citizens who, unlike Jason, know how to be private (*Pol* 1277a24–25) understand that the political community provides the means by which they may enhance life, not create it.[26] This is why "concord is found among good men" (*NE* 1167b4–5). Each, being of one mind with himself, enjoys spending time in private, and thus agrees that privacy is a good (1166a23–24, 1167b5–6). What good men argue for in public, then, is the protection and provision of the private, opportunities and means to cultivate virtue.

Rule: Friendship between Rulers and Ruled

As citizens can be friends of a sort, so can rulers and ruled (*NE* 1161a11–14, 32–34). To establish the nature of ruling and the nature of the relationship between rulers and ruled, I next examine Aristotle's main thoughts on ruling, consider the ways his thoughts on justice inform and illuminate his understanding of ruling, and, with a view to clarification, compare his understanding of ruling with a prevailing modern conception.

Ruling Defined

Although the whole of the *Politics* concerns ruling, several statements in particular note its essential nature and fundamental features. In Book I, chapter 5, in his introduction to a discussion of slavery, Aristotle observes that ruling and being ruled are natural and confer benefits (1254a21–22). Moreover, "wherever something rules and something is ruled there is a certain work belonging to these together. For whatever is constituted out of a number of

---

[26] As different as they are in other respects, Aristotle and Nietzsche both recognize that the political realm cannot be a source of true fulfillment; see, for example, Friedrich Nietzsche, *On the Genealogy of Morals*, ed. Walter Kaufmann, trans. Walter Kaufmann and R. J. Hollingdale (New York: Random House, 1967), 136.

things—whether continuous or separate—and becomes a single common thing always indicates a ruling and a ruled element" (1254a27–31). Here Aristotle provides a kind of operational definition. There is ruling going on, so to speak, if there are "a number of things" (for example, body parts) and there is a recognizable unity or harmony about those things (for example, a human being). That he does not say what the certain work (*ergon*) belonging to the ruling and the ruled together is would seem to be because one cannot do so without knowing what kind of things the ruler and the ruled are. If, for example, the ruler is the intellect and the ruled the desiring part of the soul, then the work belonging to them is the satisfaction of both parts, or the best condition of the soul.

In the remainder of the fifth chapter of Book I, Aristotle gives the following examples of parts that constitute wholes and so evidence that ruling is at work: the soul and the body; the rational and the nonrational parts of the soul; man and other animals; male and female; and naturally superior and inferior human beings, generally speaking. Notably absent from this list are political rulers and citizens. Why does Aristotle leave out this apparently most obvious example? Evidently because "political rule is over free and equal persons" (*Pol* 1255b20). In the other cases, the natural superiority of one party over the other makes possible and desirable the activity of ruling.

What, then, makes possible the phenomenon of the free ruling the free? And what is the "certain work" belonging to and conferring benefits on both the ruling free and the ruled free? According to Aristotle, "among similar persons nobility and justice are found in [ruling and being ruled] in turn, for this is something equal and similar" (*Pol* 1325b7–8, 1287a16–18). To recall from my Chapter 3, he suggests, however, that political rule need not be rotational in order to be political rule; rulers may take into account the wishes of the ruled and in this sense "be ruled in turn" by them.[27] The reciprocal aspect of political rule helps make it acceptable to the

[27] Mary P. Nichols, *Socrates and the Political Community: An Ancient Debate* (Albany: State University of New York Press, 1987), 159. In fact, if one considers that human beings are much more likely to be unequal than equal to each other, the latter situation being a matter of chance or divine benevolence (*Pol* 1276b37–38, 1295a28–29, 1331b21–22), Aristotle seems to be cautioning against establishing rotational rule in claiming that "[to assign] what is not equal to equal persons and what is not similar to similar persons is contrary to nature, and nothing contrary to nature is noble" (*Pol* 1325b8–10).

ruled free. Reciprocity is the certain work that confers nobility and justice on both the ruled and the rulers.

The Status of Common Opinion

Although political rule requires reciprocity, it depends even more on the exceptional virtues of rulers. Indeed, it might be observed that prudence, temperance, and justice precede and preside over reciprocity. They make ruling the noble and just institution of inequality. In other words, correct political rule confers more authority on the judgment of rulers than on the opinion of the ruled.

On the one hand, Aristotle seems to make the case that political rule requires mostly listening to the ruled, that this is what makes rulers and ruled friends. First, as I noted in Chapter 6, he implies that rulers should have the characteristics of the ruled, for ruling well presupposes having been ruled (*Pol* 1277b7–13). Likewise, a ruler's familiarity with particulars (*hekasta gnōrizein*) (*NE* 1141b14–15, 1142a14) implies familiarity with common opinion. Finally, Aristotle seems to say that a ruler should be sympathetic to common opinion; to see what is fair, one has to show consideration for others (*NE* 1143a21–22).

On the other hand, he modifies these points. First, although ruling well presupposes having been ruled, only the prudent should rule (*Pol* 1277a14–16, 27–28) because only they recognize that the point of view of the ruled is only one of the two points of view that should be taken into consideration when ruling (1277b15–17). The other point of view is that of the ruler—the point of view of what is best for everyone in practice (*NE* 1141b12–14, 1140b4–6, 20–21). So, although Aristotle indicates that judging what is equitable requires sympathy or consideration for others (*suggnōmē*), he immediately elaborates, pointing out that showing true consideration for others means discerning what is really equitable, not what they believe to be so (*NE* 1143a23–24). Rulers must take common opinion or the opinion of those involved in a particular situation into account, for prudence requires holding in view all particulars before issuing a decree; but in that prudence also requires meeting to the extent possible the demands of the good life in general, rulers must be willing to compromise, even abandon, opinion.

Thus, it is mistaken to suggest, as Ronald Beiner does, that judging what is equitable requires in Aristotle's estimation yielding to the viewpoint of those concerned. The source of Beiner's mistake is his assumption that citizens are in Aristotle's estimation normally morally virtuous or just. He regards as the usual case for Aristotle what Aristotle takes to be the exception. Hence Beiner writes: "A theory of political judgment leads irresistably to the formulation of a corresponding theory of friendship. To judge is to judge-with, to judge-with is to be a friend. To judge well is a staple of politics." Only when all citizens have prudence will judgment be judgment-with. As Beiner himself acknowledges at the beginning of his account, prudence moves back and forth between the universal and particular; it does not conjoin with the particular.[28]

Rulers: Representatives or Parents?

It will be noticed that Aristotle's view of ruling contravenes the modern Western democratic view according to which what is best for the community necessarily represents common opinion. Ascertaining to what extent it contravenes this view, and its merits as an alternative, calls for a brief consideration of the modern concept of political representation.

There appear to be two conceptions of representation: disinterested and protective mediation. The first reflects the Latin origin of the word, *repraesentare*, which means "to make present or manifest or present again."[29] I may represent you at the town meeting by simply repeating your views. But if three referenda are put forth, to continue to represent you I must judge which one you would support on the basis of the views you have expressed to me. This judgment would necessarily be, however, a judgment as to which referendum you *should* support. I cannot know which one you would support if you were there; I can only reason on the basis of your expressed views X, Y, and Z which one you should support. Such representation cannot, then, be disinterested mediation. It must always involve the judgment of the representative. Accordingly, the original Latin meaning of representation "had nothing to do with agency or government."[30]

Nonetheless, if the views put forth by a representative have little

<hr />

[28] *Political Judgment* (Chicago: University of Chicago Press, 1983), 73, 79–82; quoting 82.
[29] Hanna Fenichel Pitkin, *The Concept of Representation* (Berkeley: University of California Press, 1967), 241.
[30] Ibid., 241; see also 209.

or nothing to do with the wishes of particular persons, then, according to Hanna Fenichel Pitkin, "we leave the realm of representation altogether, and end up with an expert deciding technical questions and taking care of the ignorant masses as a parent takes care of a child."[31] That Aristotle does not think of rulers as experts deciding technical questions is evident from his arguing that their task is to prescribe not the legally just but the equitable. Almost anyone can merely apply laws, but it takes education, experience, and natural endowment to recognize and remedy their deficiencies. Aristotle's rulers represent the true interests of a community rather than the wishes of citizens,[32] like good parents, but so do modern representatives. In other words, the question as to whether Aristotle's rulers are more like representatives or parents is misguided insofar as it presupposes a difference between their intentions.

Aristotle did not, then, fail to conceive the ruler as a representative in the strict sense because his linguistic repertoire lacked such a word, or because the age in which he lived was politically unsophisticated, but because he recognized the impossibility of neutral mediation.[33] His work presupposes this rather than debates the possibility and merits of neutral mediation, because one cannot, as he says, deliberate about what cannot be otherwise (*NE* 1140a31–32); ruling and being ruled are natural (*Pol* 1254a21–22).

Aristotle reveals not only the naturalness but the desirability of ruling and being ruled (*Pol* 1254a22). Governing should go beyond merely re-presenting opinions because they may not be reputable. The task of rulers is to rid politics of unreputable opinions.[34] In Hannah Arendt's view, this definition degrades politics by precluding civic participation, the essence of freedom.[35] Aristotle would perhaps respond that mandating respect for ignorance and turpitude is not freedom.

---

[31] Ibid., 210.

[32] This means, it should be noted, that they would consider the true interests of noncitizens as well.

[33] According to Pitkin, the ancient Greeks had no word or concept corresponding to the word "representation" (*Concept of Representation*, 241).

[34] Rulers thereby serve philosophers, who begin inquiry by considering reputable opinions (see Chapter 8, "Philosophical Inquiry," pp. 202–4).

[35] *The Human Condition* (Chicago: University of Chicago Press, 1958), 196, 222–29; for the same contention, see Stephen Taylor Holmes, "Aristippus in and out of Athens," *American Political Science Review* 73, no. 1 (1979), 119.

Ruling and the Private

Aristotle's view of the political role of common opinion brings the discussion to the familiar debate as to whether his political ideal is totalitarian, as Arendt and others charge.[36] Aristotle would refute this charge at least by highlighting three features of his conception of ruling.

First, as noted, prudence compels rulers to listen to common opinion. Their aim is, not to impose their own views on all, but to discover and prescribe what is best for all. What is best may well incorporate the views of many or all. In any case, rulers do not aim to stifle the opinions of citizens, since they may be of help in the discovery of what is best for the political order.

Second, with political decision making the responsibility of rulers, not citizens, Aristotle's conception of ruling allows citizens to attend to their private affairs. Unlike rulers, they have the privilege of withdrawing from participation. Indeed, rulers have a responsibility to secure this privilege by preserving privacy and the means to use it well. Attending to private activities displays knowing how to be ruled, a virtue (*Pol* 1277a24–27, b25–27). A good citizen promotes the self-sufficiency of the whole by attaining self-sufficiency. Political participation is not the only way to make a civic contribution. Aristotle's conception of ruling thus opens a wider range of options to citizens than do political philosophies that conceive the political order as dependent on civic participation.

Third, although Aristotle does not grant rulers the prerogative of living private lives (*NE* 1130a2–3), he advocates their attending to some extent to their private concerns by noting that prudence includes doing what is good for oneself as well as what is good for the whole (*NE* 1141b29–1142a10). A person who does not exercise virtue in relation to himself will not be of service to the community. In sum, Aristotle argues that political friendship between rulers and ruled requires acknowledging and fostering the private.

---

[36] See, for example, Holmes, "Aristippus."

8

PHILOSOPHY: RECIPROCITY BETWEEN THE MOST PRIVATE AND THE PUBLIC

According to the account given in the previous chapter, true friendship entails being morally virtuous to oneself and to others. But because Aristotle advocates exercising intellectual virtue at least as much as moral virtue, one wonders whether he thinks a human being can exercise moral and intellectual virtue at the same time. Can a human being engage in the activity of philosophy or lead the contemplative life and maintain human relationships? Can friends even philosophize together? Finally, one wonders, is friendship perhaps even necessary to philosophy? In this chapter I try to answer these questions and, more generally, to explain what Aristotle means by the activity of contemplation or philosophy.[1] Thus, it begins with his discussion of the intellectual virtues.

INTELLECTUAL VIRTUE AND CONTEMPLATION

The intellectual virtues fall into two categories: faculties and qualities (*NE* VI). The intellectual faculties are mechanical aptitude, which may develop into technical skill (*technē*); scientific aptitude or knowledge (*epistēmē*), the ability to understand and use scientific, including mathematical, truths in problem solving; prudence (*phronēsis*); wisdom (*sophia*); and intuitive reason, or mind (*nous*), the last two faculties of which require some discussion (*NE*

---

[1] See Chapter 6, note 55, pp. 159–60.

1139b16–17). The other intellectual virtues may characterize these faculties: deliberative excellence (*euboulia*) should characterize prudential decision making; understanding or comprehension (*sunesis*) allows one to follow reasoning and can thus supplement both scientific aptitude and prudence; and judgment (*gnōmē*), a sense for what is fair in human matters, is an aspect of prudence (*NE* 1142b31–33, 1143a11–24, 29–31).

Nature ranks the faculties according to what each grasps. The faculties that concern what varies rank lower in nature than those that apprehend what does not vary, for in nature that which is constant maintains order, whereas that which comes into being and passes away merely shares in it; and what maintains order partakes more directly in the divine or supreme good (*to ariston*) (*Met* 1075a11–15). The lower intellectual virtues, then, are technical skill and prudence, for the variable includes "both things made and actions done" (*NE* 1140a1–2). The higher virtues are scientific knowledge, wisdom, and intuitive reason, for the objects of these do not come into being and pass away: the object of scientific knowledge is that in nature which, demonstrably, never changes (for example, the life cycles of plants and animals, the constellations of the stars, the composition of air); intuitive reason apprehends "the first principle from which what is scientifically known follows"; and wisdom is intuitive reason and scientific knowledge combined (*NE* 1139b22–24, 31–32, 1140b33–34, 1141a18–20). A human being must, it appears, have and engage these higher virtues in order to be by nature excellent.

There is, however, a natural hierarchy even among the higher intellectual virtues; hence, to be truly excellent one must have the highest of them—wisdom (*NE* 1141a16–17). Since scientific knowledge is a part of wisdom, it is probable that some understanding of modern science, such as its findings on human health and longevity (since nothing incomplete belongs to happiness;[2] *NE* 1177b25–26), would be subsumed under wisdom. But knowledge of the demonstrable constants of nature is knowledge of only one kind of constancy, and not of the most honorable kind (1141b2–3). Indeed, scientific knowledge is defective by its own measure: it establishes truth by revealing the cause or rational ground of every effect, but

---

[2] See also Chapter 7, note 9, especially p. 178.

it must itself presuppose the rational ground of this method, that is, of reason (1139b28–29), as Kant also observed. And although intuitive reason apprehends the source of all scientific constancy, which is not itself demonstrable, and therefore ranks higher in nature than scientific knowledge, what accounts for scientific constancy is still in some sense only a part of nature. To be wise is to have knowledge of the whole of nature, of what is demonstrable and indemonstrable (1140b33–1141a8).

But to indicate that one can know what is indemonstrable contravenes the widely accepted modern epistemological claim that one can have knowledge only of what exists and can know what exists only by demonstrating its existence. What, according to Aristotle, both has being and is indemonstrable? One might infer that the answer is God—that is, Aristotle's prime mover. Aristotle explains, however, that wisdom is not concerned "with the causes described in the *Physics*. It is not concerned with the final cause; for this is the Good, and this belongs to the sphere of action and to things which are in motion; and it is this which first causes motion. . . . but there is no Prime Mover in the sphere of immovable things" (*Met* 1059a34–38).

According to Aristotle, speculative reason itself *is*, and yet it is not of the physical world. Intuitive reason is the ability to think about thinking (*noēsis noēseōs*). In contrast to "scientific knowledge [*epistēmē*] and perception [*aisthēsis*] and opinion [*doxa*] and [calculative] thought [*dianoia*]" which "are apparently always of something else, and only incidentally of themselves," the object of intuitive reason is thinking itself (*Met* 1074b35–36).[3] Although intuitive reason is the only always self-conscious faculty—the only faculty whose sole work is to understand or define reason— scientific knowledge or aptitude, the other speculative faculty, is self-reflective insofar as its object is theory, definition, or truth. Similarly, if one abstracts the matter from the objects of the non-speculative or productive faculties, one is left with pure thought or definition (for example, the perception of Argos the dog becomes the concept of dog). When definitive knowledge is the object of thinking, one is thinking about thought (*Met* 1074b37–1075a5).

[3] The human mind ordinarily "knows itself [only] in so far as it is conscious of its object"; see Klaus Oehler, "Aristotle on Self-Knowledge," *Proceedings of the American Philosophical Society* 118, no. 6 (1974), 498.

As both Richard Bodéüs and Klaus Oehler stress, Aristotle thinks that a human being can become one with the divine being or prime mover *only* insofar as the activity of thinking thought is also its activity. One can transcend human consciousness only by imitating, not "grasping" or "beholding," the divine[4] (this is what Aristotle means by saying that wisdom is not concerned with the prime mover). As Oehler explains, "the mistaken view" is "that the self-reflection of the Nus [*nous*], since as actualized Nus it is identical with the intelligible forms, consists in the thinking of those intelligible forms." In fact, "[Aristotle] is not saying . . . that when the Nus is thinking itself it is thinking some particular content; he is saying that the Nus, in thinking its objects, experiences the self-reflection inherent in all thinking and so experiences itself."[5]

One cannot remain like the divine—and thus become divine, or immortal—because "happiness is a kind of activity; and an activity clearly is something that comes into being, not a thing that belongs [to one all the time], like a piece of property" (*NE* 1169b29–30). "Human finitude does not allow us to remain, like the Prime Mover, in a permanent state of Energeia." We can only aspire to, never attain, "la Vie de Dieu."[6]

Yet earthly existence does not entirely handicap the activity of thinking about thinking, for consciousness is not possible without the world of action and objects. The intellect cannot perceive that it is perceiving unless it has something outside itself to perceive. As Oehler puts it, "the perceptible seems to be prior to perception" (and thus to awareness of perception or consciousness). Insofar as the intellect cannot either perceive or perceive itself without the world—and thus without being in such a world—the intellect and body are for Aristotle one (he is thus not the ancestor of Descartes).[7]

---

4 Bodéüs, "Notes sur quelques aspects de la conscience dans la pensée aristotélicienne," *Phronesis* 20, no. 1 (1975), 73.
5 Oehler, "Aristotle on Self-Knowledge," 497–98; see also 495–96. Bodéüs makes the same point at "Notes," 73.
6 Oehler, "Aristotle on Self-Knowledge," 499; Bodéüs, "Notes," 73–74.
7 Oehler, "Aristotle on Self-Knowledge," 496. See also Bodéüs, "Notes," 68: "It is important to observe that consciousness can accompany the most banal of actions: walking, for example . . . and that all acts are not automatically conscious." Hence, Aristotle says, "we *can* perceive that we are perceiving."

Ordinary consciousness differs from the consciousness of the wise man who thinks about being conscious. In being aware of his ability to think about his thinking, he is conscious of "his own perfection."[8] As Aristotle explains,

> there is something which perceives [*to aisthanomenon*] that we are active. Hence, if we are perceiving, we perceive that we are perceiving; and if we are thinking [*noōmen*], we perceive that we are thinking. Now perceiving that we are perceiving or thinking is the same thing as perceiving that we are, since we agreed that being is perceiving or thinking [*to gar einai ēn aisthanesthai ē noein*]. (*NE* 1170a30–b1)

But why should we think about thinking? Because it is living, not only according to what is highest in us, which is the human function, but engaging what is highest with what is highest, namely, itself (*Met* 1072b18–24; *NE* 1098a7–17, 1170a16–19). This self-engagement is superior to the activity of thinking about anything else because reason's function is to be active (*energei*), and it is most active and thus functioning best when contemplating itself (*theōria*).[9] Thus, Aristotle points out, it is the *activity* of thinking about thinking, not the *capacity* to think about thinking, which is divine, or approaches divinity. Strictly speaking, possession of a human mind does not make human beings worthy of the characterization 'part-divine'; only their exercise of that mind to its capacity, in contemplation, does. And only contemplation bestows true happiness. As Bodéüs explains, the realization that we are equipped to think about thinking—that we are in this sense perfect beings—gives us immense pleasure. *Actualizing* our perfection in noetic activity thus makes us happy.[10]

Human beings should aspire to experience perfection also because it illuminates the range of human virtue. To understand the possibilities of human virtue and demonstrable nature's resistance to them is to have wisdom, "the most exact of the forms of knowl-

---

[8] Bodéüs, "Notes," 70.
[9] Oehler explains: "The Nus knows itself by means of its participation in the nature of its object. The nature of its object is to be knowable. When the Nus participates in it, it assumes the nature of its object, which thereby becomes common to both" ("Aristotle on Self-Knowledge," 499).
[10] "Notes," 69–70.

edge" (*NE* 1141a17) and the knowledge that should guide political order.[11]

THE RELATION BETWEEN MORAL AND INTELLECTUAL VIRTUE

If happiness lies in engaging *nous*—not only the intellectual part of us but a part of that part—then how can happiness be also "an activity of the soul in accordance with complete virtue [*kat'aretēn teleian*]" (*NE* 1102a5)? Happiness can be both, it seems, only if exercising the speculative intellect somehow presupposes or entails exercising the remaining virtues—prudence and the virtues of character.

Aristotle seems to give two contradictory accounts. On the one hand, he claims that the exercise of *nous* is itself complete—it is self-sufficient (*autarkes*). It seems to be necessarily so, since the excellence of the mind is separate from matter, or the body (*hē de tou nou kechōrismenē*), and "nothing incomplete is proper to happiness" (*NE* 1178a22, 1177b25–29). Contemplative activity, its object not being human beings or divisible, does not evidently need assistance from prudence. Nor does it need the assistance of the other various moral virtues—such as generosity, courage, and moderation—since it does not require, and even seems to exclude, interaction with human beings (1178a9–14). In particular, it seems not to need moderation, since thinking is the most active and thereby extreme of all activities (*Pol* 1325b16–21; *NE* 1177a19–21, b20–21).

On the other hand, Aristotle suggests that exercising *nous* does in fact presuppose the moral virtues. He claims that prudence aims to bring wisdom into being as medical science aims to bring health into being (*NE* 1145a6–9) and that prudence "cannot reach its fully developed state without virtue" (1144a29–30, 1178a16–19)—since moral virtue "makes us aim at the right mark, and prudence makes us take the right means" (1144a7–9). It can be inferred that a human being led by appetites and desires cannot think about thought. But what is equally clear and makes Aristotle's claims problematic is that a human being cannot, according to Aristotle's

---

[11] See Chapter 6, "Leisure: Public and Private Good," pp. 163–64.

description, contemplate and simultaneously exercise the moral virtues toward others. Thus, as A. W. H. Adkins explains, Aristotle's meaning must be as follows:

> The *theoretikos* will indeed possess all the *aretai:* they are needed to render him a good specimen of human being (1144a1 ff.), and an absence of well-established moral dispositions would distract him from his *theoria*. However, any *arete* can exist in a state either of *hexis* or of *energeia;* one cannot exercise both *theoria* and any practical *arete* at the same time; and for the well-being of the *theoretikos* it suffices that he possess the other *aretai* in a state of *hexis* for so long as he is able to exercise his *theoria* uninterruptedly.[12]

We must speculate, however, about why Aristotle thinks that philosophers should be good specimens of human being. It seems that a philosopher should have at least a good reputation, that is, should be a good citizen and morally virtuous enough to teach. A philosopher who does not obey the laws risks, as does any other person, incarceration, ostracism, or execution. But such a philosopher also risks the reputation of all philosophers and philosophy. Indeed, one instance of a philosopher being uncivil might be sufficient for a political order to prohibit philosophy. A philosopher who is not civil enough to teach, to whom no one listens, fails to provide for the future of philosophy. The Socratic question Aristotle perhaps wishes to bring to mind is, to what extent can one appear morally virtuous without being so?

Aristotle suggests that a philosopher needs more than a good reputation insofar as he needs friends to philosophize well: "The solitary person has a hard life; for by oneself it is not easy to be continuously active, but with others and toward others it is easier" (*NE* 1170a5–6). Being excellent, a philosopher naturally seeks another excellent person for a friend, since excellent people find what is good by nature "good and pleasant in itself" (1170a13–16, 1179b21–23); the philosopher seeks companionship that facilitates rather than impedes philosophizing (1177a34).

Two can pursue wisdom together because, although thinking is a divine activity, it is also a human activity; as with any other human activity, one who engages in it well can help another do so. Indeed,

---

[12] "*Theoria* versus *Praxis* in the *Nicomachean Ethics* and the *Republic*," *Classical Philology* 73, no. 4 (1978), 301.

the more often the good meet, the greater friends they become, for they not only share the same activities but correct and learn from each other, each imitating "what in the other he approves of" (NE 1172a10–13). One who seeks to think correctly about thought or to find truth chooses a friend, then, not for moral sustenance or because of his moral virtue but because of his intellectual virtue. Moreover, if excellent men agree that the best way to spend their lives is in philosophizing together (sumphilosophousin) (1172a1–8), then they are willing to suspend or reconsider their differences, convictions, or individuality. Thus, to philosophize together must be to try to persuade not for the sake of one's own convictions but for the sake of truth. A genuine philosopher is, then, prepared to abandon or modify his claims.

By indicating that "sharing in discussion and thought [koinōnein logōn kai dianoias]" characterizes both friendship (NE 1170b10–12) and philosophy, Aristotle implies that friendship can be the midwife of truth. And in this way he, like Socrates, "calls philosophy down from heaven." What is more, in establishing friendship as a means to truth, Aristotle intimates that truth concerns what is good or right for human beings. In other words, one can, beyond thinking and sharing thoughts, partake in and share the truth with others.[13]

Yet does not truth's human accessibility indicate its variability over time? Would not the continuous mediation of the truth by human reason distort the truth? Would not 'the truth' come to reflect in fact the needs and concerns of every age? According to Aristotle, truth's safeguard against distortion is its accessibility only or fully to select human beings. Truth seems to lie somewhere between heaven and earth (NE 1134b18–1135a5), to be "the quotient of the simply good and the ancestral."[14] Aristotle is admitting, in the spirit of the philosopher who returns to the cave, "that what is intrinsically or by nature the highest is not the most urgent for man, who is essentially an 'in-between' being—between the brutes and the gods."[15] The philosophical truth, or natural right, is

[13] Aristotle belongs to the Socratic tradition in that "Socrates is said to have been the first who called philosophy down from heaven and forced it to make inquiries about life and manners and good and bad things. . . . he is said to have been the founder of political philosophy"; Leo Strauss, Natural Right and History (Chicago: University of Chicago Press, 1953), 120.

[14] Ibid., 153.

[15] Ibid., 152.

political in that it lends itself to political adaptation.[16] But it is also political in being elusive.

Philosophers following Aristotle challenge his view of natural right. Kant's moral philosophy attempts to redignify or impute greater moral weight to reason.[17] Aristotle and Kant agree that the domain of reason is more real than practical experience in that contemplation is experience of the whole. Kant leaves Aristotle, however, in arguing that moral choice must occur at the noumenal level: to be moral, human beings must follow directives issuing from the domain that is independent of conditional constraints; they can apprehend those directives by hypothetically universalizing human conduct.

But what compels a person to apprehend them? Kant answers, belief in the Idea of freedom. Belief in an unconditioned totality is the law of all moral laws, for the Idea provides the connection of ends pure reason demands and is thus in the service of pure reason. Standing as a regulative principle of reason, the unconditioned totality is not thinkable as are the categories over which it presides. Being unthinkable, man can never *know* the Idea—for example, through the activity of philosophy—and so must hold the conviction that a perfect unity exists.

Belief in the perfection of the noumenal requires a human being to imitate it in conduct, not in thought, by enacting universalizable principles. Overcoming the tension between the noumenal and the phenomenal by way of the noumenal is the passage to freedom.

---

[16] Put another way, "there is no fundamental disproportion between natural right and the requirements of political society, or there is no essential need for the dilution of natural right. . . . A right which necessarily transcends political society, [Aristotle] gives us to understand, cannot be the right natural to man, who is by nature a political animal" (Strauss, *Natural Right*, 156). Likewise, as Richard Kennington observes, the "concreteness" of the instantiation of natural right defeats eliciting an "abiding and univocal meaning." Classical natural right thus contrasts with Stoic natural law, which "is problematic because it is trans-political and therefore politically useless, at least in its undiluted form; and because its theological and teleological requirements are not easily satisfied by philosophy"; see "Strauss's Natural Right and History," *Review of Metaphysics* 35, no. 1 (1981), 59, 78–79.

[17] The following remarks on Kant derive from his *Critique of Pure Reason*, unabridged ed., trans. Norman Kemp Smith (New York: St. Martin's Press, 1965); "On the Common Saying: 'This May Be True in Theory, but It Does Not Apply in Practice,'" and "Perpetual Peace: A Philosophical Sketch," in *Kant's Political Writings*, ed. Hans Reiss, trans. H. B. Nisbet (Cambridge: Cambridge University Press, 1970), 61–72, 116–30; and *Foundations of the Metaphysics of Morals*, trans. Lewis White Beck (New York: Bobbs-Merrill, 1959).

Being the commands of reason, freedom is knowable to all.[18] Aristotle maintains not only that most human beings cannot understand wisdom but that prudence must mediate or transform its dictates into conduct. So, although he thinks that the commands of wisdom should guide political order, he does not think that they can, as Kant hopes, replace judgment.

This is not to say that Kant does not recognize the need for judgment. But he finds the need in matters of justice, where the upholding of principles often fails and calls for response to the advisement of hypothetical imperatives. This implies, according to Kant, in contrast to Aristotle, that in the realm of justice one cannot err. Yet Kant presents the contrast between the realms of justice and morality, not in order to encourage us to lower our standards for political life, but to persuade us not to exchange duty for expediency. In his view, justice should not overrule morality, prudence should not overrule duty.[19]

One might say that Kant, in advocating the direct application of pure reason in practice, advocates collapsing the public-private distinction. Private standards (of reason) should become public standards (of conduct). Disjunction signals failure on the part of the public, or politics, to meet the imperatives of reason. By contrast, Aristotle argues that wisdom is recognition and preservation of the tension between the requirements of the truly private, thought thinking itself, and those of the public. Wisdom, or natural right, is not so much the compromise between private perfection and public imperfection as the understanding of public perfection or political goodness through private perfection.[20] Knowledge of the unchanging standards of human excellence includes the insight that the ultimate standard is good judgment.

PHILOSOPHICAL INQUIRY

Aristotle differs conspicuously from Kant on topics other than natural right as well. Kant believes that we must begin with pure

---

[18] Kant, *Metaphysics of Morals*, 20; see also 47–49; Ronald Beiner, *Political Judgment* (Chicago: University of Chicago Press, 1983), 66.

[19] "Perpetual Peace," 115–16, 122–25, 130; "On the Common Saying," 62, 80–83. See also Beiner, *Political Judgment*, 63–66.

[20] Similarly, Kennington says that "the emphatically political character of classic natural right required that the wisdom of the highest human type, for which the society has the greatest need, be harmonized with the inability of the non-wise to recognize that wisdom" ("Strauss's Natural Right," 77).

reason and aim toward its practical employment; Aristotle thinks that we should begin with opinion and aim toward truth or pure reason. Not all opinions are worthy of dialectical inquiry, of course. Opinions that are not accepted either "by the majority or by the wise" are not "reputable" but merely "contentious" (*Top* 100b1–101a4, 104a4–15). Moreover, generally speaking, reputable opinions take the form of ethical, logical, or scientific propositions (105b19–25). Just as a doctor does not employ every method to heal, so a philosopher does not pursue every opinion (101b5–10, 104b3–5). By the same token, the philosopher should not overlook or dismiss any possibly reputable opinions (101b9–10). The philosopher must begin with what is available and accessible and has a great ability *(nous)* to see the truth; but he cannot see it all at once, all of a sudden. As Socrates demonstrates in the *Republic,* only by pressing opinions to their conclusions can one ascend out of the realm of opinion and into the realm of truth, thereby acquiring a different perspective of the former.

If opinion or the city is the subject of or feeds philosophy, then must not philosophy be subordinate to it? On the one hand, insofar as philosophy must begin with ethical propositions or politics and philosophers must be educated in the city, politics holds architectonic supremacy over even philosophy. On the other hand, philosophical activity becomes self-sufficient the moment it questions opinion. Moreover, insofar as philosophers arrive at an understanding of the whole that citizens, rulers, and legislators cannot have, they are superior to them. Hence, Aristotle concludes, to say that politics rules philosophy because philosophers are human beings is like claiming that because human beings rule the city they rule the gods (*NE* 1145a10–11). At the same time, in pointing out that the subject of philosophy includes the political Aristotle reveals that, from the theoretical or comprehensive vantage point of the philosopher, a dynamic equilibrium between politics and philosophy exists.

Aristotle would perhaps point out at this juncture that dialectical inquiry cannot proceed without skepticism. The philosopher's epistemic privilege should not be mistaken for possession of the truth or omniscience.[21] According to Aristotle and Socrates before

---

[21] Aristotle does not attribute omniscience to even the most perfect being of all, the prime mover. Oehler speculates that this is because Aristotle "noticed the tremendous numbers of complications connected with the question, whether immutability and omniscience are logically consistent or not, and for him there were no

him, the genuine philosopher does not claim to have certain knowledge, being keenly aware that, as part political and part divine, he is not wholly suited for truth seeking. The philosopher's skepticism is then both auxiliary and nemesis: it simultaneously prompts relentless questioning after certainty *and* encourages the dismissal, as unreasonable, of any understanding of certainty. In Aristotle's eyes, a philosopher who forecloses the possibility of truth becomes, thereby, a naysaying cynic.

What enables a philosopher to be at once skeptical and open to the possibility of truth? The experience of appearances should be sufficient to compel skepticism, whereas dialectical discovery should compel an openness to the possibility of truth. Again, such openness must mean, operatively, acceptance of appearances (which may take the form of reputable opinions) as possible guides to truth. The constant apparently provides only the changing as means to its discovery. A philosophical disposition, then, keeps the world of appearance as its friend and ally while quietly resisting its attempts to seduce and divert it.

An inescapable desire to find coherence between the moral and the intellectual, the practical and the theoretical, the human and the divine, thus keeps alive a philosophical disposition. Philosophy insists on the evidential appeal of its dialectical discoveries. Yet, according to Aristotle, being unable to resolve completely the dissonance between the human and the divine does not discourage the genuinely philosophical human being; in fact, it assures that the divine is still in sight, that the philosophizing continues.

PRIVACY

In Book X, chapters 7 and 8, of the *Nicomachean Ethics*, Aristotle makes clear, with liberal use of superlatives, the exceptional nature of the philosopher. The philosopher exercises the highest (*kratistēn*) (1177a13, 19–20, 1177b34, 1178a5–6), divinist (*theiotaton*) (1177a16), and best (*aristǭ*) (1179a26) virtue, and in doing so engages in the most continuous (*sunechestatē*) (1177a21–22) and most pleasant

---

theological reasons which would have obliged him to accept these complications which are necessarily connected with the thesis of omniscience" ("Aristotle on Self-Knowledge," 503).

(*hēdistē*) (1177a23, 1178a6) activity; of all human beings, he is the most self-sufficient (*autarkestatos*) (1177b1), the happiest (*eudaimonestatos*) (1178b23, 1179a31, 1177a6), and the most beloved by the gods (*theophilestatos*) (1179a30, 1178b22). In fact, the philosopher strives to attain immortality (*athanatizein*) (1177b33). This all corroborates the earlier finding that a philosopher does not need or want to associate with any human beings except the philosophical. Aristotle makes the similar observation in Book IX that the good man (philosophical and otherwise) not only does not mind being alone but enjoys it, at least in part because it offers an opportunity for reflection (1166a23–27); Aristotle also indicates in the *Politics* that a good man knows how to be a private individual (*idiōtēs*) (1277a24–25).

One thus wonders why Aristotle places his discussion of the philosopher in a section of the *Nicomachean Ethics* that serves as a transition to the *Politics*. Could it be that the philosopher represents—by his excellence, self-sufficiency, and solitude—the epitome of privacy, and that cities should not forget to provide for privacy? Privacy, being a moral, philosophical, and political good, provides a thematic link between ethics and politics narrowly understood. The good man enjoys it, the philosopher requires it, and the political order must provide it to cultivate not only diversity, a requirement of political unity (*Pol* 1261a23–30), but diversified excellence, a requirement of the best political order (*Pol* 1332a29–38, *NE* 1176b26–28).[22] Mastering the violin, understanding a mathematical proof, running a marathon, and composing a poem may each conceivably be done in the company of others, but they do not require an audience and are not collective enterprises. Aristotle would disagree with Arendt that "neither education nor ingenuity nor talent can replace the constituent elements of the public realm, which makes it the proper place for human excellence." He would thus be surprised to find himself implicated as an advocate of this view:

Excellence itself, *aretē* as the Greeks, *virtus* as the Romans would have called it, has always been assigned to the public realm where

---

[22] Thus Aristotle is, if anything, reacting against, not endorsing, the alleged view of his contemporaries and Homer that "the public realm . . . was reserved for individuality"; see Hannah Arendt, *The Human Condition* (Chicago: University of Chicago Press, 1958), 41.

one could excel, could distinguish oneself from all others. Every activity performed in public can attain an excellence never matched in privacy; for excellence, by definition, the presence of others is always required, and this presence needs the formality of the public, constituted by one's peers, it cannot be the casual, familiar presence of one's equals or inferiors.[23]

In sum, Aristotle makes clear that human beings are not simply political animals (in the sense of inclined toward others) but, insofar as they have a divine element in them, also intensely private beings. "Happiness extends just so far as contemplation does" (*NE* 1178b28–29). Of course, "the happy person is a human being, and so will need external prosperity also"—that is, "bodily health, food, and [human] attention [*tēn loipēn therapeian*]" (1178b33–35). Nature compels the philosophical and all those who aspire to happiness to use the resources of both the public and the private. But in contrast to the noble citizen or ruler, who draws on the private to serve the public, the philosopher draws on the public to serve the private.

[23] Ibid., 48–49.

CONCLUSION

I begin this book by suggesting that proponents of liberalism should pay attention to Aristotle's political philosophy because it defends privacy as vigorously as liberalism, but better. Liberalism, by conceiving privacy as a set of rights forming a protective bubble around every individual, enabling them to do whatever they like within it, justifies privacy only from the point of view of the individual, not from that of the public. Moreover, it is questionable whether this justification is in the interest of the individual. Aristotle offers a corrective to liberalism's conception of privacy in that he conceives the private to be virtuous activities that discount popular opinion; the private thus benefits the individual and, thereby, the public.

In Aristotle's account, privacy is not a right to do as one pleases but an opportunity to do as one ought. In private one can cultivate virtues one cannot in public, because the private offers activities the public cannot. Raising a family, for example, gives adults opportunity to practice temperance and judgment and children opportunity to develop moral virtues. Economic transaction calls for self-restraint and reciprocity and thereby teaches the inevitability of self-interestedness and the meaning of distributive justice. Genuine friendship challenges human beings even more by expecting the exercise of full moral virtue over time. Engaging in the liberal arts fosters directly or inspires through reflection dispositions and conduct such as moderation, trustworthiness, prudence, justness, and nobility. At the same time, the liberal arts induce appreciation for activities having no end beyond themselves, and thus for philosophy. Finally, philosophy itself demands supreme virtue.

Aiming at excellence, private activity cannot accommodate prevailing values (except in the best regime). This is in fact fortunate from the point of view of the regime; by resisting what is merely fashionable or politically necessary, private activity embodies a standard of excellence that political activity can aspire to uphold. But just as the public cannot flourish without the private, so the private needs the public. There is a natural reciprocity between public and private, just as there is a natural ruling relation among all things (*Pol* 1254a32–33). Hence a human being trying to live a wholly private life, as much as a city trying to be wholly public, will not succeed. The public and the private are like a man and a woman insofar as the self-sufficiency of each presupposes the other. That one is superior is, then, not clear in either relation. Yet, insofar as a regime cannot aspire to excellence without the insights only philosophy can yield, Aristotle may be intimating that the private should prevail. At the same time, he reminds us that philosophy's predominance can occur only in a regime in which all members are sympathetic to it. Ordinarily, then, a regime should seek not the supremacy of the private but a dynamic equilibrium between public and private. And as with a relationship between a man and a woman, there is no formula for achieving such equilibrium. In both cases, nature supplies only obscure guidelines, leaving us to figure out how to achieve harmony.

If Aristotle lived in the twentieth-century Western world, he might agree with communitarian critics that disequilibrium between the public and the private exists. But he would attribute this not to citizens retreating to private life but to their reserving it largely for letting go of virtue. As a consequence of their using the private in this way, the private has little to offer the public. Moreover, Aristotle would perhaps point out that the unpreparedness of people today to engage properly in private activity is in part the result of laws and educational institutions failing to encourage the proper use of privacy.

What then is the solution to this predicament? Aristotle directs his most significant advice on the achievement of harmony between the public and the private to the individual, exhorting one to recognize and pursue the vast opportunities the private offers for cultivating virtue and to draw support from public life selectively. One should eschew practices, customs, opinions, trends, and relationships that handicap the furtherance of one's own virtues and accept or undertake those that foster them.

Dynamic harmony between the public and the private results, according to Aristotle, when individuals make the whole excellent by each of them being excellent (*Pol* 1332a30–38). Individual excellence entails envisioning a perfectly harmonious complete life, for it is only after a person has lived that the life can be judged a happy one (*NE* 1098a18–20, 1100a35–b3)—that is, one lived knowing how to be private. Nonetheless, the public can facilitate the virtue of citizens and thereby help to bring about harmony between the public and the private. The main task of laws, schools, and office holders in this respect is to help individuals appreciate that their private conduct bears heavily on that harmony and thereby on the health of the political order. But the public can foster such harmony more directly by introducing or increasing 'aristocratic' provisions—procedures, policies, institutions, and practices that encourage virtue, what we sometimes call talent or expertise but which is not quite captured by these terms.

From Aristotle's work several such measures may be inferred. They pertain on the one hand to citizens and on the other to rulers, and they either mandate or encourage the upholding of certain standards. Aristotle would, for example, encourage government to promote the liberal arts through education, perhaps by even requiring some proportion of schools to adopt liberal arts curricula, and by sponsoring culture—libraries, museums, and theater—with the understanding that the liberal arts by definition maintain their own standards. Aristotle would also recommend discouraging or prohibiting activities that impede the exercise of virtue on the part of the agent and diminish the prospect of others around the agent practicing virtue; this calls for rethinking the notion of self-regarding and other-regarding activities that shapes civil and criminal law in contemporary liberal societies. He would counsel societies to adopt or increase electoral and political appointing processes, for such processes entail evaluating candidates. Here education directly serves the community. Accordingly, he would recommend establishing educational requirements for political office.

In this way, societies could protect their electorate from being seduced by those whose only qualification to rule is a professed love for the people or country.[1]

Moving regimes in the direction of aristocracy would help to establish a proper equilibrium between public and private because those empowered, having become so by way of their own efforts, would understand the importance of private initiative to human happiness and to the well-being of the whole. Seeing the many ways private endeavor could contribute to the whole, they would promote in their regimes both opportunities and rewards for private endeavor.

In this bias- and discrimination-conscious time, it should be noted that Aristotle's political proposals do not encourage the political domination of a particular socioeconomic class, as he is often charged with doing. He makes clear that there is a difference between oligarchy and aristocracy: "The only regime that can be justly called an aristocracy is one where the members are the best simply on the basis of virtue, not good in relation to some supposed standard" (*Pol* 1293b3–5). He goes on to say that any regime that elects people to office on the basis of desert, whether or not it also establishes other qualifications for office, is aristocratic (1293b10–21, 1273a41–b1); nonetheless, kinds of regime that establish other qualifications fall short of "the true and first form" of aristocracy (1294a24–25), his political standard (1273a31–32, 1293b18–19). As individuals should envision perfection, so should a regime. Aristotle wants, then, to promote genuine moral and intellectual virtue and is fully cognizant of the hazards of establishing only qualifications of birth and wealth for political office. Indeed, his recognition of the insufficiency of these for meriting political office is one of the reasons he endorses publicly supported education and political offices in circumstances in which the virtuous are not well off (1273a32–39).

But why should we think that contemporary liberal societies might be willing and able to assimilate Aristotle's proposals? They might be willing because the proposals maintain the sanctity of privacy. They should be able because Aristotle directs his proposals

---

[1] See Socrates' description of the demagogue (Plato, *Republic*, 558c).

to "middling regimes," what liberal societies are;[2] although he derives his precepts from "the regime that one would pray for," he tailors them so that they do not require special advantages for their fulfillment (*Pol* 1328a35–41, 1295a25–40).[3] Insofar as Aristotle's political objective is to bring about polities that border on aristocracies, and not aristocracies, his political advice is apt for contemporary liberal societies.

[2] As Pierre Pellegrin explains, "a *middling constitution* . . . [is one] that does not institutionalize the domination without recourse of one group of citizens over another"; see "La 'Politique' d'Aristote: Unité et fractures éloge de la lecture sommaire," *Revue Philosophique de la France et de L'étranger* 177, no. 2 (1987), 141.

[3] See the Appendix, "The Composition of Aristotle's *Politics*," pp. 221–26.

Appendix

Premises of Interpretation

The question of Aristotle's teaching on privacy or freedom continues to engage the attention of scholars and to call for a return to the texts. Investigation of the problem is heavily affected by the premises or principles of interpretation assumed or adopted by the interpreter. For example, as is well known, Werner Jaeger and his followers insist on a developmental or genetic interpretation that presents a young Aristotle whose views on certain subjects are generally Platonic and a mature Aristotle whose thoughts are original.[1] By this account, the critical distinction is the one between the stages in Aristotle's understanding. My own study attempts to show that the most important difference is the one between the Aristotle of the common conception, which sees him as time- and culture-bound and thus thoroughly backward or reactionary, and the Aristotle whose point of orientation is the meaning and possibility of human goodness in and out of political society.[2] On this very point there is also scholarly debate. Aristotle's relation to Platonism implicates the issue of Aristotle's idealism or utopianism

[1] Werner Jaeger, *Aristotle: Fundamentals of the History of His Development*, 2d. ed., trans. Richard Robinson (Oxford: Clarendon, 1948).
[2] This is not to say that Aristotle's relation to his culture ought to be dismissed, as this book tries to show, but rather that we must rely on Aristotle to prompt our interest in investigating aspects of his times and cannot assume that he unreflectively assimilated prevailing ideas.

(his position, for example, on the distinction between the best and the best possible or second-best regimes) as well as his understanding of privacy. In the present discussion I attempt to address some of the general issues raised by interpretations that regard Aristotle as essentially a product of his times or of his teacher or of both.

Among those who insist that Aristotle's texts cannot be understood without an appreciation of the culture in which he lived is A. W. H. Adkins. According to him, for example, the *Nicomachean Ethics* and the *Politics* can be properly understood only if they are read together because the former concerns excellence (*aretē*) and the latter describes the socially determined tasks (*erga*) to which excellences are *always* relative. The *Politics* gives excellence, which is devoid of "moral content" in the *Nicomachean Ethics*, further definition by linking it "with the different roles of different citizens in the polis." Furthermore, according to Adkins, Aristotle appeals to the "virtues recognized by . . . his audience"—to their view of excellence "in politics and ordinary life." Accordingly, "excellence" in Aristotle's works always means excellence at a task or job that contributes to successful living, or means successful living itself, and living successfully is having the *aretai* that Aristotle and his (adult Greek male) audience acknowledge as being most conducive to living successfully.[3]

There are at least two difficulties with Adkins's understanding of the two texts. For one, in arguing that Aristotle endorses ancient Greek values Adkins ignores the plethora of instances in both texts in which Aristotle explicitly criticizes common opinion or practices. Adkins contends, for example, that a good man according to Aristotle is a "good Greek male citizen"—one who rules, deliberates, and defends his city. But the distinction between the good man and the good citizen implies that no society alone determines the nature of the good man. Even if one rejects with Adkins that metaphysical biology informs human *erga* and thus sees the good man as simply a product of the best regime, the centrality of leisure to the best regime and the difficulty of a human being combining, even seriatum, a politically active way of life with a philosophical one, suggest that the philosophical life is an alternative to active citizenship. Indeed, as Adkins admits, only by setting *theōria* on

---

[3] "The Connection between Aristotle's *Ethics* and *Politics*," *Political Theory* 12, no. 1 (1984), 33–47.

one side can one conclude that the definition of the good man derives "from Greek political practice from Homer onwards."[4]

Aristotle not only promotes the activity of philosophy but also teaches about the relation between politics and philosophy, or that between the practical and the theoretical. Thus, although, as Adkins claims, both the *Nicomachean Ethics* and the *Politics* aim to develop the practical *aretai*, the works convey a theoretical teaching as well.[5]

Like Adkins, Richard Bodéüs argues that both works are fundamentally practical in their intent. Unlike Adkins, however, Bodéüs does not maintain that Aristotle is presenting a merely logical or formal account of human excellence; rather, he maintains that in the *Nicomachean Ethics* Aristotle explains what ethical conduct or complete virtue is and in the *Politics* explains how to cultivate it in a populace. Both works, then, are addressed to the legislator, who cannot know what sorts of law to establish without understanding what they should accomplish.[6] Bodéüs is arguing against the view, held by Eric Voegelin, René-Antoine Gauthier, and Jean Yves Jolif, for example, that the *Nicomachean Ethics* expounds "an autonomous moral science" that articulates "the wisdom of the excellences independent of the problem of its political actualization."[7] Attributing an essential Platonism to Aristotle, he argues that "man's excellence, in Aristotle's eyes, can be realized effectively only under the aegis of the right coercive norms, that is of just laws. . . . most of the moral virtues analyzed by Aristo-

---

[4] Ibid., 41–44, quoting from 44.

[5] Ibid., 30–31. This is also Carnes Lord's claim: "Aristotle's enterprise is not so much 'political philosophy' as it is 'political science' in its original sense—the practical 'art' (*technē*) or expertise of the statesman or legislator"; see "The Character and Composition of Aristotle's *Politics*," *Political Theory* 9, no. 4 (1981), 463. See also Leo Strauss, *The City and Man* (Chicago: University of Chicago Press, 1964), 12–29.

[6] Bodéüs, *Le philosophe et la cité: Recherches sur les rapports entre morale et politique dans la pensée d'Aristote* (Paris: Société d'Édition "Les Belles Lettres," 1982), 16, 47–51, 57–59, 77, 92, 96, 135. Pierre Pellegrin endorses Bodéüs's "ends-means" explanation of the relations between Aristotle's ethical and political works and agrees that what unifies the *Politics*, especially Books IV–VIII, is its practical nature; see "La 'Politique' d'Aristote: Unité et fractures éloge de la lecture sommaire," *Revue Philosophique de la France et de L'étranger* 177, no. 2 (1987), 143, 158.

[7] Bodéüs, *Le philosophe et la cité*, 85; Eric Voegelin, *Plato and Aristotle*, vol. 3, *Order and History* (Baton Rouge: Louisiana State University Press, 1957), 303; René-Antoine Gauthier and Jean Yves Jolif, *L'éthique à Nicomaque: Introduction, traduction, et commentaire*, 2d. ed., vol. 2 (Louvain: Publications Universitaires, 1970), 89–168; P. A. Vander Waerdt, "The Political Intention of Aristotle's Moral Philosophy," *Ancient Philosophy* 5, no. 1 (1985), 77.

tle . . . suppose an organization of the life in common according to precise rules."⁸ Bodéüs's argument derives from the correct premise that, according to Aristotle, one does not possess complete knowledge of the virtues unless one understands how to actualize them.

In support of his argument, Bodéüs points out that at the end of the *Nicomachean Ethics* (1181b12–15) Aristotle is saying that the "philosophy of human affairs" is not lacking ideas for or conceptions of the perfect regime (previous generations have supplied these) but recommendations for implementing these ideas. Aristotle announces that what remains for him to do is to explain how to put these ideas into practice—to explain how to legislate what has already been discovered.⁹

The main difficulty with Bodéüs's "ends-means model" of the relation between the two texts is its assumption that, if legislators know what a virtuous human being is or what the best way of life is for an individual, then they have the basis for bringing about a virtuous city or the best way of life for the whole. This presupposition is unwarranted because, as P. A. Vander Waerdt points out, "if the city is capable only of an analogue of the highest activity of the individual *(philosophia theōrētikē)*, then the best way of life for the city and individual will diverge, and even in the case of the best regime the statesman will not simply attempt to establish the best way of life for the individual." More precisely, "the philosophy to which the best regime devotes itself is not theoretical contemplation but rather the leisured culture which constitutes the closest approximation to the philosophical life possible on the level of politics." In brief, Vander Waerdt explains, Bodéüs consistently disregards "the tension between the city and man which necessarily arises from the fact that man's highest end and perfection lies in the non- or trans-political activity of theoretical contemplation."¹⁰

⁸ *Le philosophe et la cité,* 85–86.
⁹ Ibid., 152–54.
¹⁰ "Political Intention," 84–85. Vander Waerdt cites Carnes Lord, "Politics and Philosophy in Aristotle's *Politics," Hermes* 106: 336–57, and refers the reader to Strauss, *City and Man,* 25–29, 49. A second criticism of Bodéüs by Vander Waerdt is that, since the natural character of citizen bodies varies, the legislator would need knowledge of the best way of life not only for those capable of complete virtue but also for those incapable or less capable of complete virtue. Thus, Vander Waerdt remarks, "in the case of inferior regimes . . . the question of how the statesman will employ his knowledge of the ethical writings is even more complex" ("Political

Moreover, "if it be true that the best way of life possible for the city and individual diverge, it is difficult to resist the conclusion that each of the components of political science—practical wisdom, economics, and political science—is partially autonomous or sovereign in its own sphere." Bodéüs, Vander Waerdt continues, fails "to explain why Aristotle had to treat the individual, the household and the city independently of and in partial abstraction from one another."[11] Vander Waerdt's implied answer is that Aristotle does so to persuade us that the actualization of virtue is not simply dependent on the right coercive norms, just laws, or precise rules. Virtue may flourish between friends or in the household, for example. Vander Waerdt seems to be saying that Aristotle recognizes that the various entities on the public-private spectrum—the individual, the household, the economy, the laws—can sustain different kinds and levels of virtue. Legislators should not expect, then, to cultivate the same amount and kind of virtue in all entities on all points of the spectrum.

In addition to overlooking Aristotle's recognition of private activities and the respective virtue they can sustain, Bodéüs's account of Aristotle's political science fails, like Adkins's, to acknowledge its theoretical dimension.[12] Political science requires more than knowledge of how to rehabilitate individuals. A legislator should know, not only what virtue consists of and how to cultivate it, but something about the relation between *praxis* and *theōria*, between the realm of justice and the realm beyond justice, or between convention and nature—the concerns of political philosophy. The legislator does not need to be able to perceive what nature intimates but should understand that it circumscribes the general character

---

Intention," 84; see also 87). It should be acknowledged, however, that although the *Nicomachean Ethics* does not provide complete knowledge of the characters of inferior human beings it does not neglect them altogether: Aristotle notes the difference between the virtues of a slave and a master, speaks of various kinds of friendship, and indicates that all other human beings are inferior to philosophers (1161a24–b8; VIII–X). He thus provides legislators with some insight into the kinds of people they will most likely legislate for.

[11] "Political Intention," 85.

[12] Carnes Lord does acknowledge it: "Aristotelian practical science indeed appears to renounce the search for the principles of moral and political phenomena . . . yet the possibility of an adequate theoretical account of those principles is nowhere explicitly denied, and to some degree seems taken for granted" ("Character and Composition," 463).

of the good life.[13] Such understanding inclines him to heed the wisdom of those who grasp nature's dictates and consequently to transform, by way of prudence, this wisdom about nature's dictates into legislation. Or, similarly, Vander Waerdt explains, "knowledge of the theoretical sciences, although an end *kat'hauto*, may be useful *kata sumbebēkos* . . . and . . . one of the tasks of the statesman is to be a good judge of when *theōria* is relevant, i.e., of when it is useful *kata sumbebēkos* and when not ([*EE*] 1216b35–1217a7). So even if Bodéüs is correct in holding that the purpose of political science is solely practical . . . theoretical philosophy must play an integral role in the statesman's education."[14]

With a view to clarifying further the premises of my study, a consideration of Manfred Riedel's arguments may be helpful. According to Riedel, political philosophy for Aristotle is characterized by the quest not for natural right[15] but for the requirements of the possibility of rational action and speech—for *koinōnia* itself. In other words, political philosophy seeks to perceive that condition that is conducive to, or necessarily gives rise to, living well—namely, the confluence of *praxis* and *logos*. Or, to use Riedel's Heideggerian illustration, a political philosopher seeks to understand the merging or focalization of historical occurrence and Being, which is the polis itself. The polis is the institutionalization of *koinōnia*, the interchange of language and activity within the right order of communal life. A political philosopher, then, seeks the paradigm that embodies *koinōnia*, a certain kind of communal life. According to Riedel, the *Nicomachean Ethics* and the *Politics* describe this paradigm.[16]

Riedel's view mischaracterizes Aristotle's project in that it fails to appreciate the private dimensions of the polis. Riedel, much like Hannah Arendt, seems to think that Aristotle believes that human beings fulfill themselves qua human beings only by way of speech and rational action and thus that a political philosopher seeks the conditions most conducive to them. But, as this study attempts to

[13] See Leo Strauss, *Natural Right and History* (Chicago: University of Chicago Press, 1953), 127.

[14] "Political Intention," 86.

[15] Strauss maintains it is in *Natural Right*, 156–63.

[16] *Metaphysik und Metapolitik: Studien zu Aristoteles und zur politischen Sprache der neuzeitlichen Philosophie* (Frankfurt am Main: Suhrkamp Verlag, 1975), 37, 90.

show, Aristotle indicates that the most fulfilling activity is contemplation and thus implies that a philosopher seeks the political
conditions that are most advantageous to the preservation and
practice of contemplation. A philosopher seeks, then, to discover
the dynamic equilibrium between public and private, which, because it preserves the quest for natural right, is necessarily an
aspect of natural right.

Joachim Ritter offers yet another characterization of Aristotelian
political philosophy. In Ritter's understanding, Aristotle is saying
that the distinctively human activity is contemplation of the divine
order—but divine order that is to be found not in another world
but in this one. Thinking must take place in the context of society
and its practices. Indeed, theoretical wisdom presupposes human
praxis: "Knowledge of practice and of ordinary life" renders accessible the theory of the divine order because "the object to which
theory is devoted is already present in the knowledge appertaining
to the life fulfillment of all men." In other words, "free theoretical
cognition elicits and frees knowledge from the world, knowledge
which is already included in and present in all practical and poet-
ical knowledge."[17] On this account, a true understanding of the
world requires seeing, not only the divine order, but necessarily
the divine order as it is lodged in or emanates from *praxis.* Ritter
further explains that

> the object which theology has always contemplated and referred
> to is the divine as the totality of the world system present in all
> that is. This "totality" as the all-encompassing and controlling is
> called "being" in philosophy. Thus, "theory concerns being."
> (Met. XII, 1.1069a18: *peri tēs ousias hē theōria.*) However, while
> theory becomes science [in the broadest sense of organized
> knowledge], it applies itself to "being," to the extent that being is
> present in things which, in their causes and reasons, are part of
> practical existence. The theory of "being" becomes science, in that
> it becomes a theory of "the things which are" (*ta onta*). However,
> the 'things which are' are the very things whose "reasons and
> causes" the formation of the active life of individuals and society
> develops and knows.[18]

---

[17] Joachim Ritter, *Metaphysik und Politik: Studien zu Aristoteles und Hegel* (Frankfurt
am Main: Suhrkamp Verlag, 1969), 28.
[18] Ibid., 28–29.

If theory concerns being, and being lies within the causal structure of practical existence and must therefore be gained access to through that existence, then one cannot philosophize apart from that existence. Further, since *praxis* occurs by definition at a particular time and place, the activity of philosophy can never be, according to Ritter's account, historically neutralized. To neutralize historically the activity of philosophy—to abstract it from its historical setting—is in Ritter's view to Platonize it.[19] This seems to imply, in turn, that we should not abstract Aristotle's political philosophy from its historical setting—that to grasp Aristotle's account of the divine order we need to appreciate or have knowledge of the *praxis* through which he gained access to it. Yet, Ritter claims that we (presumably the modern democratic West) have inherited the political structures of Aristotle's time, and because we have we can gain access to or understand Aristotle's thought. If we did not have this political inheritance, then we could not understand Aristotle.

Ritter is not arguing, as Adkins does, that knowledge of the values, attitudes, and practices of fourth-century Greece is essential for understanding Aristotle's texts. His view does imply, however, that our intellectual link to Aristotle is historical, which suggests that it is fragile and precarious. Should human beings someday be robbed of the Western political legacy, their minds would in turn be robbed of their potential to understand Aristotle. Ritter would perhaps reply that humanity is not at risk of being severed from Aristotle because reason will continue to preserve throughout history the political structures through which it manifests itself. This Hegelian account nonetheless leaves our historical context as the medium through which we can grasp Aristotle's thoughts.

Ritter's understanding of Aristotle's notion of philosophy is correct insofar as Aristotle does indicate throughout his texts that the divine order manifests itself in the world—in nature and thus in human beings. But contrary to Ritter's view, Aristotle does not say or imply that theoretical wisdom presupposes *praxis*.[20] Thought

[19] Ibid., 106, 109.
[20] Amélie Rorty offers an interpretation of Aristotle's idea of contemplation similar to Ritter's in "The Place of Contemplation in Aristotle's *Nicomachean Ethics*," in *Essays on Aristotle's Ethics*, ed. Amélie Oksenberg Rorty (Berkeley: University of California Press, 1980), 377–94.

thinks itself; *nous* does not require a medium through which to grasp the divine. It is the nature of (divine) truth that it does not need to be mediated. It follows that Aristotle's teachings do not depend for their transmission on a historical medium. They depend primarily on his written words and secondarily on an understanding of the aspects of his intellectual heritage to which his texts explicitly or implicitly refer.

According to Günther Bien, we should read Aristotle neither for historically independent teachings nor (as Arendt, for example, tends to do) for historical truths; for, in the first place, Aristotle is a representative of the Hellenistic tradition and, in the second place, he is a critic of that tradition. His texts do not reveal unaided the truth of his own time. Thus, Bien concludes, Aristotle's texts are valuable for their contributions to and place in intellectual history—more specifically, valuable insofar as they illuminate through intellectual criticism ancient Greek schools of thought and thereby the foundation of the European tradition of practical or political philosophy.[21]

Bien's main interpretive premise is that we can understand Aristotle's texts best if we understand his motive for writing them and can understand his motive only if we understand his intellectual heritage, "his own presuppositions which have now become foreign." Bien reminds us that "through every philosophical writing, there is a certain polemical thread, even when it is only barely evident. The one who does philosophy is not one with the conceptualizations of his predecessors and contemporaries." He goes on to explain that, just as the dialogues of Plato are directed against the poets (as H. G. Gadamer argues), so we should understand Aristotle's thought to reflect "a critical-polemical" relationship with Plato.[22] But, although Bien is correct to maintain that appreciation of Aristotle presupposes an understanding of the critical nature of philosophy and that Plato is among those Aristotle criticizes, two points should be kept in mind. First, one should recognize and keep in view the 'Plato' that Aristotle is from time to time criticizing. In the second book of the *Politics*, for example, Aristotle is evidently attacking the common interpretation or overt teachings of Plato's *Republic*. More precisely, he is criticizing the "city in speech" that Socrates builds with the other interlocutors; but, one should realize, Plato too criticizes (via the dialogue and dramatic action) this communal city (indeed, the conversation reveals that it contains the seed of its own destruction). Plato, like Aristotle, suggests that this city is mostly absurd. Why then does Aristotle bother to attack it? Perhaps lest readers miss Socrates' often ironic critique—lest they fail to see the absurdities of the city. When Aristotle criticizes Plato, he does not, then, as Pierre Pellegrin claims, "most often miss Plato's point";[23] rather, he is criticizing the surface or exoteric Plato, using Platonic imagery or Socratic statements as a straw man.[24]

Second, even though Aristotle may at other times criticize the esoteric Plato (for example, his explicit critique of the Idea of the Good and the Forms in the *Eudemian* and *Nicomachean Ethics;* his implicit critique in the *Politics* of the philosopher-king), it would be mistaken to assume with Bien and Jaeger that entire works of Aristotle are directed against Plato or that Aristotle's perspective is best understood as primarily a reaction against Plato—to assume, in other words, that Aristotle fails to go beyond merely writing against another argument. As Bodéüs explains, for example, when Aristotle announces his intention at the end of the *Nicomachean Ethics* to investigate legislation, he is not disavowing Plato's *Laws,* as Jaeger claims, but proposing to go beyond the work his predecessors have accomplished, to investigate what has not been investigated.[25]

THE COMPOSITION OF THE *POLITICS*

Carnes Lord begins his article "The Character and Composition of Aristotle's *Politics*," by lamenting that scholarly discussions of the "literary character" of the *Politics* "too frequently lack opera-

---

[23] *Aristotle's Classification of Animals: Biology and the Conceptual Unity of the Aristotelian Corpus,* trans. Anthony Preus (Berkeley: University of California Press, 1986), 40.

[24] Arlene W. Saxonhouse characterizes Aristotle's treatment of Socrates' statements in this way; see "Family, Polity, and Unity: Aristotle on Socrates' Community of Wives," *Polity* 15, no. 2 (1982), 205.

[25] Bodéüs, *Le philosophe et la cité,* 152–54, 136–37.

tional significance for the interpretive effort." Yet, as Lord notes, the problem of the literary character and composition of the *Politics* is "an area where all is hypothesis."[26] There is an interpretive risk, which others may recognize, in bringing a hypothesis regarding the character and composition of the *Politics* to bear on its interpretation: a temptation arises to make the text support the hypothesis. Pierre Pellegrin, for one, cautions against succumbing to this temptation: although it is perfectly legitimate, he says, to have the conviction that a certain order of the books of the *Politics*, the traditional one, for example, makes sense, one should not regard this order as a hypothesis or a proposition capable of sustaining or holding up an interpretation. One can end up, but not begin, with a thesis about the order of the books.[27] In other words, as Lord states, "an interpretation of the *Politics* . . . must depend importantly on the interpreter's view of the kind of work it is and the audience for which it was composed," but the interpreter must arrive at an understanding of the character of the *Politics* "only by a comprehensive interpretation of the work as a whole."[28] Any claims about the character and order of the books of the *Politics* should be ventured on the basis of and substantiated by an analysis of its content.

Accordingly, the thesis of this book does not emerge from but is fortified or complemented by a hypothesis as to its composition which grew out of investigation of my thesis on privacy. My hypothesis regarding the composition of the *Politics* is unorthodox and has not, as far as I know, been previously proposed. It challenges "the old view that Books VII and VIII have been displaced from their proper position and belong between Books III and IV"[29] and the *reasons* given for the more recent Jaegerian view that the books are in their proper order as they have come down to us. According to Jaeger, Aristotle inserted Books IV–VI between Books III and VII to correct or mitigate the Platonic idealism of the flanking books (I–III and VII–VIII), which he had written earlier.[30]

It is plausible, I contend, to attribute to Aristotle the present order of the books, but not on the grounds of an alleged intellec-

<hr/>

[26] "Character and Composition," 459, 460.
[27] "La 'Politique' d'Aristote," 133.
[28] "Character and Composition," 459, 469.
[29] Ibid., 460.
[30] *Aristotle*, 263–75.

tual development; rather, the books as they are ordered present a logical sequence of ideas. Books I–III concern two broad themes: the naturalness of the city, and the moral significance of the household. Within each of these themes are two subtopics. In discussing the naturalness of the city, Aristotle notes (a) the naturalness of ruling—that it is advantageous and good to rule and be ruled (Book I)—and (b) the difference between conventional or citizen virtue and full virtue (Book III). In discussing the household, he makes clear that (a) private relationships and (b) private things are essential for the cultivation of virtue or moral well-being. Although I do not dispute the general view that Books I–III cohere with Books VII and VIII in that they describe features of the best regime, I think that they are placed where they are, and apart from Books VII and VIII, because they are features not only of the best regime but *also* of the best possible or second-best regime and of the lesser regimes described in the middle books.

In other words, in Books I–III Aristotle is arguing that both ruling and the household are essential features of any regime (they must be preserved for a regime to be viable) and that the good or correct forms of ruling and the household can be maintained within a less than ideal regime. In cases where the same cannot always rule—the ideal—there can be "at least an imitation of this" (*Pol* 1261a38–b4). And even tyranny is not wholly bad (*Pol* 1315b4–10, V.11). Further, Aristotle's discussion of the good household in Books I and II serves to explain his claim in the *Nicomachean Ethics* that individuals may cultivate moral virtue independently of the regime in which they live.[31]

Books I–III, then, are introducing neither "a general theory of the state" (as Jaeger claims Book I is) nor "an ideal state" (as Jaeger claims Books II and III are) but essential and ideal features of all regimes.[32] That Books I–III recommend provisions for both the second-best and the best regimes is one of the reasons the line between the two kinds of regime is not as distinct as Jaeger and others claim. A second reason is that Aristotle is teaching legisla-

---

[31] As Vander Waerdt remarks, "there is no suggestion in *EN* x 9 that a father who lives in an inferior regime should educate his children in accordance with its inferior ends" ("Political Intention," 87).

[32] Jaeger; *Aristotle*, 267, 273; that is, Aristotle is introducing ruling and the household as necessary features of all regimes but at the same time promoting correct forms of rule and the best household.

tors in the middle books not only to preserve the regime they have at hand but to better it (in ways besides preserving households and ruling). As Vander Waerdt explains,

> the statesman will be guided by the double teleology which underlies the program of political science announced in iv 1: his minimal aim will be the regime's preservation, but his higher aim will be to turn it toward the good life and *eudaimonia,* so much as circumstances permit. . . . the purpose of the statesman's architectonic science is not merely to legislate in the interest of the regime in force, as Bodéüs concludes, but to foster the good life and *eudaimonia* for others as far as possible through political virtue.[33]

To summarize with Harry V. Jaffa, it might be said that the line between the best and the lesser regimes is blurred because "the best regime is the implicit subject of every book."[34]

Pierre Pellegrin is, then, correct to argue that Aristotle intends his unqualifiedly best regime to be neither purely speculative nor a blueprint for all regimes. More precisely, Pellegrin goes on to say, Aristotle is advocating that legislators transform all regimes into the best regime (*l'aristè politeia*) but at the same time suggesting that the best constitution can take many forms. The absolutely best regime, the city "one would pray for," can arise only if the proper equipment (*chorēgias*) is available (*Pol* 1325b37). But this regime is only one of Aristotle's four best regimes, according to Pellegrin. Aristotle is arguing that, where the proper material or equipment does not exist, legislators should aim to bring about the best regime possible given the circumstances. Pellegrin describes the three general ways legislators can bring about the best regime according to

---

[33] "Political Intention," 87–88.

[34] Jaffa goes on to explain that "in Book I, the understanding of the generation of the *polis* implied an understanding of its perfection—*i.e.,* the best regime—because to understand the generation of anything that exists by nature means to understand the activity of that thing when it has attained its perfection. . . . Book II examined a number of regimes . . . and they were found wanting. But the principle in virtue of which Aristotle noted those deficiencies was the principle of the best regime. Book III culminated in the examination of the principal rival claims to supreme power in the *polis.* . . . The reconciliation of these claims . . . itself constituted the principle of the best regime. Books IV, V, and VI demonstrate the different manners in which this reconciliation or harmonization takes place when external conditions forbid its full implementation"; "Aristotle," in *History of Political Philosophy,* 2d ed., ed. Leo Strauss and Joseph Cropsey (Chicago: University of Chicago Press, 1972), 125–26.

Aristotle. Encountering a badly functioning regime, a legislator should change the constitutional form itself—not all at once to the absolutely best form, but to a better form; that is, the legislator should reform the regime, changing it piecemeal in the direction of the best to the extent that circumstances allow. In situations in which it is not possible or desirable to change the existing form, a legislator should (simply) improve it—either by replacing a deviant form with its corresponding correct form (oligarchy with aristocracy) or by better adapting the existing (correct) form to the circumstances (in effect replacing, for example, one kind of aristocracy with another). Still other circumstances may require a legislator to give power to and establish laws that benefit the middle class (*Pol* 1296b35–1297a13). Aristotle, Pellegrin correctly notes, is not here advising the legislator to transform the regime into a particular *kind* of regime; rather, he is giving the legislator "valuable principles for all the particular forms of constitution."[35]

Aristotle never says, according to Pellegrin, that legislators should rest content with less than perfect regimes. All legislators should know how to bring about the best form of regime that circumstances allow. This view makes evident that Aristotle as much as Plato is a partisan of the ideal regime. In short, Aristotle "assigns to the legislator only a single goal *in all possible situations:* the best constitution. . . . in each case there is only one form (kind?) of constitution that is 'naturally the best,' having taken into account the conditions." Therefore, Pellegrin reasons, in Books VII and VIII Aristotle does not present a particular form of regime but a perspective from which to judge all regimes. At the same time, Aristotle suggests or leaves open the possibility that the city that "one would pray for" could be endowed with or embodied by a specific form, "une constitution *déterminée.*"[36]

This very point seems, however, to undermine Pellegrin's thesis that Books IV–VIII are more unified than Books IV–VI on the one hand and Books VII–VIII on the other. Although it is true that Books IV–VIII are united by their intention to promote the best regime circumstances allow, including the best of circumstances (again, it seems that all of the books are so united), the observation that Books VII and VIII present not only a standard or vision for

[35] "La 'Politique' d'Aristote," 137–41.
[36] Ibid., 141–58.

other regimes but also the foundations for an actual regime indicates that they cannot be wholly integrated with, but—as Pellegrin says about Books I–III—should be annexed to, Books IV–VI.[37]

My view of the rationale behind the order of the books is, as noted earlier, supported substantially by the contents of the *Politics*. It is also, however, generally supported by the passage at the end of the *Nicomachean Ethics* which allegedly lays out the plan of the *Politics* (1181b12–21). In that passage Aristotle proposes that we (1) "in general study the question of the constitution" (the phenomenon of ruling and being ruled?) (Book I); (2) review what "has been said well in detail by earlier thinkers" (Book II); and (3) study what preserves and destroys cities in light of the constitutions we have collected, as well as what makes them ill or well administered (Books IV–VI); after studying these subjects, (4) "we shall perhaps be more likely to see with a comprehensive view, which constitution is best" (Books VII–VIII).[38]

The view that the order of the books is the original and intended order also has historical support: "Almost alone among the major works, the *Politics* is cited by name and assigned the correct number of books in all of the ancient lists. There is a strong presumption, therefore, that the *Politics* existed in something closely approaching its present form prior to the edition of Andronicus—indeed, in the lifetime of Aristotle himself."[39]

---

[37] Ibid., 155, 159.

[38] I am aware of the claim that this paragraph was not written by Aristotle and refers not to Aristotle's but to Theophrastus's *Politics*. As Lord acknowledges, there is evidence on both sides ("Character and Composition," 473).

[39] Ibid., 467; however, Lord goes on to argue that the traditional arrangement of the books resulted not from "the work of Aristotle" but from "a mechanical accident"; he maintains that "Books VII–VIII do indeed belong between Books III and IV" (470, 471).

Bibliography

Works by Aristotle

The "Art" of Rhetoric. Trans. John Henry Freese. Loeb Classical Library, 1926.

The Athenian Constitution. Trans. H. Rackham. Loeb Classical Library, 1952.

———. Trans. P. J. Rhodes. New York: Penguin Books, 1984.

Eudemian Ethics.Trans. H. Rackham. Loeb Classical Library, 1935.

Generation of Animals. Trans. A. L. Peck. Rev. ed. Loeb Classical Library, 1963.

Historia Animalium. Ed. Leonardus Dittmeyer. Leipzig: B. G. Teubner, 1907.

———. Trans. A. L. Peck. 3 vols. Loeb Classical Library, 1965.

Magna Moralia. Trans. G. Cyril Armstrong. Loeb Classical Library, 1935.

Metaphysics. Trans. Hugh Tredennick. 2 vols. Loeb Classical Library, 1933, 1935.

[Nicomachean Ethics]. L'éthique à Nicomaque: Introduction, traduction, et commentaire. Trans. René-Antoine Gauthier and Jean Yves Jolif. 2d ed. 2 vols. Louvain: Publications Universitaires, 1970.

Nicomachean Ethics. Trans. Terence Irwin. Indianapolis: Hackett, 1985.

———. Trans. H. Rackham. Rev. ed. Loeb Classical Library, 1934.

———. Trans. W. D. Ross. Oxford University Press, 1925? Rpt. in Introduction to Aristotle. Ed. Richard McKeon. New York: Modern Library, 1947.

———. Ed. Franciscus Susemihl. Leipzig: B. G. Teubner, 1903.

Oeconomica. Trans. G. Cyril Armstrong. Loeb Classical Library, 1935.

On the Soul. Trans. D. W. Hamlyn. Clarendon Aristotle Series, 1968. Sel.

rpt. in *A New Aristotle Reader*. Ed. J. L. Ackrill. Princeton: Princeton University Press, 1987.

——. Trans. W. S. Hett. Loeb Classical Library, 1935.

Parts of Animals. Trans. A. L. Peck. Loeb Classical Library, 1937.

Physics. Trans. P. H. Wicksteed and F. M. Cornford. 2 vols. Loeb Classical Library, 1957.

Politics. Trans. Ernest Barker. Oxford: Clarendon, 1968.

——. Ed. Alois Dreizehnter. Studia et Testimonia Antiqua VII. Munich: Wilhelm Fink Verlag, 1970.

——. Trans. Carnes Lord. Chicago: University of Chicago Press, 1984.

——. 4 vols. Ed. W. L. Newman. Oxford: Clarendon, 1887–1902. Rpt. Arno Press, 1973.

——. Trans. H. Rackham. Loeb Classical Library, 1944.

Topics. Ed. Maximilianus Wallies. Leipzig: B. G. Teubner, 1923.

——. Trans. W. A. Pickard-Cambridge, rev. J. Barnes. Revised Oxford Aristotle, 1984. Sel. rpt. in *A New Aristotle Reader*. Ed. J. L. Ackrill. Princeton: Princeton University Press, 1987.

SELECTED SECONDARY WORKS

Adkins, A. W. H. "The Connection between Aristotle's *Ethics* and *Politics*." *Political Theory* 12, no. 1 (1984): 29–49.

——. "*Theoria* versus *Praxis* in the *Nicomachean Ethics* and the *Republic*." *Classical Philology* 73, no. 4 (1978): 297–313.

Ambler, Wayne H. "Aristotle on Acquisition." *Canadian Journal of Political Science* 27, no. 3 (1984): 486–502.

——. "Aristotle on Nature and Politics: The Case of Slavery." *Political Theory* 15, no. 3 (1987): 390–410.

——. "Aristotle's Understanding of the Naturalness of the City." *The Review of Politics* 47, no. 2 (1985): 163–85.

Annas, Julia. "Plato and Aristotle on Friendship and Altruism." *Mind* 86, no. 344 (1977): 532–54.

Arendt, Hannah. *The Human Condition*. Chicago: University of Chicago Press, 1958.

Arnhart, Larry. *Aristotle on Political Reasoning: A Commentary on the "Rhetoric."* DeKalb: Northern Illinois University Press, 1981.

Barker, E. *The Political Thought of Plato and Aristotle*. New York: Dover, 1959.

Barnes, Jonathan. *Aristotle*. New York: Oxford University Press, 1982.

Beiner, Ronald. *Political Judgment*. Chicago: University of Chicago Press, 1983.

Bien, Günther. *Die Grundlegung der politischen Philosophie bei Aristoteles*. Frieburg/Munich: Verlag Karl Alber, 1973.

Bodéüs, Richard. "Notes sur quelques aspects de la conscience dans la pensée aristotélicienne." *Phronesis* 20, no. 1 (1975): 63–74.

———. *Le philosophe et la cité: Recherches sur les rapports entre morale et politique dans la pensée d'Aristote.* Paris: Société d'Édition "Les Belles Lettres," 1982.

Booth, William James. "The New Household Economy." *American Political Science Review* 85, no. 1 (1991): 59–75.

———. "Politics and the Household: A Commentary on Aristotle's *Politics* Book One." *History of Political Thought* 2, no. 2 (1981): 203–26.

Broadie, Sarah. *Ethics with Aristotle.* New York: Oxford University Press, 1991.

Brunschwig, Jacques. "Du mouvement et de l'immobilité de la loi." *Revue Internationale de Philosophie* 34, no. 133–34 (1980): 512–40.

Carter, L. B. *The Quiet Athenian.* Oxford: Clarendon, 1986.

Castoriadis, Cornelius. "From Marx to Aristotle, from Aristotle to Us." *Social Research* 45, no. 4 (1978): 667–738.

Clark, Stephen R. L. *Aristotle's Man: Speculations upon Aristotelian Anthropology.* Oxford: Clarendon, 1975.

———. "Aristotle's Woman." *History of Political Thought* 3, no. 2 (1982): 177–91.

Coby, Patrick. "Aristotle's Four Conceptions of Politics." *Western Political Quarterly* 39, no. 3 (1986): 480–503.

Cooper, John M. *Reason and Human Good in Aristotle.* Indianapolis: Hackett, 1986.

Cropsey, Joseph. "Justice and Friendship in the *Nicomachean Ethics.*" In *Political Philosophy and the Issues of Politics.* Chicago: University of Chicago Press, 1977. Pp. 252–73.

Develin, Robert. "The Good Man and the Good Citizen." *Phronesis* 18, no. 1 (1973): 71–79.

Dobbs, Darrell. "Aristotle's Anticommunism." *American Journal of Political Science* 29, no. 1 (1985): 29–46.

Elshtain, Jean Bethke. "Aristotle, the Public-Private Split, and the Case of the Suffragists." In *The Family in Political Thought.* Ed. Jean Bethke Elshtain. Amherst: University of Massachusetts Press, 1982. Pp. 51–65.

———. *Public Man, Private Woman: Women in Social and Political Thought.* Princeton: Princeton University Press, 1981.

Farrar, Cynthia. *The Origins of Democratic Thinking: The Invention of Politics in Classical Athens.* Cambridge: Cambridge University Press, 1988.

Finley, M. I. *The Ancient Economy.* 2d ed. Berkeley: University of California Press, 1985.

———. "Aristotle and Economic Analysis." In *Ethics and Politics,* vol. 2 of *Articles on Aristotle.* Ed. Jonathan Barnes, Malcolm Schofield, and Richard Sorabji. London: Gerald Duckworth, 1977. Pp. 140–58.

———. *Democracy Ancient and Modern.* Rev. ed. New Brunswick: Rutgers University Press, 1985.

Fortenbaugh, W. W. "Aristotle on Slaves and Women." In *Ethics and Politics,* vol. 2 of *Articles on Aristotle.* Ed. Jonathan Barnes, Malcolm

Schofield, and Richard Sorabji. London: Gerald Duckworth, 1977. Pp. 135–39.

Fraisse, Jean-Claude. "*Autarkeia* et *philia* en EE VII 12, 1244b1–1245b19." In *Untersuchungen zur Eudemischen Ethik: Akten des 5. Symposium Aristotelicum*. Ed. Paul Moraux and Dieter Harlfinger. Berlin: Walter de Gruyter, 1971. Pp. 245–51.

———. *Philia: La notion d'amitié dans la philosophie antique*. Paris: Librairie Philosophique J. Vrin, 1974.

Fustel de Coulanges, Numa Denis. *The Ancient City*. Baltimore: Johns Hopkins University Press, 1980.

Gadamer, Hans-Georg. *The Idea of the Good in Platonic-Aristotelian Philosophy*. Trans. P. Christopher Smith. New Haven: Yale University Press, 1986.

———. *Truth and Method*. 2d rev. ed. New York: Crossroad, 1989.

Gagarin, Michael. *Early Greek Law*. Berkeley: University of California Press, 1986.

Galston, William A. *Justice and the Human Good*. Chicago: University of Chicago Press, 1980.

Gauthier, R. -A. *Magnanimité: L'idéal de la grandeur dans la philosophie païenne et dans la théologie chrétienne*. Paris: Librarie Philosophique J. Vrin, 1951.

Grene, Marjorie. *A Portrait of Aristotle*. Chicago: University of Chicago Press, 1963.

Hagen, Charles T. "The '*Energeia-Kinēsis* Distinction and Aristotle's Conception of *Praxis*." *Journal of the History of Philosophy* 22, no. 3 (1984): 263–80.

Havelock, Eric A. *The Liberal Temper in Greek Politics*. London: Camelot, 1957.

Holmes, Stephen Taylor. "Aristippus in and out of Athens." *American Political Science Review* 73, no. 1 (1979): 113–28.

Horowitz, Maryanne Cline. "Aristotle and Woman." *Journal of the History of Biology* 9, no. 12 (1976): 183–213.

Huxley, George. "On Aristotle's Best State." *History of Political Thought* 6, no. 1/2 (1985): 139–49.

Irwin, T. H. "Moral Science and Political Theory in Aristotle." *History of Political Thought* 6, no. 1/2 (1985): 150–68.

Jaeger, Werner. *Aristotle: Fundamentals of the History of His Development*. 2d ed. Trans. Richard Robinson. Oxford: Clarendon, 1948.

Jaffa, Harry V. "Aristotle." In *History of Political Philosophy*. 2d ed. Ed. Leo Strauss and Joseph Cropsey. Chicago: University of Chicago Press, 1972). Pp. 64–129.

———. *Thomism and Aristotelianism*. Chicago: University of Chicago Press, 1952.

Kennington, Richard. "Strauss's Natural Right and History." *Review of Metaphysics* 35, no. 1 (1981): 57–86.

Kenny, Anthony. *Aristotle's Theory of the Will*. London: Gerald Duckworth, 1979.

Keuls, Eva C. *The Reign of the Phallus: Sexual Politics in Ancient Athens*. New York: Harper & Row, 1985.

Keyt, David. "Three Fundamental Theorems in Aristotle's Politics." *Phronesis* 32, no. 1 (1987): 54–79.

Lacey, W. K. *The Family in Classical Greece*. Ithaca: Cornell University Press, 1968.

Lear, Jonathan. *Aristotle: The desire to understand*. Cambridge: Cambridge University Press, 1988.

Lloyd, G. E. R. *Science, Folklore, and Ideology: Studies in the Life Sciences in Ancient Greece*. Cambridge: Cambridge University Press, 1983.

Loraux, Nicole. *Les enfants d'Athena: Idées athéniennes sur la citoyenneté et la division des sexes*. Paris: François Maspero, 1981.

Lord, Carnes. "Aristotle." In *History of Political Philosophy*. 3d ed. Ed. Leo Strauss and Joseph Cropsey. Chicago: University of Chicago Press, 1987. Pp. 118–54.

———. "The Character and Composition of Aristotle's *Politics*." *Political Theory* 9, no. 4 (1981): 459–78.

———. *Education and Culture in the Political Thought of Aristotle*. Ithaca: Cornell University Press, 1982.

MacDowell, Douglas M. *The Law in Classical Athens*. London: Thames and Hudson, 1978.

MacIntyre, Alasdair. *After Virtue: A Study in Moral Theory*. Notre Dame: University of Notre Dame Press, 1981.

Mansfield, Harvey C., Jr. "Marx on Aristotle: Freedom, Money, and Politics." *Review of Metaphysics* 34, no. 2 (1980): 351–67.

———. *Taming the Prince: The Ambivalence of Modern Executive Power*. New York: Free Press, 1989.

Mara, Gerald M. "The Role of Philosophy in Aristotle's Political Science." *Polity* 19, no. 3 (1987): 375–401.

Meikle, Scott. "Aristotle and the Political Economy of the Polis." *Journal of Hellenic Studies* 99 (1979): 57–73.

Mele, Alfred R. "Choice and Virtue in the *Nicomachean Ethics*." *Journal of the History of Philosophy* 19, no. 4 (1981): 405–23.

Miller, Eugene F. "What Does 'Political' Mean?" *Review of Politics* 42, no. 1 (1980): 56–72.

Morrall, John B. *Aristotle*. London: George Allen & Unwin, 1977.

Morsink, Johannes. "Was Aristotle's Biology Sexist?" *Journal of the History of Biology* 12, no. 1 (1979): 83–112.

Mulgan, Richard. "Aristotle and the Value of Political Participation." *Political Theory* 18, no. 2 (1990): 195–215.

———. *Aristotle's Political Theory: An Introduction for Students of Political Theory*. Oxford: Clarendon, 1977.

Nannery, Lawrence. "The Problem of the Two Lives in Aristotle's Ethics: The Human Good and the Best Life for a Man." *International Philosophical Quarterly* 21, no. 3 (1981): 277–93.

Newell, W. R. "Superlative Virtue: The Problem of Monarchy in Aristotle's 'Politics'." *Western Political Quarterly* 40, no. 1 (1987): 159–78.

Nichols, Mary P. "Aristotle's Defense of Rhetoric." *Journal of Politics* 49, no. 3 (1987): 657–77.

———. "The Good Life, Slavery, and Acquisition: Aristotle's Introduction to Politics." *Interpretation: A Journal of Political Philosophy* 2, no. 2 (1983): 171–83.

———. *Socrates and the Political Community: An Ancient Debate.* Albany: State University of New York Press, 1987.

Nussbaum, Martha Craven. *The Fragility of Goodness: Luck and Ethics in Greek Tragedy and Philosophy.* Cambridge: Cambridge University Press, 1986.

———. "Shame, Separateness, and Political Unity: Aristotle's Criticism of Plato." In *Essays on Aristotle's Ethics.* Ed. Amélie Oksenberg Rorty. Berkeley: University of California Press, 1980. Pp. 395–435.

Oehler, Klaus. "Aristotle on Self-Knowledge." *Proceedings of the American Philosophical Society* 118, no. 6 (1974): 493–506.

Okin, Susan Moller. *Women in Western Political Thought.* Princeton: Princeton University Press, 1979.

Ostwald, Martin. *From Popular Sovereignty to the Sovereignty of Law: Law, Society, and Politics in Fifth-Century Athens.* Berkeley: University of California Press, 1986.

———. "Was There a Concept *agraphos nomos* in Classical Greece?" In *Exegesis and Argument: Studies in Greek Philosophy Presented to Gregory Vlastos.* Ed. E. N. Lee, A. P. D. Mourelatos, and R. M. Rorty. Assen: Van Gorcum, 1973. Pp. 70–104.

Owen, G. E. L. "Aristotelian Pleasures." In *Ethics and Politics,* vol. 2 of *Articles on Aristotle.* Ed. Jonathan Barnes, Malcolm Schofield, and Richard Sorabji. London: Gerald Duckworth, 1977. Pp. 92–103.

Pellegrin, Pierre. "La 'Politique' d'Aristote: Unité et fractures éloge de la lecture sommaire." *Revue Philosophique de la France et de L'étranger* 177, no. 2 (1987): 129–59.

Polanyi, Karl. "Aristotle Discovers the Economy." In *Primitive, Archaic, and Modern Economies: Essays of Karl Polanyi.* Ed. George Dalton. Boston: Beacon, 1968. Pp. 78–115.

Randall, John Herman, Jr. *Aristotle.* New York: Columbia University Press, 1960.

Rees, D. A. "'Magnanimity' in the Eudemian and Nicomachean Ethics." In *Untersuchungen zur Eudemischen Ethik: Akten des 5. Symposium Aristotelicum.* Ed. Paul Moraux and Dieter Harlfinger. Berlin: Walter De Gruyter, 1971. Pp. 231–43.

Riedel, Manfred. *Metaphysik und Metapolitik: Studien zu Aristoteles und zur politischen Sprache der neuzeitlichen Philosophie.* Frankfurt am Main: Suhrkamp Verlag, 1975.

Ritter, Joachim. *Metaphysik und Politik: Studien zu Aristoteles und Hegel.* Frankfurt am Main: Suhrkamp Verlag, 1969.

Romilly, Jacqueline de. *La loi dans la pensée grecque: Des origines à Aristote.* Paris: Société d'Édition "Les Belles Lettres," 1971.

——. *Problèmes de la démocratie grecque.* Paris: Hermann, 1975.

Rorty, Amélie Oksenberg. "The Place of Contemplation in Aristotle's *Ethics.*" In *Essays on Aristotle's Ethics.* Ed. Amélie Oksenberg Rorty. Berkeley: University of California Press, 1980. Pp. 377–94.

Ross, W. D. *Aristotle: A Complete Exposition of His Works and Thought.* New York: Meridian, 1959.

Salkever, Stephen G. *Finding the Mean: Theory and Practice in Aristotelian Political Philosophy.* Princeton: Princeton University Press, 1990.

Saxonhouse, Arlene W. "Classical Greek Conceptions of Public and Private." In *Public and Private in Social Life.* Ed. S. I. Benn and G. F. Gaus. New York: St. Martin's Press, 1983. Pp. 363–84.

——. "Eros and the Female in Greek Political Thought: An Interpretation of Plato's Symposium." *Political Theory* 12, no. 1 (1984): 5–27.

——. "Family, Polity, and Unity: Aristotle on Socrates' Community of Wives." *Polity* 15, no. 2 (1982): 202–19.

——. "From Tragedy to Hierarchy and Back Again: Women in Greek Political Thought." *American Political Science Review* 80, no. 2 (1986): 403–18.

Schmidt, James. "A Raven with a Halo: The Translation of Aristotle's *Politics.*" *History of Political Thought* 7, no. 2 (1986): 295–319.

Sherman, Nancy. *The Fabric of Character: Aristotle's Theory of Virtue.* Oxford: Clarendon, 1989.

Smith, Steven B. "Goodness, Nobility, and Virtue in Aristotle's Political Science." *Polity* 19, no. 1 (1986): 5–26.

Solmsen, Friedrich. "Leisure and Play in Aristotle's Ideal State." *Rheinisches Museum für Philologie* 107 (1964): 193–220.

Sorabji, Richard. "Aristotle on the Role of Intellect in Virtue." In *Essays on Aristotle's Ethics.* Ed. Amélie Oksenberg Rorty. Berkeley: University of California Press, 1980. Pp. 201–19.

Stocks, John Leofric. *Aristotelianism.* Boston: Marshall Jones, 1925.

——. "*Scholē.*" *Classical Quarterly* 30 (1936): 177–87.

Strauss, Leo. *The City and Man.* Chicago: University of Chicago Press, 1964.

——. *Natural Right and History.* Chicago: University of Chicago Press, 1953.

Vander Waerdt, P. A. "Kingship and Philosophy in Aristotle's Best Regime." *Phronesis* 30, no. 3 (1985): 249–73.

——. "The Political Intention of Aristotle's Moral Philosophy." *Ancient Philosophy* 5, no. 1 (1985): 77–89.

Vernant, Jean-Pierre. *The Origins of Greek Thought.* Ithaca: Cornell University Press, 1982.

Voegelin, Eric. *Plato and Aristotle*, vol. 3 of *Order and History*. Baton Rouge: Louisiana State University Press, 1957.

———. "What Is Right by Nature?" In *Anamnesis*. Trans. and ed. Gerhart Niemeyer. Notre Dame: University of Notre Dame Press, 1978. Pp. 55–70.

White, Michael, J. "Aristotle's Concept of *Theōria* and the *'Energeia-Kinēsis* Distinction." *Journal of the History of Philosophy* 18, no. 3 (1980): 253–63.

Wilson, John F. "Power, Rule, and Politics: The Aristotelian View." *Polity* 13, no. 1 (1980): 80–96.

Winthrop, Delba. "Aristotle and Theories of Justice." *American Political Science Review* 72, no. 4 (1978): 1201–16.

———. "Aristotle on Participatory Democracy." *Polity* 11, no. 2 (1978): 151–71.

Wolff, H. J. "'Normenkontrolle' und Gesetzesbegriff in der attischen Demokratie," *Sitzungsberichte der Heidelberger Akademie der Wissenschaften, philosophisch-historische Klasse*, no. 2. Heidelberg: Jahrgang, 1970.

Yack, Bernard. "Community and Conflict in Aristotle." *Review of Politics* 47, no. 1 (1985): 92–112.

———. "Natural Right and Aristotle's Understanding of Justice." *Political Theory* 18, no. 2 (1990): 216–37.

Zuckert, Catherine H. "Aristotle on the Limits and Satisfactions of Political Life." *Interpretation: A Journal of Political Philosophy* 2, no. 2 (1983): 185–206.

INDEX

Abortion, 47n, 66n, 110
Acquisition, natural. *See* Agriculture; Household management
Acquisition, unnatural. *See* Money
Action, voluntary versus involuntary, 176
Adkins, A. W. H., 199, 213–14, 219
Adultery, 107
Aeschylus, 48n
Agamemnon, 48n
Agathocles, 182
Agriculture, 23n, 72n, 76–82, 89–90, 140n; political rationale for, 90–91n
Ambition, 61–62, 146. *See also* Recognition, desire for
Anaxagoras, 48n
Ancient and modern views, compared: on church and state, 117; on civic friendship, 180, 182–84; on democracy, 129n; on division of labor, 80; on embryology, 46; on friendship, 165; on household, 20; on institutions, 145; on political order, 96n; on political rule, 124, 190–91; on reason, 120n, 195; on rights, 122, 168–69 (*see also* Rights, natural); on science, 194–95; on the sexes, relations between, 25, 171n; on virtue, 152n; on will, 135. *See also* Classical liberalism; *entries for specific authors* (*e.g.,* Hobbes)
Androdamas of Rhegium, 96n
Andronicus, 226
Animals: compared to slaves, 34–35; disposition of, 16; and man, 23n, 81, 188; and music, 153; negative sense of, 35n
Annas, Julia, 176–77, 179n
Apollo, 48n

Appetites. *See* Desires
Aquinas, Saint Thomas, 181
Arendt, Hannah: on Aristotle and the Greeks, 1–2n, 31n, 205–6, 220; on courage, 9, 20–21, 29n, 108; on economics, 70–71, 82n, 93n, 94n; on freedom and necessity, 3, 9–10, 31, 45n, 191–92; on law, 96; and liberalism, 5n; on male and female, 45n; on political participation, 9–10, 191; on privacy as idiotic, 1n; on the private as the household, 1–3, 9–11, 15, 30; on public realm, 9–10, 19n, 205–6; on slavery, 31–32, 41
Areopagus, 102n
Aristocracy: defined as political standard, 7–8, 125–26, 210; means to, 90–91n, 108, 129, 161n, 209–11; succession in, 121
Armstrong, Cyril G., 37n, 70n
Army: control of, 117–19; financing of, 88n; need for, 106, 115. *See also* War
Arnhart, Larry, 123nn
Artisans, 81
Asian race, 138
Athena, 48n
Athenian Stranger: on education, 148–51, 161; on familiarity, 109n; on spiritedness, 138–39; virtues ranked by, 108n. *See also* Plato; Socrates
Athens: Areopagus, 102n; economy of, 87, 90; jury selection in, 122n; laws of, 102–3n, 132n; oligarchs of, 102–3n; payment for political participation in, 90, 102n, 130n; populism of, 102–3n; quietism (*apragmosunē*) in, 155; women in, 65–67
Augustine, Saint, 180–84

Library of Congress Cataloging-in-Publication Data

Swanson, Judith A. (Judith Ann), 1957–
  The public and the private in Aristotle's political philosophy /
Judith A. Swanson.
        p.   cm.
  Includes bibliographical references and index.
  ISBN 0-8014-2319-8 (alk. paper)
  1. Privacy, Right of.   2. Privacy—Moral and ethical aspects.
3. Public interest.   4. Aristotle—Contributions in political
science.   I. Title.
JC596.S93   1992
320'.01—dc20   91-55528